FROM MODEL T TO P-38 LIGHTNING

*Celebrating The Life of
William Frank Schottelkorb,
August 30, 1918 to January 23, 1943*

by Robert W. Schottelkorb

Pictorial Histories Publishing Co. Inc.
Missoula, Montana

COPYRIGHT © 2003 ROBERT W. SCHOTTELKORB
All rights reserved. No part of this book
may be used or reproduced without written
permission of the publisher.

LIBRARY OF CONGRESS
CONTROL NUMBER No. 2003 100406

ISBN 1-57510-100-9

First Printing March, 2003

Typography and layout by Jack G. Schwartzman

Cover Graphics by Mike Egeler, Egeler Designs

*Printed by Walsworth Publishing Co.
Marceline, Missouri*

PICTORIAL HISTORIES PUBLISHING CO., INC.
713 South 3rd Street West, Missoula, Montana 59801
Phone (406) 549-8488 FAX (406) 728-9280
E-Mail—phpc@montana.com
Website—pictorialhistoriespublishing.com

TABLE OF CONTENTS

DEDICATION..v

ACKNOWLEDGEMENTS...vi

ABOUT THE AUTHOR..vii

INTRODUCTION...ix

GROWING UP IN WESTERN MONTANA..1

PRIMARY FLIGHT TRAINING..27

BASIC FLIGHT TRAINING...37

ADVANCED FLIGHT TRAINING...47

MARCH FIELD, CALIFORNIA..57

NAVAL AIR STATION, NORTH ISLAND...67

CALIFORNIA TO ENGLAND...91

COMBAT TRAINING IN ENGLAND...105

ENGLAND TO NORTH AFRICA..139

COMBAT IN AFRICA...159

ONE SURVIVED..183

BEYOND AFRICA...191

2nd Lieutenant Bill Schottelkorb, March 1942, San Diego, California

Dedicated to

Bill Schottelkorb and his close friends, Mark K. Shipman, Wallace A Sorensen and John A Stege who flew with him as Aviation Cadets and as P-38 Fighter Pilots. They were assigned to the 48th Fighter Squadron of the 14th Fighter Group. On July 25, 1942, they departed for England in their P-38's. After further training they were assigned to the Twelfth Air Force and on November 11, 1942, they flew to Gibraltar to join in the invasion of North Africa, Operation Torch. They fought against veteran combat-trained German Fighter Pilots and gave a good account of themselves.

This is also dedicated to all of the members of the 48th and 49th Fighter Squadrons, 14th Fighter Group, Twelfth Air Force. The ground support units as well as the pilots, all had to endure very primitive conditions, scarcity of equipment, food and shelter, especially in the early months of the invasion. They did their best to "Keep Em Flying".

They all deserve our thanks.

Acknowledgements

First of all I thank my wife, Shirley, for putting up with me for well over a year while I attempted to get "The Book" finished. Too many times I said I couldn't go some place because I might make some progress on it. Certainly my good friend, Jack Schwartzman, deserves much credit for encouraging me early on to publish Bill's diaries. The delay may have had some benefit, however as I later decided to include Bill's life as a youth before he joined the Army Air Corps. It gives insight into a time in our country's history when life was simpler with fewer regulations and less crowded living conditions.

A very special thanks to Donald F. Tomlinson of Missoula who was a good friend of Bill's since high school days and while they were in the service. Don has been very helpful with suggestions and assistance at every opportunity.

Mark K. Shipman has helped immensely with his support and by giving us permission to quote from his own wartime diary, with the 48th Fighter Squadron. Mark's diary account of Bill's last mission is a vital link in the story.

It is a pleasure to thank John A. Stege for his part in Bill's life both as a cadet in Primary Flight School and onward into combat in North Africa. Thanks for your input and encouragement.

Joseph Onesty, the Secretary-Treasurer of the 48th Fighter Squadron Association, has volunteered information as well as being a source to call on.

For any others who I may have failed to recognize for their assistance, I apologize.

Last but not least, my thanks to Mrs. Ken (Rea) Walker of Missoula for her proficient review, advice and proof reading of this book.

The actual diaries utilized were modified only for clarity.

RWS

Most of the photographs were taken from Robert Schottelkorb's collection of photos. Bill had sent some of them home and others Mark Shipman and Wally Sorensen had returned to Bill's parents when they brought some of his personal effects and diaries to them. A few of the pictures are from the internet and didn't list any credits with them.

About the Author

On the way to Goose Bay, Labrador

Robert W. Schottelkorb, Bob, was born in Missoula, Montana on October 25, 1922 and was four years younger than his brother Bill. Each had his own friends, but Bill had considerable influence on his younger brother. When Bill left for the Army Air Corps in April 1941, Bob became the proud-owner of Bill's beloved "**Dynamiter**". Bob also took the car to Canada and on an extensive trip to Mexico with two of his friends in the summer of 1942; as Bill had done two years earlier.

Bob enlisted in the Army Air Corps in May 1942, after completing the Primary Course of the Civilian Pilot Training program at Missoula, as Bill had encouraged him to do. Bob's call to active duty came a little earlier than he expected, but he managed to leave Missoula for San Antonio, Texas shortly after he received his notice on September 1, 1942.

After pre-flight training Bob completed his Primary Flight Training at Pine Bluff, Arkansas, flying the Fairchild PT-19A. Then on to Basic at Winfield, Kansas where he flew the Vultee BT-13A. He graduated from Advanced Training at Altus, Oklahoma, where he flew the Cessna AT-17. He received his commission as a 2nd Lieutenant and received his wings on June 26, 1943, with the class of 43-F. Bob was assigned to the B-24 Bomber Transition School at Liberal, Kansas, and then to combat training. The first phase was at Tucson, Arizona, where he was assigned a crew. Second and third phases were at Biggs Field, El Paso, Texas. After this the crew joined the 493rd Bomb Group at McCook, Nebraska where they trained as a unit.

Departing on May 13, 1944, the aircrews flew their B-24s to England, by way of Goose Bay, Labrador, Iceland, Scotland and to their home field at Debach, England. The 493rd Bomb Group became operational on D-Day, June 6, 1944. Bob flew 32 combat missions to France and Germany. He completed his last mission to Hamburg, Germany on his 22nd birthday. He was awarded the DFC and Air Medal with 3 Oak Leaf clusters.

After returning to the United States he continued flying on various assignments until he was separated from the service on October 18, 1945. He stayed in the Air Force Reserve and retired as a Lieutenant Colonel. He graduated from the University of Montana in 1948 and was active in several small businesses until he retired in August 1987 at age 65. He married Shirley Lee in 1948 and they have a son, Bill, and daughters Bette Clark and Bobbi Combs as well as six grandchildren. All reside in Western Montana at this time.

Winter in Western Montana

Introduction

Bill was my "Big Brother" and he is still my hero even though he died nearly 60 years ago. He had definite ideas of what was important in life and he had a desire to share his positive attitude with others. Good fellowship with his numerous friends was high on his priorities and he enjoyed it most when he could explore the great outdoors with them. Fortunately we both grew up in Western Montana and Bill took full advantage of that. We were also blessed with good health and a stable family life.

Bill was 5 ft. 11 in. tall and well proportioned. He kept in good physical condition working hard at his jobs, as they required a lot of manual labor. Outdoor activities of hiking, swimming and skiing also contributed to his well being. He didn't smoke nor did most of his friends. Pepsi Cola was the favored drink for years but later beer increased in popularity. He believed in the inscription over the entrance to the men's gym, at the University, "Health is the First of all Liberties".

Adventure and exploration of the unknown was an exciting idea. He read about William R. LaVarre, a professional adventurer, who wrote about seeking gold, diamonds and orchids in South America in his book, "Exploring for Profit". Great! Adventure combined with a nice income! Richard Halliburton was another professional adventurer who he admired. Before he could fulfill these dreams he had to get an education and mature. For the time being he could explore the great outdoors in Western Montana and Northern Idaho.

Bill's natural mechanical ability led him to bond with several buddies who shared his interests and they became life long friends. They enjoyed working on their cars starting with Model T Fords, then progressing to Model A's and V-8's. These gave them the means to travel and explore the natural beauty of the area and not to just drive around sight seeing. They hiked, climbed Forest Service lookout towers, climbed cliffs, swam, skied and whatever else they could think of doing as an adventure.

Owning a car was an expense, and they worked hard at low wages to get the necessary money to be able to have one. They also wanted to get a good education, which they successfully accomplished, but that proved difficult for Bill because of all the other activities in his life. He knew the value of a good education but had a hard time applying himself when it came to studying.

He had an active imagination and from an early age on, he was interested in a wide range of activities. Charles Lindbergh's solo flight to Paris in 1927 heightened his desire to fly. He was a regular reader of the monthly aviation magazines, "Flying" and "Popular Aviation". He readily attended any meeting in high school that promoted the idea of forming a light plane club or a glider club. None of these groups went past the discussion phase mainly due to lack of money.

While at the University, Bill had a close group of friends who liked to get together and socialize. Since few of them joined a fraternity they decided to have their own social group and they called it "The Brawl". Joe "Ed" Halm was one of the prime leaders and Fred Barrett was secretary and the two of them worked closely together in the planning of the "Brawls". Ed often hosted them at his home where all of the guys were welcomed and had the freedom to use the kitchen and living room. There was usually a lot of food that they would enjoy. The menu varied, depending on the theme and location. They usually had lots of desserts and of course Pepsi. Activities included taking photos, showing ones taken previously, ping pong, card games and a lot of storytelling. Also they would plan for upcoming "Brawls" and future outings in the area. Later girls were often invited and dancing became popular. The girls also helped in the preparation of a more varied menu.

Introduction

Bill was fortunate to achieve his goal of flying by qualifying to be an Army Air Corps Flying Cadet. From this he progressed through training to become a proficient P-38 Combat Fighter Pilot. His life ended on January 23, 1943 when he was shot down by enemy ground fire when his flight inadvertently flew over a German airfield in Tunisia, North Africa, while flying under low clouds.

It was a blow to his squadron buddies, family and friends but in wartime many others had to bear the same burden. Ironically, his squadron was to be relieved and returned to the United States after two more missions. Fortunately Bill and two of his closest friends, Mark Shipman and Wallace Sorenson had made a pact that if any of them were killed the survivors would bring the personal effects back to the pilot's family, even though this was against regulations.

Our parents and I were so grateful that Mark and Wally did this and especially so, because his two diaries that he had kept since leaving the US for overseas duty were among his effects. These diaries along with one he kept in 1939 and 1940 while he was at home and a student at the University in Missoula as well as his letters to and from his family are the main basis for this book. The remainder of the book is from my memory and knowledge of our family life.

Bill was not perfect, as he did make mistakes, but he could be counted on and was very loyal to his friends.

I feel considerable regret that I have waited so long before publishing Bill's story. I know that many combat veterans, pilots and others would have enjoyed reading about his exploits. Many of his associates and World War II buddies have died and continue to do so at a rapid pace. I'm sure Bill would have wanted his story told and he would want to honor all who served their country in its hour of need.

Lastly, I would like to say Bill was a brother who anyone would have been proud to have. I certainly was.

We love you Bill. We will always remember.

Bob Schottelkorb

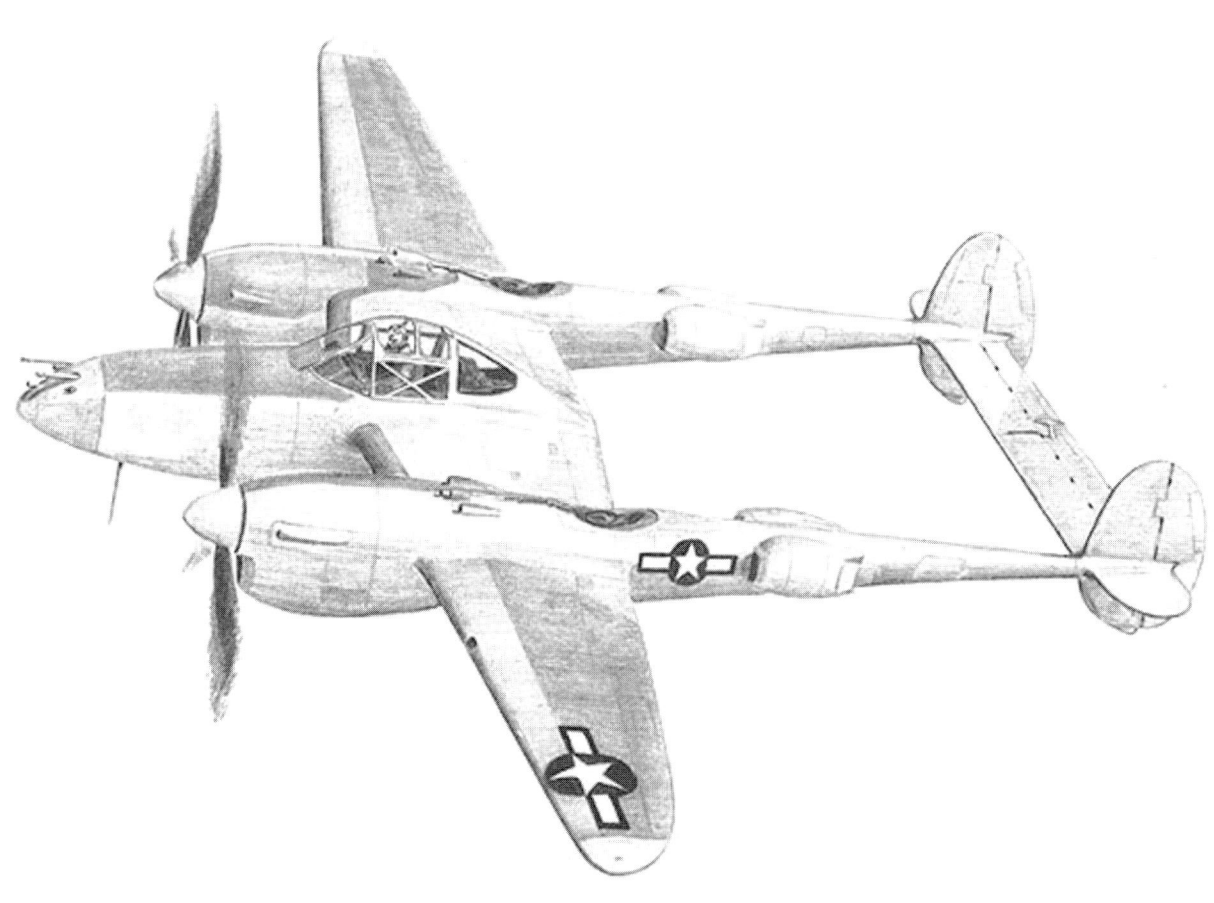

48TH FIGHTER SQUADRON

Bill and Ed Halm on the running board of the "T". It had a Ruckstell 2-speed rear axle with a low range that enabled it to climb the hills around Missoula.

Bud Blanchette and Bill mountain climbing with the "T"
Photos by Joe E. Halm

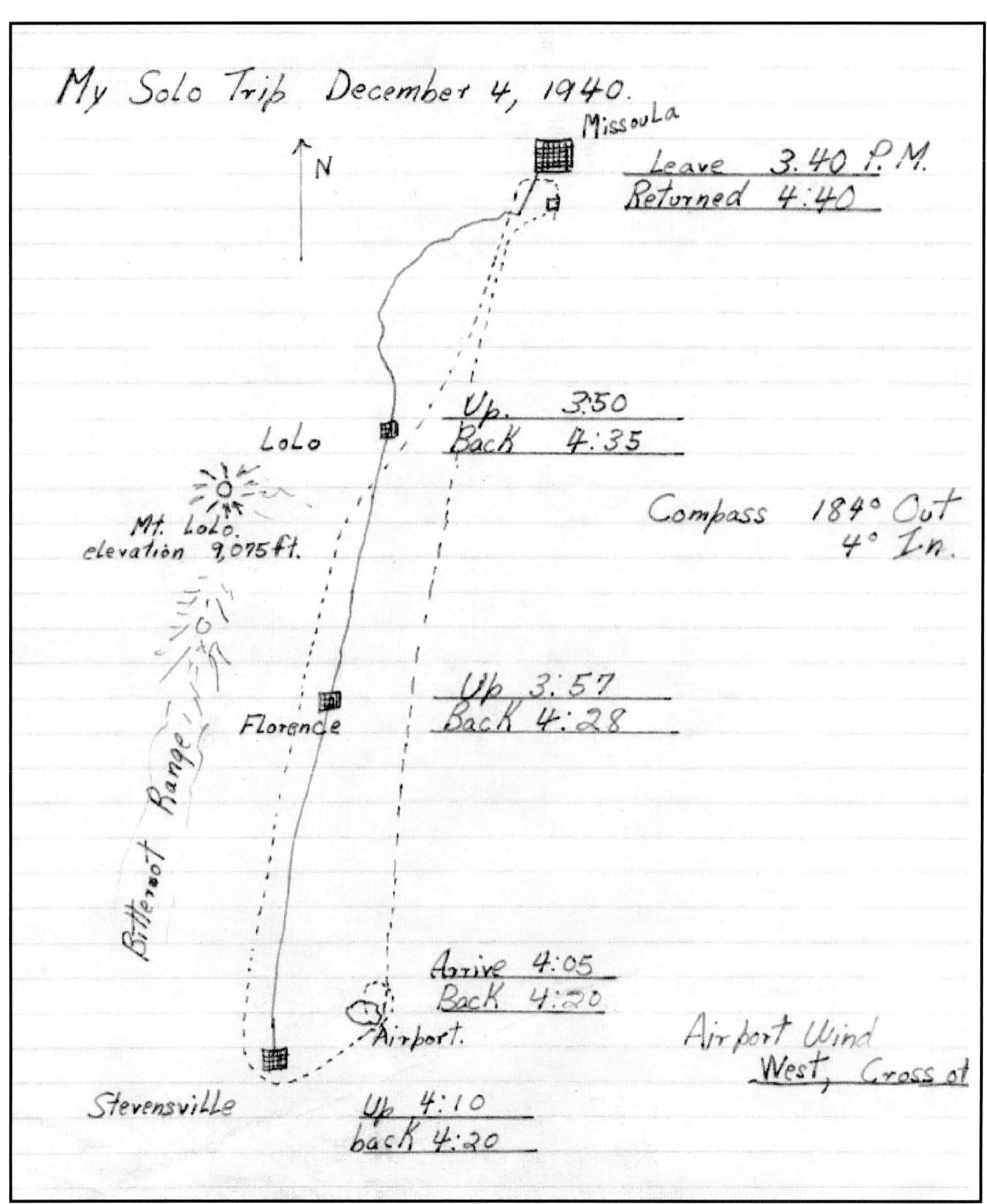

Bill's first cross-country flight, while a CPT student at Missoula, Montana

Growing up in Western Montana

This is the story of Bill, a young man who was born in western Montana and lived there until he enlisted in the Army Air Corps as an Aviation Cadet on April 25, 1941. Bill had dreamed of flying since his youth and his golden opportunity came when he signed up for the Primary Course of the Civil Aeronautics Administration's, Civilian Pilot Training, better know as CPT, in September, 1940.

Montana State University from J-3 Cub

Bill was in his senior year at Montana State University, later known as the University of Montana, in Missoula at the time. The program was designed to give students a brief entry into aviation as a prelude to military flying. The university provided basic courses on Meteorology, Navigation and Civil Air Regulations.

Johnson Flying Service was the local civilian school, which had the contract to teach the students how to fly a J3, Piper Cub. To complete the course the students had to log about 40 hours of flying time, and then were awarded a Private Pilot's License. Bill did complete the course under his instructor Dick Ogg, who later became a pilot for Pan American Airways. Bill loved every minute of it and he especially enjoyed the cross-country flights where he put his new-found skills to use.

The following is an excerpt from a page Bill wrote about his first cross-country:

One of Johnson's J-3 Piper Cubs

"My first cross-country ………..
Flight number one…On the 30th of November 1940.

Don Worden and Dick Ogg flew ship number four and I followed in number two. We left Missoula at 2:30 PM and arrived at Stevensville, in about 20 minutes. The field was much harder to find than I had thought it was going to be. I followed them in for the landing. Then we each made a practice turn around the field.

On the way back I flew with Ogg in number four and Worden brought number two back. The field in Stevensville is fairly rough and I had to stall it off on the take off when the bounces built up. Total time was 55 minutes from Missoula to Stevensville and return."

Bill, William Frank Schottelkorb, was born on August 30, 1918 in Stevensville, Montana, a small rural town in Western Montana. His father, William John Schottelkorb, was born in 1887 in Corning, Ohio and moved to Montana with his family when he was a young man. He became an automobile mechanic after training in Kansas City, Kansas. Bill's mother, Eva Hooper, was born in Springfield, Missouri in 1892. The family moved to Stevensville, by covered wagon when she was a young girl. She was a telephone switchboard operator in Stevensville when she met her husband to be. At this time William was a mechanic at the local Ford garage.

Growing up in Western Montana

When Billy was about a year old the young family moved to Missoula, a much larger town, 30 miles north of Stevensville. Dad continued to work as a mechanic for the H. O. Bell Company, the local Ford dealer, and remained there for the rest of his working career.

In 1922 our family built a comfortable two-bedroom home, in a nice neighborhood, at 315 Blaine St., near the Missoula County High School. I was born on October 25, 1922 and was named Robert Warren. I was called Bobby and was Bill's only sibling.

On left, Schottelkorb's house, 315 Blaine St.

Our family liked to visit with other families and often times we shared meals together, with plenty of good food and desserts. Mom liked to cook and share her recipes with friends. Both Dad and Mom were ardent fishermen in the streams and rivers nearby, and usually enjoyed good success. They would load up the old Model T Touring Car with a tent, cookware, and bedding and of course us kids. Sometimes we were accompanied with other friends and their kids. Meals were cooked over an open campfire and the freshly caught fish were fried in a skillet for all to enjoy.

Medicine Hot Springs was 90 miles south of Missoula and it was a favorite spot for camping and swimming in the large covered pool. Sparkling clear streams nearby provided good trout fishing. In the late summer, before the first snowfall, Huckleberry picking was a yearly event that was enjoyed, and provided our family with berries for pies, jam and pancakes later in the year. The best areas for this were in the

Family camping in the Bitterroot

mountains of Western Montana or Northern Idaho. It was especially good if it was in the burnt over areas of old forest fires where there was a lot of light and the bushes could really grow. This usually made for a trip of at least two days and entailed camping out. If one continued upward on the Forest Service roads they would usually lead to one of the fire lookout towers. If you climbed up on the towers you would be rewarded with a magnificent view of the surrounding peaks and mountainsides. Bill appreciated such beauty and serenity.

July 23, 1939 our family loaded up our 37 Ford V-8 sedan and started an 18-day trip to California. Bill drove much of the time and traded off with his dad. We went by way of Pocatello, Idaho and spent some time in Salt Lake City, Utah. Then on to Zion National Park and from there to Las Vegas, where it was very hot.

Growing up in Western Montana

Bill was impressed with Boulder Dam, later known as Hoover Dam. We left Las Vegas at 5 AM to beat the heat and arrived at Grandmother Schottelkorb's place in Los Angeles. Most of Mom and Dad's families had moved to California when they were young adults so there were many relatives to visit. The beaches, movie studios, parks and beautiful homes were sights that were enjoyed. The majority of relatives were near San Francisco and they were great hosts and showed the family around the area. Bill was to take advantage of their hospitality one year later while on a 6-week trip with two of his friends.

Zion National Park

San Francisco World Fair from the air

The World's Fair on Treasure Island was one of the highlights of the trip and there was much to see and do. Bill and Bob got to take a flight in an amphibian aircraft and were able to view the bay area from the air. Bob was "wowed", when the family attended the "Follies", and in one scene a curtain "opened accidentally" and exposed a scantily clad showgirl up on a stepladder. The curtain closed as a stagehand hurriedly removed her from the stage. All of the many relatives treated our family royally.

Amphibian plane at World Fair

Bill kept a brief diary of each day and on August 5th he wrote, "Aunt Dolores really has a nice place in Milpitas. She also has a dog, a horse and a husband" (Dr. Al Currlin). After 5 days in the bay area our family headed north through the Redwood Forest and up the coast to Oregon, crossed the Columbia River by ferry and on to Seattle. After looking around there, we headed east to Grand Coulee Dam and Spokane. When we reached Montana we stopped briefly at the ranger station at Haugan and visited with Ed Halm at his summer job with the Forest Service, arriving back in Missoula on August 10th and all had wonderful memories of the trip.

Bill was an ambitious youth and started working to earn money at an early age. He began with lawn mowing jobs and other small chores.

One of his classmates, in the Paxson Grade School, was Walter "Bud" McLeod, Jr. Bud's father, Walter McLeod, and grandfather, C.H. McLeod, were the manger and president, respectively, of the Missoula Mercantile Company. This was the largest mercantile

Growing up in Western Montana

establishment in western Montana and was one of the largest employers in the area. Bill was a

The McLeods, Walter, Bud and CH

friend of Bud and he spent enough time at their house so Bud's parents became acquainted with him. In 1935 after Bill's sophomore year in high school they offered him a summer job at their family's summer place. This was located on the shore of Seeley Lake 55 miles northeast of Missoula.

He had a variety of duties with many of them being new to him. The family usually ate on the screened porch, which had a nice view of the lake. Bill would set out the dinnerware and serve the meal to the family. Of course his duties included cleaning up afterward and then wiping the dishes. He said that he didn't mind doing this except when they had company. Having twelve or more people made his job that much harder. He mentioned that they used two forks and bread and butter plates and he thought that was a little too much, but didn't complain to them.

After dinner he would clean the stable and then attend to the horses. The family kept a few horses so that they could ride on the trails that led to nearby mountain peaks, Forest Service lookouts, small lakes and waterfalls that were in the area. In the afternoons Bill had about two and half free hours and usually spent this time swimming in the lake, which he thoroughly enjoyed. Being a strong swimmer was one of his attributes. In a letter to his family, Bill said, "The McLeods are sure nice to me and I sometimes get to ride along on their horses with them. I am just beginning to learn to ride and I sure like it."

Clara Marsh McLeod, Bud's younger sister

Driving their Ford V-8 was a treat and one day he got to drive it to Cottonwood Lakes and back, a round trip of 21 miles over mountain roads. He took five other people and supplies there for a picnic. They reached there safely and he wrote, "I only shifted into second gear three times". He was very impressed with this part of his job. In a postscript he added, "How is your dandy little Norge refrigerator doing, bet you wouldn't trade it for anything now". It was only recently that his folks had purchased an electric refrigerator after years of using an "icebox", which relied on a block of ice to keep food cool. After returning to Missoula that fall he resumed his normal routine and school life. No doubt he was glad to be with his family and friends again. He really enjoyed fellowship with his friends, as he was a very social person.

Working outside of school hours continued to be an important part of his life and he felt the necessity of it, in order to have a car and "spending" money. Pay was low but the cost of living was also low in those days. On July 16, 1940, Mr. C. H. McLeod had a talk with Bill and

Growing up in Western Montana

told him that he had learned the value of work and the dollar and he had everything necessary to succeed in life. Bill remarked, "That really pepped me up". Most of Bill's employment until the time that he entered the Army in 1941 was at the Missoula Mercantile as it was with many other people in the area.

Bill spent a lot of time working for Mr. Frank Jones who had a cleaning contract with the "Merc", as it was known. Usually there would be a crew of 2 or 3 young fellows and Jones himself would often work right along with them. He was a fun gentleman to be around but he expected everyone to work hard and you earned your pay. The work would include washing windows, mopping floors and waxing, cleaning restrooms, vacuuming carpets and a lot of other chores. Mr. McLeod and Mr. Bunge also paid Bill to keep their cars clean and he continued to do personal jobs for the McLeods. This was the part of the job that he liked as he got to drive family members around from time to time. He was also able to get his friend Cliff Stephenson to work on some of these jobs and sometimes they were able to work together on projects.

Later on Bill spent more time working directly for the "Merc" in various departments, but the one that eventually was his mainstay was the night watchman job at the store. His shift usually ran from midnight to 8 a.m. and sometimes included a cleaning job or two. At times he could do a little studying if he could make himself settle down to it.

Quite often he was short on sleep and his grades suffered. He enjoyed some of his classes but others were just something that was required and he skipped more classes than he should have. His problems were also multiplied by his craving for getting together with his friends. He loved to go to the shows, as they were called back then, and many were double features.

The outdoors had a strong appeal and he and his friends drove around in the hills near Missoula. Sometimes they would roast hot dogs over an open fire or take a lunch with them on their driving excursions. In the winter, skiing was a favorite pastime. On January 7, 1939, Bill wrote, "I put the harnesses on my new skis. Went up to the Pattee Canyon Ski Course in the afternoon with Ed Halm. First I had to fix a flat tire but had a nice trip up. Pulled it up, all in high gear. Poor skiing. You can't do anything without climbers. Nearly ruined our skis". "A foot of snow, measured horizontally", Ed said. The ski areas were just cleared hills without lifts. They had to climb up and then could ski back down.

Feb 2, 1939 Monday: Cliff Stephenson and I went skiing up Sawmill Gulch at 1:00. Met a car and had to back quite a distance. The other fellow got a kick out of my driving (skill). I skied down hill across country toward Grant Creek. That's what I like – outdoors! Wonderful. Home at 4:00.

Getting ready to ski in the Rattlesnake

Mar 17, 1939 Friday: Ed and I plan to go to the Lolo Pass on the Montana/Idaho border, on Sunday. I worked on my car most of the day and fixed the windshield so it would lay flat. Then I greased it and soundproofed the doors by sticking newspapers in them. It helped no end.

Mar 18, 1939 Saturday: Worked all day getting ready for the trip tomorrow. Ed and I waxed our skis. Later Dad and I went to the garage and tightened the steering post and aligned the wheels.

US Forest Servcie cabin at Lolo Pass

Mar 19, 1939 Sunday: Up at 2:45 am. Put things in the rumble seat and picked up Ed. He and Merl Brunsvold had been up all night developing pictures, (Merl was living with the Halm family while he attended the University). It took us two hours to drive to the Mud Creek Ranger Station, about 1 mile west of Lolo Hot Springs. This was as far as we could drive due to the snow. It was about 7 miles to the Forest Service cabin at the pass and this took 3 hours of uphill skiing. A hard crust wore the wax off our skis. Mick Thieme and his dad were already there. We made a jump and took pictures of the action.

Mick Thieme jumping

The skiing really wasn't perfect but we had a good time. A wonderful day; it was sunny with 10 feet of snow. I will always remember this day. I called the folks on the telephone from the ranger cabin. It took three and a half-hours to come home. Rough Road. Ed and I were fagged. Bed at 9:00.

In the spring when the weather warmed up they could get out and do some hiking. On April 25, 1939 he picked up Bud Blanchette and Cliff Stephenson and drove up to the Franklin Ranger Station in the Rattlesnake valley. They then hiked 3 miles to Rattlesnake Falls and ate their lunches and hiked on up to the top of the saddle. They saw great rock cliffs and slid down crusted snow banks, "just like on skis, we took a lot of pictures and everyone had a perfect day".

Bill and Bud sliding on crusted snow

By the time Bill entered high school in the fall of 1933 he was already thinking about owning his own car. He soon found several friends that shared his passion for cars. Joe "Ed" Halm and Don Tomlinson were the first to buy Model "T" Fords and were eager to put them in good running condition.
The garage at Ed's home had a small forge, tools and there was lots of room out back to park cars. It was the favorite hangout for the guys for many years and they were welcomed there.

Growing up in Western Montana

Ed's T, no seats no seat belts!

Bill's first car was a Model T pickup with a small pickup bed. When two or three of the guys could get together with their Model T cars they had a lot of fun exploring the surrounding country side. Bicycling was a forgotten thing for most of them, except for Cliff.

Cliff and his bike

Bill and Ness with Bill's T

Joe B. Halm

Ed's dad, Joe B. Halm, was on the staff of Region One Headquarters of the U. S. Forest Service in Missoula. He had shown remarkable skill and courage during the Great Fire of 1910, in leading his fire crew to safety when the fire in the mountains of northern Idaho trapped them. He was a real gentleman and encouraged the boys with their mechanical endeavors.

After a couple of years, they traded their old Model T cars for Model A Fords of the 1928-31 era. They had a friendly rivalry to see who could outdo the others in looks and good running engines. The Model A Roadster with rumble seat, was the favorite. If the factory equipped canvas top was missing they had to improvise or do without. Usually they drove them with the top down or completely removed when the weather was good.

Growing up in Western Montana

Bill's pride and joy, Model A, Mick Thieme In rumble seat and Cliff Stephenson in front At Lost Trail Pass

The Model A had a 40 horsepower engine and they were much more modern and dependable than the Model T. Bill enjoyed working on his Model A Roadster and he didn't hesitate putting it up on blocks to work on it. While doing this he could usually borrow his folks' 37 Ford, V-8, four-door sedan or just ride along in one of his friends car, on their frequent rides. On March 25, 1939 he took all the wheels and hubs off his car and said, "It's about time I got some brakes on the hack". On September 7, 1939 he removed the old shock absorbers and pulled out the transmission and clutch assembly. By the end of the next day he had it almost completely disassembled and ready to work on.

L to R, Bud Blanchette, Fred Barrett, Bill and Ed Halm

Bill graduated from high school in 1937 and that fall enrolled at the Montana State University in Missoula. This later became the University of Montana and the school in Bozeman became Montana State University. He majored in history and political science. At this time the University required two years of participation in the basic Army ROTC program. Bill enjoyed this for the most part and it helped prepare him for his entrance into the Army Air Corps in 1941. Many of Bill's buddies stayed in Missoula and entered MSU as well, including Ed, Don and Cliff, Bud Blanchette, Fred Barrett and Charles Luedke.

In 1939 the Missoula County Fair sponsored an old car race for the 4th of July celebration. Bill decided it would be fun to enter an old Model T in this, but had to scrounge around to get it built from old Model T parts and abandoned cars around the area. He didn't have much time to get it running and tuned up, but with help from his friends he was determined to do it. His personal diary for Thursday, June 29 said, "Now settling down to business for the Model T. We are stripping it completely and have removed all but two leaves of the rear springs. Bed early.

Bill in his racing machine

June 30 Friday—worked on the "T" all day. Cliff and I made a mounting on the dash for the coil box—installed the gas tank in the cowl—lowered the steering gear—fixed a flat tire. Had a lot of trouble. Had to take the head off a couple of times. Bed early.

July 1 Saturday—Well, still another day on the "T". When we did get it running, it would only

Growing up in Western Montana

hit, on about two cylinders. That was funny because Dad had ground the valves. We went over all the coils, the timer wires; by means of wires from my Model "A's battery. At last we discovered that there wasn't any compression on number four cylinder. Valves OK that means rings are bad. Looks pretty discouraging because the race is at 1:30 tomorrow.

Showing off after the race

July 2 Sunday—I was pretty discouraged this morning. Dad wanted to call the whole thing off, said that I might get hurt. I almost gave in and then rallied and said "I'll do or die". Worked two hours as watchman at the Missoula Mercantile. Dad worked on the car all morning. I also fixed steering, radiator, etc. Cliff, Mick, Fred and I went out to the grounds on the "T". My hopes kind of faded when I saw the competition. 1st race = 4 qualifying heats, I placed 2nd in the 3rd heat. Beat by a Chevy. I got a poor start. Terrible dust in eyes, lost in loose dirt. Finally learned to take the curves, but then it was too late. A Willys was first (A 29 model strangely let in). Model "T" 2nd and an Essex 3rd. Then the free for all – I was in the 1st heat, 5 laps. I took 1st against 3 other "T's". In the finals I ran against the Chevy, Essex and another "T". I got the lead and held in for 12 laps. (Running start used) Then the thing started getting hot and the Chevy passed me. Took 2nd, 10 seconds behind. Winning time, 14 minutes 10 seconds, winning time for 10 miles, 20 laps. Averaged about 40 mph. Certainly a lot of fun and I won $20.00.

Don Tomlinson was the first of his buddies to "upgrade" to a 1933 Ford V-8, which needed considerable work to put it in running condition. Ed Halm decided at this time to install a Ford V-8 engine in his Model A. This proved to be no small undertaking. He, Bill and Don found a 1935 V-8 engine in a wrecking yard and the cost was $85.00. Ed worked diligently on his new project with help from his buddies from time to time.

5 Fords, L to R, Cliff's Model A coupe, Bill's "Dynamiter", Ed's "Dynamiter", Bob with family 37 V-8, and Don's 33 "Hammering Hearse"

Both Don and Bill were also working on their cars and other projects as well and later Don said that their grades in school suffered. After working on the cars they would end up grimy with grease in their hair. "Lying on your back trying to drill into the frame with a dull bit was no fun", Bill's personal diary said on February 10, 1940, "The work is progressing nicely on Ed's conversion". Bill helped him start it on March 24th and said, "It runs swell". After a ride in Ed's car on April 12th, Bill wrote, "God, but it has power". This was the reason for Bill naming his car "The Dynamiter", after he installed a V-8 in his Model A roadster later on.

On April 14, 1940, Ed drove Bill and Ness Calkins around in his car up the Rattlesnake and Blackfoot valleys, putting 80 miles on the wonder car. In town if any young fellow would challenge them from a standing start, they would show him up or "larn him" with the car's great acceleration. Later he took brothers Cliff and Bits Stephenson for a ride and they also marveled at its performance.

Bill and Cliff with the "Dynamiter"

Two months later Bill decided he had to have his "A" changed to a V-8 also. On June 12, 1940 he bought a 1933 Ford V-8 engine from the H. O. Bell Company for $55.00. There were a lot of problems to overcome and it was a tight fit to get the larger V-8 engine into the cramped engine compartment of the Model A. Like Ed, Bill wanted to preserve the appearance of the Model A, so he used the original radiator and outer shell. This entailed much work to match it to the requirements of the V-8 engine. The radiator proved to be rather inadequate to efficiently cool the engine, but it did work. A new frame cross member was needed as well as, new, home made motor mounts and a few other components. This required innovative engineering that was done at home. Bill's dad worked hard on it at every opportunity he had, as did several of Bill's friends, when they could and their work was much needed and appreciated. It was finally completed in the afternoon of July 31st.

Bill and fellow classmates, Fred Barrett and Walter "Mickey" Thieme had been planning a trip to Mexico for two years or more. They each had taken Spanish classes during this period and had eagerly discussed this exciting adventure many times. On December 15, 1939, when his Spanish professor, Mr. Thomas, got off the subject and started talking about Mexico; Bill wrote in his diary that night "swell Spanish class today". Earlier that year, on July 14, 1939, Bill and Cliff had gone to the movie "Juarez" and he had thought it was very good. "LaPaloma" was sung beautifully in the movie, and Bill said, "and they asked me why I want to go to Mexico!"

At 6 PM that evening they left for a six week trip to Mexico in his new "A-V-8", without so much as a trial "shake-down" period. They only drove the car at 35 mph at first to break in the newly overhauled engine, and the car "ran perfect". They went east about 100 miles and camped on top of Mac Donald Pass, 6,320 feet, on the first leg of their journey.

Aug 1, Packed up and wrote letters atop McDonald Pass. Helena to Three Forks, 1st hot stage tests on V-8. Water put in every 35 miles kept it well. Between Bozeman and Yellowstone Park, leaking water pump kept us putting in water. Changed water pump in West Yellowstone. Nite at Old Faithful.

Aug 2, Friday—saw Old Faithful and the lodge. Drove through park noting usual sights, Canyon Junction, Tower Falls. Car heated half way up Mt. Washburn and had to halt. Saw Mountain Sheep. Started up Cook City Highway, left half of the hood up. Halfway up, heat caused us to take the whole hood off, now it was fine. Beautiful drive. Car had loads of power. Ate at Joliet, on to Laurel.

Aug 3, Saturday – Up at 7 and over to Aunt Georgia's farm. Ate a swell breakfast washed and shaved. Had a nice little visit. Georgia gave us fried chicken for our lunch. Left at 9 and went on to Billings, gassed up, had refreshments and oil changed. Started out over bad country and had it all the way through Wyoming. 1st gear locking started at Sheridan. Light trouble. Spent night at Kaycee.

Growing up in Western Montana

Aug 4, Woke up at 8:00 on the barren Wyoming flat. Made a good little breakfast on our gas stove. Drove through Casper to Cheyenne. Casper not nice at all, an oil center. Cheyenne very nice and modern. Not much larger than Missoula. On into Colorado's bordering mountains. Denver just a plain city, I was disappointed. South to Colorado Springs, very nice. We got a cabin, washed, showered and had a very good 10 hours of sleep. 450 Miles today.

The usual sleeping arrangement

Yellowstone Falls in Yellowstone Park

Aug 5, Gave up idea of going up Pike's Peak. Letter writing in morning. Took car to garage. South New Mexico nice, over Raton Pass. Slept just over Texas line.

Aug 6, I certainly enjoyed Texas. Amarillo is a perfect modern little city of about 40,000. In northern Texas there are lots of small farms, well laid out, neat and well cared for. Along the highway there is an attempt for gardening, parks and such. The southern part we found to be more scrub forests, and more tropical. I still liked it. Slept out of San Angelo after having a grease job on the car. Told of snakes but saw none.

Aug 7, Drove to San Antonio, a nice city. We noticed a great increase in the southern accent. Terrible heat wave. We drove to Laredo. Arrived terribly burned by wind and very dirty. Secured cabin and took showers. Looked over town, a mixture of Mexican and American. Wrote letters. Bed 10:00.

Aug 8, Up at 8:00 in Laredo. Hot already. Loaded up and did some letter writing. Got the Mexican entrance papers. Left about 2 for Mexico. Nearly had trouble over fact of V-8 cylinder engine. Drove to Monterey. Had to buy water for the car. Drove all night.

Mexico City

Aug 9, I was asleep in the rumble seat at 6 this morning when the fellows stopped the car in a clearing off the Pan-Am Highway, somewhere between Victoria and Tomaso Charlie. We had a breakfast of Tomato soup and fried potatoes.

Growing up in Western Montana

Then we helped some women in a Dodge up the hills past the town. Poor gas seemed to be their trouble. Beautiful curved road. Arrived Mexico City at 5:00. Got lost uptown. Camp after camp of poor people.

Aug 10, Up at 8 and took care of personal items and such until about 10. Then went uptown in Mexico City. Went through the Palace of Fine Arts, then to the bank to cash a Travelers Check. We got $49.50 for $10.00 of our money. Walked all over. Went to Travel Club. Saw all kinds of conditions. Had a huge meal for $1.50 - $.30. Went to pyramids, and climbed on one, the sun home to Aztec. Cabin. Bed 9:00. Fred and Mick sang and danced with members of a bike-touring club. I felt tired and sick from my sunburn and cold.

Aug 11, We got up and Mick sensing indecision, something against his liking, suggested we get moving. Started before noon for Vera-Cruz. Climbed over 10,300-foot pass, beautiful view of Popo and Isxt. Beautiful farming land and Pine trees. Spent night under a huge tree without fear of snakes and such. Still in highlands. Supper in Pueblo.

Aug 12, Up and played a little baseball and had a breakfast from our canned goods. Soon we dropped out of the highlands on a curvy, bumpy, paved road. Good old steaming tropics is just what I wanted to see. Hot and moist, uncomfortable but still easy enough to tolerate. Butterflies flies and many things stirring. Saw Pan American Airport. 454 Kilometers we reached Vera Cruz. Went to port, watched a ship being loaded. A tropical pest hold port. Much quaintness and nice things but many things lacking. Made good use of our Spanish with a lady at a Banana stand.

Aug 13, Went uptown and got a gas pump line for car. Shopped a little and saw a little more, then left. Drove inland and the mountain air felt good. Oil changed and grease job on car in Jalapa. Mexican service is very inefficient. Had to put in 20 oil because that was as light as they had. Have not yet added a quart. Drove on to Tehucian. Got a large good dinner, we were starved. Bed on airport. Mick kind of sick.

Mick and Fred bartering

Aug 14, Up just as a monoplane made a landing on the port. Before taking off, the pilot taxied over and talked to us. He spoke good English. Marveled at our car. Thought we were miles from home. To railway station and got tickets to Oaxaca, after storing our car, a Peso a day. Train left 2 hours late, 12 to 8 at nite. Narrow gage – 2nd class, bang, jolt. Got awfully tired. There we stayed at Hotel Paris, nice room, and 20 cents apiece. Much sleep.

Aug 15, Thursday - - up at 8 in Oaxaca. Breakfast of cocoa and bread. Explored markets, bartered. A beautiful quaint city. 36 V-8 drove us to the top of the hill for 5 Pesos, where we saw the Monte Albun Ruins, very nice. Ate good meal in good hotel at 2:00, our hotel, the Paris. Afternoon, wrote many letters and cards. Bought a tablecloth for Mother. Small supper. Bought 1st class train passage this time, left at 9 and arrived at 5 in the morning.

Aug 16, Friday - - Waiting at the station in Tehuscan at 6:00 in the morning, talking Spanish with some little kid. Got our car, stored it in a patio 2 days for 40 cents or 2 Pesos. Then drove to Puebla and then Mexico City, 150 miles. Cashed a Travelers Check and went to Aztec cabins. Slept on lawn this time. Cleaned up and went to town and had a huge meal at Gorman's for 30 cents. Walked and drove all through Chupatepec Castle and woods. Got a letter from home and one from Cliff. Went to Alameda Showhouse. The clouds above town and store very nice, soda and talked and kidded.

Aug 17, Saturday. Up at 7:30. Washed myself and some of my clothes. Had breakfast at a small quick lunch café. Went to Cuernavaca. Beautiful drive. More Montana like, mountain scenery. Able to see whole Mexican valley. Beautiful curvy road on each side. Cuernavaca is one of the cleanest of Mexican towns. Many beautiful Spanish style summer homes. A lot of tourist shops. Spent several hours looking around. Saw Xochimilco, dirty place, no beauty.

Aug 18, Sunday - - Had ham and eggs for breakfast at a small downtown restaurant. Then we went through the museum of Natural History and the big downtown museum. Both average nice, dealt more with Mexican culture. Lunch, Mick and I had a liter of milk and cookies. Fred didn't want any. Went to bullfight 6 to 7. Not very lively. Somewhat lacking in sportsmanship. Talked to Ohio girls in evening.

The bullfight

Mt. Popocatepetl, elevation 17,887 ft.

Aug 19, Monday - - Up at Aztec Cabins at 8:00. Cooked ourselves a breakfast on the stove. Changed tires around to distribute wear. Tightened bolts. Wrote letters and cards. Generally took it easy till 2:00. Aztec main lodge is very nice, very light. Then downtown to dinner. A nice reasonable one, beefsteak at a Chinese place. Bought camera supplies and food. Had a soda. Then drove to Amecameca. Took dirt road, a steep climb to 12,500 feet level. Mt. Popocatepetl, 17, 887 ft., gleaming at our right. Bed 9:00.

A village fountain

Aug. 20, Tuesday. Didn't sleep too well because of the rain. Somehow it got into our beds and caused discomfort. Up at 5:30. Ate a lunch, that we had prepared. Left for a little climbing, altitude does rob you of strength. Fred and I climbed to around the 14,000 foot level. Mt. Citaltepeti, 18,701 ft., across the way didn't look much higher. Took several pictures. Mick went ahead and climbed far into the snowline. Some wealthy folks from Pleasantville, NY walked up after their driver didn't want to go farther. We gave them a lift down. Ate meal at Gorman's. Travel day, picked up silver coins. Left city at 5.

Storm approaching

Aug 21, Drove right on through. I drove 1st. At 10 we stopped and had chicken at Jalpan, a tourist sucker hole. I drove over mountains. Rain and fog slowed us up. Animals lay right in the road. We ate at 7 in the morning in Victoria then 4 hours to Monterey, ate again, swell meal, low cost, then to Laredo. Easy coming thru customs. On to San Antonio, cabin. Swell to be in US, milkshake, and bed 11:00.

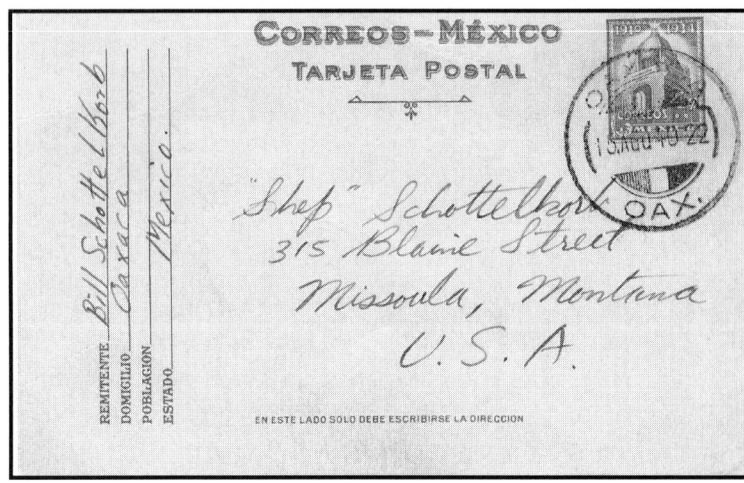
Postcard to Shep

Aug 22, Thurs. Up at 8:00, after heavy sleeping. Drove a small distance into town and had breakfast at a small home cooking café. Perfect. I had a double order of ham and eggs, toast, milk and orange juice. Cost 40 cents. Then spent a good part of the morning at the Ford garage. Had

Back in the USA

front wheels aligned and packed. 2 drag links tightened, an overflow pipe made for the radiator cap. Car greased and oil changed, $5.10 cost. Found out both water pumps were cracked. Drove to cabin. Fellows sent stuff home. Had a milkshake and foot long hot dog. Drove out to Kelly Field. Left at 3 drove till 1:00. Slept in a roadside park.

Aug 23, Today we got up and had a small breakfast of Orange Juice and Coffee. Then spent a good part of the morning writing signs on the car. Got going by 11:00. About 12 we stopped at a desert inn and had a fried ham sandwich and a bottle of pop. Day was not excessively hot till along in the evening. We went past El Paso, a nice place. Mick continued driving until 1:00 at nite. Spent the nite in the open range, 1 block from highway, near Deming, New Mexico.

Growing up in Western Montana

Aug 24, I drove 1st after a good sleep, still feeling sleepy, to Lordsburg. Had a good breakfast for 30 cents. Continuing we took a short cut between highway 70 and 80. This saved us about 100 miles. The 1st part was perfect. The last part was quite rough and we had to go very slow. The springs are overloaded as it is. Into Arizona. For noon we had sandwiches and a milkshake at Tucson, a nice desert place. Afternoon was quarts of beer. On to Yuma, another nice place. California entrance and inspection. Onward till 12 at nite. Cold wind struck us past El Centro. Bed 12:00.

News for Shep

Aug 25, Sunday - - Slept under a tree on soft leaves, perfect. I got up at 6 in morning and wrote letters. Others slept. Had a wonderful drive of 65 miles into San Diego on perfect roads. Stopped and got some peaches. Ate 5 for breakfast. Woke Chuck Luedke out of a sound sleep at 10:30. Met Jimmie Gamble and his very nice wife, Jean. Cooked up a meal of corn at Chuck's. All 6 of us went to Mission Beach in the "Dynamiter". Traffic not bad. Swam and played in sand. Rode roller coaster. Jean cooked us a waffle supper. Cleaned up. Watched Chuck do his magician act at the Paris Inn. Drank 35-cent drinks. Bed 1:00 after much talking.

Aug 26, Monday - - Up at 8:00 and went down to a small store. Bought bread, milk eggs, jam and grapefruit. Again at Chuck's place had a swell breakfast. Fred cooked eggs and hot cakes. Cleaned up cabin and washed clothes. At 12:00 we started walking and saw Balboa Park, lawns, cannons, old Exposition grounds of San Diego 1936 show and Ford Bowl. Chuck made us laugh there. 25 cents we went to the zoo, one of the largest. I especially enjoyed the snakes, huge constrictors. Also the Gorillas. Supper, each went his way. I had Beef roast in a small place. Went to "Barber of Seville", small opera. Perfect. Bed 11:00.

Aug 27, Tuesday - - Spent the morning mostly cooking a huge meal and sitting around talking. Afternoon we went to Coronado by ferryboat, expensive place. Spent an hour in the library. Evening we furnished the grub and ate in Gambles' apartment with them. Then we went to Tijuana. Saw all including Del Rio and radio station. Milkshake and to bed 12:00.

Aug 28, Wednesday - - Morning had a breakfast of hot cakes and coffee, 16 cents. I worked on water pump problem while Mick and Fred painted on car. Chuck packed his trunk of a 100 pounds and joined us for the rest of the trip. Over at Ford garage the foreman advised me to put in

Mick and Fred painting on the "Dynamiter"

thermostats instead of filing pump blades. Drove to Long Beach with 4 of us and our equipment.

Growing up in Western Montana

Went to the Coney Island. Found a place to stay out on flat. Bed 11:30.

Aug 29, Thursday - - Slept between Long Beach and Los Angeles. Spent some time in Exposition Park, looking at museum and the stadium. Spent the afternoon on the beach at Santa Monica with our own little lunch. Evening we drove around Hollywood and to the Observatory in Griffin Park. Spent nite in Santa Monica on the beach.

Aug 30, Friday - - Arrived at Aunt Rose Clark's place in Glendale at 11:30. She fixed us a perfect lunch. After a short rest we went to Tujunga where Fred stayed with his aunt over nite. Had car greased, over to Pasadena and back to Rose's. Three of us and Rose and Julian had a perfect supper. Chuck performed. Stories told. Much laughter. My birthday – 22.

Aug 31, Up, had a shower and shave. Had

Barbara Van Housen

breakfast. Packed up and left about 10:30. Then to Tujunga and out. Saw 2 big airports. Then to Santa Monica. Up the coast to Santa Barbara. Spent night outside of Santa Maria, up a small canyon.

Sep 1, Next morning we spent some time writing letters. About 9 we turned inland to Coalinga. Had dirt road for some distance and steep pulling. Saw the real California waste land. Heat wave.

Sep 2, Left at 9:00 for Fresno. Nicer country. Fresno nice. Then on to Yosemite Park. Had a water fight in the middle of the road, about derailing Mick who was trying to drive. Paid two bucks and got in. Located Aunt Carol Van Housen's place. We all went for a swim in the river, with my cousin Barbara. I ate supper with the folks and then we went to the dance. I slept there, the other fellows stayed in a camp. Bed 12:00.

Sep 3, Saw Barbara off for school in the morning. She drives 45 miles every morning. Then we left and went to Merced then on to Frisco, San Mateo and Aunt Pat Moore's home. Had a little trouble finding the place. Aunt Dolores was there. Had a good supper. Dinty drove us to town for a look around in the evening. Bed fairly late.

Sep 4, Drove to the World's Fair at Treasure Island today and saw almost everything. We each separated and saw what we wanted. But then got together again to see the Aquacade, the Follies and the Cavalcade. Drove down the Bay Shore late at night and to bed.

Sep 5, Today we stayed around a little in the morning and wrote letters. Then we drove up to the city and across the Bay Bridge, to Berkeley where we looked around the university awhile. Then drove thru Oakland in the rain and down to Aunt Dolores', where we had a barbecue when Pat and Dinty came down. Then we drove home to aunt Pat's at Redwood City late at nite.

Sep 6, Today we drove into town and looked over Chinatown, somewhat, and then to the fair. Saw what we could and left at 2:00. Spent the afternoon in Frisco, looking around. I looked up Aunt Ann and Wayne. They took us to supper on

Growing up in Western Montana

Fisherman's Wharf. Then we drove up and down Market St. Finally home, where we had a late supper with Charley and his wife, friends of Aunt Pat and Dinty's.

Sep 7, Left Redwood City at 9:30 and drove across the Golden Gate Bridge and north to Cloverdale. There we got a grease job and ate. We also saw the Italian Swiss Colony Winery. We slept outside of Eureka.

Sep 8, From Eureka we drove to Crescent City and on to Grant's Pass where we had a very nice milkshake. Then on through beautiful timbered country to Bend. Here we ate supper. A nice little place. Soon the trees began to disappear and we hit flat country. We drove on till we came to the Columbia River and made camp beside the road.

Sep 9, Then on up the river to Pasco. The weather continually was increasing in warmth. Pasco to Spokane, car ran too hot. Had to stop at a farmhouse for water. Had a swell milkshake and looked up a friend of Mick's who is in the Forest Service. On to Sandpoint thru a nice country. Then on up to Bonner's Ferry, where we had supper. On up to King's Gate, chatted with an old Englishman. Slept back of Bonner's Ferry.

Home from Mexico

Sep 10, We drove back to Sandpoint and ate breakfast. On to Missoula. Cleaned up in the river. I kept my beard but the others shaved. Then on to Thompson Falls, Ravalli, and home. Somehow we were a little disappointed with our trip on into Missoula. Things looked dried up and small time, no disrespect meant. Unpacking and dropping off guys broke up a trip that we shall never forget.

After the trip was over Bill suffered a letdown.

Sep 11 until Sep 27, After my return from Mexico, my time was devoted to loafing, reading, bloating, a period of indecision, confusion, and laziness.

Hale Field in Missoula

September 27, 1940 Friday Bill registered for the fall quarter at the University. At 3 pm he left for a visit to see Ed, who was working for the Forest Service, in the backcountry near Bovill, Idaho. Bill ate dinner in a café at Superior, Montana then continued his journey. When it began to rain hard he decided to pull off the road for the night. He made his bed under his car to escape the rain. When he arrived at Bovill, he and Ed had a good visit and spent the night. Then on Sunday he left for home, arriving just in time to make his night watchman shift at the Merc.

September 30, 1940 Monday School in the morning after spending the night on the watch

Growing up in Western Montana

shift. In the afternoon had a preliminary physical exam, passed OK, eyes all right. Bed early.

October 1, 1940 Tuesday Just beginning to become accustomed to school again. Evening had a CPT meeting at school. Met the Flight Instructor and he quizzed us. Hope I can make it.

October 7, 1940 Monday Took the thorough physical examination by Dr. Richie. He beat on me from 9 till 10:30 am. In the evening I had the first ground school class for the CPT.

October 8, 1940 Tuesday School in morning and a one hour eye examination, passed OK. Dr. Merrill of the University okayed me for the CPT course.

October 15, 1940 Tuesday Well today I had my 1st flight of the course, CPT. I sure liked it. We flew straight, made easy turns etc. Flew up near Lolo.

October 16, 1940 Wednesday Had my second flight today. We practiced rectangular course work and turns with a straight road. Evening, ground course work.

October 17, 1940 Thursday No school today. At 10 am had my 3rd flight. First time doing landings and takeoffs, some terrible. Afternoon had a shower with Cliff and Fred at the gym and then worked on my car. Evening I went to a show at the Rialto by myself.

October 19, 1940 Saturday At 10am today, I took my fourth flight, of 35 minutes duration. Everything seemed easier, even though the air was more bumpy. We made takeoffs and landings. In the afternoon I worked on my car. Now have it nearly completely tore down. Evening visited with Cliff for awhile.

October 20, 1940 Sunday Today I drove Mother and my two Grandmothers to the Skalkaho. We had a picnic lunch and ate at this very nice campground. Next we rode up to the falls. We stopped to get potatoes on the way home and dropped Grandmother off at Dennis's place in Stevensville. Evening I talked with Ed who just completed passing his Army Air Corps examination. Nite watch at 12:00.

October 21, 1940 Monday Spanish 8 to 10 am. Took my 5th flying lesson. Did quite well despite the wind currents. Couple of good landings. Slept in afternoon and CPT school at nite. Bed early. Another lesson done.

October 22, 1940 Tuesday Flying at 1:00 again. Ground school at nite. Rode around with Ed this afternoon after he had gotten his car all fixed up with a rebored engine. It sure performs well now with the high ring gear.

October 23, 1940 Wednesday Studied all day on CAA regulations. At the ground school tonight we had a test of 50 questions on CAA regulations. I missed 5.

October 24, 1940 Thursday Flew today at 2:00. Flew a new ship, No. 5. It has a tail wheel and brakes. We did 70 degree turns and power stalls. Ed and I visited. Last ground school tonite. We finished theory of flight.

November 3, 1940 Sunday Worked two hours for Jones today., At 11:00 went to the airport and waited my turn to fly. We made two good landings and Dick gave it to me for the solo flight. I went around 4 times and made good landings every time. What a thrill and responsibility. Ed brought out their deer today, that they got hunting. I stayed home this evening and went to bed early at 9:00, of course arose again at 12 to work.

November 4, 1940 Monday Had a good nite shift. I'm reading Francis Villion. Attended both morning classes and slept 2 hours. At one I was flying. Made 2 turns around with the instructor and then made 6 around by myself. Made a couple of pretty poor landings. Afternoon Ed and I rode around in his "Dynamiter". School, CPT 7 to 9. Started subject of Meteorology, OK. Then to Don's house where the "Brawl" was in session. Talked and ate heartily. Bed at 12:00

November 11, 1940 Monday Failed to make my 8:00 class this morning, because my car would not start. Slept and attended the parade later in the morning, Armistice Day. Afternoon Dick and I flew one hour dual. Today did everything in the book, spins, stalls 8's, etc. Slept this afternoon. Evening CPT class in Meteorology. Bed early, awfully tired.

November 14, 1940 Thursday Flying in the afternoon, 1 to 3:30. Did spot landings, 180 and 360 degrees. Ed and I ran around together a bit tonite after my CPT class. Bed 12:00

This was the last entry. Bill took his solo cross-country trip to Stevensville and returned on November 30, 1940.

Bill's personal diary entries for 1939 and 1940 give additional insight into his activities and his thoughts.

As mentioned in the Introduction, the "Brawl" was a lively group of Bill's friends and as it evolved it welcomed other friends and girls depending upon the occasion and the location of each event. In fact, the mothers of the main group of guys would socialize for an afternoon card game, refreshments and to share the latest news from their sons in the service. They were known as the "Brawl Mothers", but didn't advertise this or make the society page in the local paper.

The guys even had their own pet sayings or vocabulary such as "Amakil"—"You go first" or "Thanks no, I have some" this would depend on the circumstances. "Drawers"—An exclamation of incredulity or just an exclamation. "Pooperstine"—An exclamation of digust. "Store clothes"—Usually aimed at anyone daring to don a clean shirt but carrying more meaning when applied to one dressed up. "Crone"—practically anyone past 16 or older than the fellers. "Dynamiter"—a Model A body boasting of V-8 guts. "Bloated Bond Holder"—Anyone with more than average wealth enters this category.

Ed's dad drew clever cartoon figures of most of the guys and these were presented at one of the "Brawls".

**The "Brawl Mothers", from L to R,
Mrs. Thieme, Halm, Schottelkorb, Blanchette, Stephenson, Barrett and Luedke**

Cliff Stephenson

April 17, 1939 Up at 6 am. Made a map. A typical Monday, which means a big day. ROTC,

Growing up in Western Montana

our Company G, won the title as the best for the second time. Being a number one man I am a scout. Hurried through work and then went to Ed's for a meeting to ponder the brawl for Chuck's birthday. We were going to the Nine Pipes Refuge cabin as we did last year for Cliff, but Chuck has to work.

May 23, 1939 Well today is the brawl. Picked up Merl, Brad and Cliff and we left at 1:00 PM; drove to the Franklin Ranger Station, up the Rattlesnake valley. We found a swell lean-to and made a good hot fire in front of it. When the other fellows showed up we ate, hot dogs, Pepsi Cola and then roasted marshmallows. Sure good!! Chuck was sure surprised. Played baseball awhile but was stopped by rain. So we ate some more. Around 5 Fred, Merl and Cliff left to fix up Ed's house for the rest of the brawl. We all came at 6 and ate again. The scrapbook and album was presented. Chuck did magic tricks. Bed at 11:00.

Ed Halm

December 30, 1939 Saturday, worked at the store. Afterwards went over to Ed's to put up decorations. All of the fellows were there. Fixed bows on the walls and doorways. Hung silver pinecones and the lighting was perfect.

December 31, 1939 Sunday, worked hard at the Merc in the morning. At 6:30 PM George Keller and Fred picked up their dates. They arrived at 7:00, all the guys and the girls were there. Swell eats, presents, candy, dancing, ping-pong, and viewed the Brawl Book. Welcomed the New Year in by "slewing", spinning around on the ice on Higgins Avenue. Name of the brawl was, "Brawl De Los Fresco Ano". I had to leave at 2:00 AM to do my night watch job at the Merc.

February 13, 1940 Went to Ed's in the evening for a brawl business meeting. Had a swell time and we discussed a trip to Bozeman. Sorted negatives, talked aviation, told jokes, had refreshments of root beer, waffles, apples, and ice cream. I had a perfect time and outdid myself. Bed 2:00 AM.

Bill Schottelkorb

April 9, 1940 This evening I went to Cliff's for a brawl meeting. Had a good time. We flashed pictures on the wall, planned another brawl and Don gave a talk on radios. Good eats were served and then more talk. Home and bed by midnight.

November 18, 1939 Saturday Took care of personal items then worked at the Merc parking lot until 5:30 PM. Merl Brunsvold stopped by at 8 and we went to North Hall and picked up

Lucille and Anne. Went to the Sunshine Club and were joined by Chuck and Marie and Don and Peggy. Eight of us took our V-8 sedan and went to a dance at Arlee. Back at 12:15. Sat in the hall with the girls until 12:30. Then refreshments for the rest at Blackies, (a popular hamburger place on North Higgins Avenue). Bed at 2:00.

Bud Blanchette

December 1, 1939 Friday At 5 I picked up Merl and we met our dates at their dorm. He took Lucille Adamison and Louise Tommas of

A "Brawl" picnic

Roundup was mine. We went to Halm's and the gals started to get things ready. I then picked up

Chuck and Marie Brown and Ed brought Marie Cherry. The girls did pretty well cooking deer "venison" steak. Ate supper at 7, and it was very nice. Chuck went to the Wilma Theatre to handle Quiz Nite and we listened to it on the radio, and later Chuck entertained us with his magic tricks. Later all eight of us went for a ride in the V-8. Had a very enjoyable evening. Bed at 1:00.

April 21, 1940 Sunday Up at 7 and worked at the Merc until 9. Came home and got ready for a picnic. Many details and bad weather. At 12:30, Fred and I picked up Ruth Plank of Chester and Carmen Jordan. We went to Gold Creek in my car. Had to retrace and made a nice camp lower down. Soon the others joined us. Ed made 2 trips in the "Dynamiter 8". Swell time, played baseball, cooked wieners, had other goodies and sang songs. My bunch left at 9:15 and got in at 10. Bed at 10:30, then night watch at 12.

March 28, 1939 Got up at 4:30 am to help Bob deliver the Missoulian as he was sick. Only had one class today so I slept and worked around the house.

Brawl Poster

April 16, 1939 Sunday Finished my work at the Merc in one hour. Then Dad and I worked on my brakes. They are nearly done but had trouble with the emergency brake. At 1 PM we went to Stevensville to visit Great Grandmother Hooper. She is awfully thin. She likes Bob and me so much. Death is a blessing, not a curse.

April 23, 1939 Sunday Worked 4 hours at the Merc. Mopped floors in the dry goods, men's and college shop. At 2:15, Bud, Cliff and I went to Evaro in my "A". We took a steep road to a lookout that is past town about 4 miles, then took some pictures. Home by six then took the folks for a short ride up the Blackfoot Canyon. Mother picked flowers. In the evening I worked around the house. Bed at 10.

Blackfoot picnic

May 28, 1939 Sunday Did some work at the Merc in the morning, then the Halms and the Schottelkorbs went up the Blackfoot for a family picnic, Merl Brunsvold also went. We played baseball. The two dogs, Tippy and Shep, had a great time. Ed and Merl looked for flowers and called them by their scientific names. (Both were majoring in Forestry at the university.) At home I wrote a 700-word paper for English.

June 16, 1939 Friday Mother left for the Swan River country with the Halms this morning. Fishing!

June 22, 1939 Sunday Went over to Ed's to see him off for Haugan for the summer. He took his "A". Departures are always kind of sad. Dad calcimined (painted) the front bedroom. At 5 our family went to the Roxy and saw "Alexander's Ragtime Band" and "The Jones Family". Then we had our super at Blackie's. Ice cream and fireplace fire at home.

On the Cedar Creek divide

July 4, 1939 Holiday The folks, Shep, Bob and I took a trip in the V-8 to Superior then up Cedar Creek and over the mountain to Trout Creek and then back home. Beautiful country, old mining

Chuck at Roundtop lookout with a road sign that Ed made

district. At one place we encountered 3 men and a girl who had a swell little placer mine in a gulch. They were working but showed us around. 178 miles. Bed early.

November 26, 1939 Sunday Worked at the store 8-12. Fixed flat on V-8. Cleaned up garage. Dad and I put the new clutch plate and transmission back in my car. Folks went to the show. Talked to Bob about the future, studied and listened to the radio. Bed 10:00.

**Ed's summer home at Roundtop Lookout
In the Lochsa, North Idaho**

June 23, 1940 Sunday Came home from the night shift and went to Rock Creek. Merl, Glenn and Ruth rode with me. Folks rode in Halm's car. Went to Dalles Creek camp ground, slept a little and then took a hike with Merl. Swell meal. Ruth and I left for home at 2 and got back to town at 3. Slept an hour and took the night watch shift until 12. Worked my fool head off as usual doing the vacuuming, but had a satisfied feeling of work well done when finished.

July 4, 1940 4th of July Home from night watch at 8:00 am, then the family went to Stevensville for the Creamery Picnic Celebration. Picnic tables on lawn at Great Grandparents place.

Many relatives and lots of food as well as watermelon and ice cream. Slept 1:30 to 6:30. Home at 9 and to bed at 9:30 and the night watch at 12.

February 19, 1939 Sunday Up at 8. Good breakfast and to work at 9. Had to wait for Jones. I wonder if I will ever have the watchman job? We waxed accessory dept and front office, and then we cleaned the tops of the display cases. That is one more buck, $1.00. Rested in the afternoon and then discussed the advantages of coupes and roadsters with Bob's friend Ken Rigby. Studied in the evening.

June 21, 1939 Wednesday Mr. Keith told me that I could probably have the night watchman job while Bob Hamilton and Logan are on their vacations. In the evening Cliff, Bits, Jim McCray and I towed Jim's old "T" over to Halm's with my "A". We then took the body and fenders off that evening.

September 24, 1939 On Sunday C. H. McLeod called at 12 and we drove to Polson. We had a very good chicken dinner at the hotel. On the way back we stopped at the grain elevators at Ronan and Charlo. (They were owned by the Missoula Mercantile) At Charlo Mr. McLeod talked to Mr. Wamsley and at St Ignatius we visited at the George Shepard place. A happy family, seven swell kids and they get to ride horses at their nice place near the mountains. I wouldn't mind a place like that myself, sometime, someday.

September 28, 1939 Thursday Did my work early and then met Cliff at 9 for some work in the warehouse. Finished at noon after sweeping enough dust into our lungs to give everyone consumption. At 1:30 we took a shower at school. Later we went downtown with Bud Blanchette and had a milkshake, then to the Merc to get our wage vouchers. Mine 33 hours @ $ .40 per hour equaling $14.06. Evening I had the night watch job until 12. Bob did the vacuum work.

Growing up in Western Montana

December 14, 1939 Thursday Last Spanish reading class with the student teacher, Mr. Cadet. He is a nice fellow. Terribly bashful for a teacher though. If he can, I can (make it). Spent and hour cleaning both cars. Collected money from Keith and made arrangements not to work Christmas vacation. In one and a half months I have made $ 68.00 and spent $ 67.00. Polished shoes. Studied. Bed.

June 9, 1940 Sunday Up at 8:00. Drove C. H. to Seeley Lake. Cliff was already up there. They had dinner for 30 people, pitched horseshoes and did a great deal of laughing. I teased Alice about the war and she got mad. Cliff, Bud and I had great discussions. Saw my old Model T. When I arrived home I slept until 12, then got up for the night watch shift.

On mountain roads

January 17, 1939 Tuesday, 20 degrees below zero last night and I have a cold. Didn't get much out of Economics today. In Geology we had a gem stone test, where we had to identify 40 stones and crystals. Rotten! No Humanities test, Thank God! Slept most of the afternoon.

February 27, 1939 Monday Studied Economics in the library 9-10 am, also at noon and 3-6 PM, then again from 7 to 9:30. Bob did my work for me at the Merc. It is bad to do this much studying, better if you do it as you go along.

March 27, 1939 Monday No gym today. Put on my Army ROTC uniform and went to school at 3. Spent 2 hours getting organized, marching and drilling. We then had a parade from 5-6. It was a little sloppy but I did all right though and that makes me feel good. I believe that I could be an officer.

April 27, 1939 Studied some this morning then out to the airport to watch 3 Army planes come in. The Colonel overshot the field the first time. They are here to examine recruits for the Army Aviation Cadet Program.

May 31, 1939 Wednesday Last day in Geography, Dr. Rowe talked about Hot Springs. He was very humorous today. I meant to make some maps but as usual I didn't get it done. The reason being, I rode around with the fellows and had a Peps.

August 31, 1939 Today Germany actually invaded Poland. Although war has not been declared, England and France are sure to be mixed up in it soon.

September 3, 1939 Sunday After doing my work at the Merc I took Chuck, Bud and Bob out to the Tex Rankin Airshow at the new airport west of town. We got in for nothing by taking a long hike through the "badlands of British Guiana". One fellow really put a Piper Cub through its paces, down gullies, close to the ground, and landing on one wheel. Tex Rankin did all this and more.

16 October 1939 Up at 7:15 am, to school. Studied 2 hours on Economics in the morning. Two Army planes banked low over the campus in perfect formation. I was thrilled.

January 17, 1940 Wednesday School 8-12. A blizzard took the city this morning, dropping the temperature to 10 degrees. Spanish, small class, and I read a large portion in both English and Spanish, but no matter I've got Ada Nopper of

Growing up in Western Montana

White Sulphur Springs to keep me interested in life.

March 8, 1940 Friday Last day of winter quarter. Economics 8-9. Studied and read Natural Science magazine till 10. Then Humanities, music lecture till 11 with Professor John Lester, he was quite good. Last Spanish on imperative at 2:00. Ada Nopper was sure dolled up cute. Ed, Fred and I rode around in the V-8 until 6:00. Bob did my vacuuming work at the Merc. I studied and read "Popular Aviation" until 12 midnight.

March 20, 1940 Wednesday School at 8:30. Got my grades, 2 C's and a B, saved the day. Finally got registered. Bennett is my advisor. Went to Spanish, got a 90 in the final. Taking 4 subjects now, 2 histories.

April 10, 1940 Wednesday (Mike) Mansfield spent all of History Class on the present world conflict. Yesterday, Germany took over Norway and Denmark. Sleeply and inattentive in my afternoon class. Later went to the airport and saw my first close up of a Luscombe. Swell! 6-8 did my work at the Merc., and then I read my new "Popular Aviation" magazine. Personal and study, bed 10:30.

May 26, 1939 Friday Today we finished our required 2 years of Physical Education. At baseball, on my last turn to bat I struck out. In the afternoon I made one more trip to the airport, then played tennis with Bud, Cliff and Fred. It is a great game and I would like to be more proficient at it.

June 27, 1939 Tuesday My 1st day of vacation in a long time. It certainly doesn't pay to work too much; you get in a rut. Worked on the model "T" bug. Afternoon Cliff, Bits, Bob, Shep and I took the "A" to Schley and Saddle Mountain lookouts. "A" pulled wonderfully. The lookout is the steel tower type. Had an adventure with a Woodchuck. Evening worked on the "T".

May 30, 1940 Memorial Day After much quibbling Fred, Chuck, Bud, Cliff and I started for Slide Rock Lookout up Rock Creek. Long pull in low gear. Saw 2 mountain Goats. Had a perfectly swell time. Bed 10.

June 29, 1940 Saturday Slept late, until 10. Ed came home from Haugan and then we rode around until noon. Ed and I went swimming in the river by the Buckhouse Bridge. Enjoyed it greatly and it was just like we used to do in the good old days. In the evening Ed, Don and I ate supper on Halm's lawn. We then rode around in the "Dynamiter" and went to the Wilma and saw two good shows. One was "Ghost Breakers" with Bob Hope. Out in time to go on the night watch shift at 12.

Swimming at the Buckhouse Bridge

Bill enrolled for the winter quarter, 1941, at the university and upon completion in mid March he drove to Hill Field in Ogden, Utah to take his Aviation Cadet physical examination. Ed was already in training in California and Bill left for Oxnard, California on April 28th for Primary Flight School. Some of his other friends were about to enter the military service also as the armed forces were expanding as rapidly as training facilities were ready. Don left a few weeks later for the Army Air Corps Primary School at King City, California.

Growing up in Western Montana

At the university, spring 1941, shortly before leaving for active duty with the armed services in World War II.
L to R, Cliff Stephenson, Don Tomlinson, Bill Schottelkorb, Bud Blanchette
Charles Luedke and Fred Barrett

Shep

Schottelkorb family, Bob, Bill, Mother and Dad, 1937
Bill had just graduated from high school

Primary Flight Training

Bill left Missoula by train for Oxnard, California to begin his pilot's training. His first letter was written after he arrived there.

From the Air Corps Training Detachment, Oxnard, California, May 5, 1941: When we arrived in Oxnard we had to stay in a hotel overnight, as it was too late to get a bed in the barracks. We had good meals on the train but exceeded our allowance of $1.00 per day. We arrived in Oakland Wednesday morning at 8:30, too late to catch the train south. This meant that we had to spend three hours in San Francisco. All we had time for was a walk down to Market Street. We left at noon on the Southern Pacific Streamliner, this is a real train and frequently travels at 75 MPH. Twice we saw new Army Camps, which will house 20,000 soldiers per camp. You know that's about the same population as Missoula. The train made four stops on the way to Los Angeles. We got off in Santa Barbara and took a Greyhound bus to El Rio. Here we called the school at Oxnard and they sent a 41 Ford station wagon for us.

Primary Flight Training Facility

The upper-class men really gave us the works when we first arrived. It seemed awful at first but now doesn't seem bad. We had a hard first two days, marching two three hours periods a day, and I do mean marching. They of course want us to be officers and know how to march and lead. I don't mind marching but would rather be doing other things.

The barracks are very new and the rooms aren't completely finished yet. The whole camp is laid out in a circle. Everything is new and we are the very first to use the facilities. The grounds are just dirt yet, but in a few weeks they will have in the concrete walks and grass will be planted. Our cabins are modern little houses with four rooms in each one. There are two fellows assigned to a room and we share a bathroom with the fellows from another room. The walls are finished with Pine paneling.

Tommy Morris's platoon in front of barracks

Our rooms have twin beds and nice roomy closets that have drawers built into them. We have lamps and one chair. We're to receive a desk and another chair, this is the reason I haven't gotten a letter off to you. The bathroom has a shower, toilet and two washbowls. Boy! Our rooms have to be perfect. It's really hard to get the bed made to their high standards. Corners have to be square with a 45 degree fold and not a wrinkle anywhere on it. They move their hands up and down the blanket and if a wrinkle develops, you get a demerit. What I mean, it really has to be perfect.

Just got back from Sunday dinner. The large dining hall contains 40 tables, with 8 settings each. The grub is wonderful, for dinner we had ham, fruit salad, soup, baked potatoes, asparagus, gravy, milk, tea, and two kinds of bread, ice cream and cake. Everyday it's just loads of the best food and lots of vegetables.

Primary Flight Training

From a letter home dated May 10, 1941: Sure was glad to receive your letter. It's the first I've received since arriving here. I also received the War Department's letter; wanting me to consider becoming a flying cadet due to my **excellent record** in the CPT. How's that?

PT-17 In Flight

Well I soloed Friday as I thought I would. Did this at 2 hours and 44 minutes, after my instructor recommended me for check ride with the Head Flight Instructor. I had a 30 minute check ride with him. We did spins, stalls, climbing turns, landings etc. When we got back he said I was OK to solo. I went around the field twice with my instructor, and then he said, "Okay go ahead and make me three good landings". I did all right. It's some fun handling this heavy equipment. When you open up that 220 horsepower engine you really know that something is under the hood. We hold it wide open to 100 feet then cut down to half throttle, level off, look back to see that nobody is close, then throw it over on the side and make a level turn, next a steep climb to 3,000 feet. Everything is regulated, we can't do this or that. Every moment we're in the air we're working hard. I'm not worried about flying because I'm sure I can do it all right. I think that I'm going to have a tough time with ground school. It's not easy and I'm having a tough time with Math. Feel like I'm awfully weak in Algebra also.

You asked if I like my new life down here. My answer; not so well. Everything is entirely new and different from home and I'm having a heck of a time getting used to it. Inspections, drills and regulations aren't to my liking. Right now I'm in for the weekend because I got seven demerits for the week. We have an inspection everyday and almost everybody gets demerits, usually for not having some part of their room perfect. The inspectors dish out the demerits two at a time. If you end up with more than five you are restricted to the base all weekend. If just the slightest thing is out of order, they rashly say cupboard mussed, two demerits and you just have to take it. One time things will pass, the next time they don't. Seems to be a whim of the inspector who doesn't

Landing the PT-17

Primary Flight Training

weigh his words very heavy. If you receive more than nine demerits you have to march them off, out on the ramp, at one per hour. This is Saturday evening and there are some 25 of us confined to the post for the weekend. Also out on the ramp there's about 4 men pacing up and down, as they have been for the last three hours. This all might be a joke to some but it's not to me. The only way I can justify all of this is that they want to see if we can survive under pressure.

Cadets at Attention

About our daily schedule. Up at exactly 5:00 AM, which is the time the sun is coming up. The bugle sounds at 5:30 AM but we need to be up early to work on our bed and other things. At 6:40 AM we run two blocks to a field and have 15 minutes of doing sitting up exercises. **NOW'S** the best time of the morning, breakfast. Weak from lack of food we stand in line to get our grub. After breakfast we go back to our room where we get another 15 minutes to get it into shape, this isn't half enough time of course. At 6:45 AM we assemble and march to the flight line. Here one student and instructor fly the planes over to the auxiliary field while the rest ride over in the bus. We're on the flight line until noon. Another rest while we have lunch, then ground school until 4:00 PM. We don't even have enough time to brush our teeth between lunch and time for school, even if we did we couldn't use the washbowls or toilets because they've been cleaned for inspection.

About 4:00 PM they figure we need more exercise, so we march an hour or so. However they do give us 10 minutes to prepare for dinner. When dinner is over we prepare for inspection. We work hard on our beds and usually get a couple of demerits anyway. Now it's about 8:00 PM and we figure we can sit down and relax a moment, but no, we hear the upper-classmen coming around. They make us come to attention, wipe out all smiles and throw them on the floor, pick them up by the left hind leg and put them in the toilet then flush them away. Finally about 9:00 PM we're really on our own. However we have to frantically shave, shower and try to get letters written. Lights out at 9:30 PM and we're ready for bed as we're completely worn out. Of course everything isn't as bad as I describe as there are some awfully funny things happening and we do have some fun.

Look at that Determination

Primary Flight Training

I really miss home and all that it stands for. Here we don't have a car to drive, have to walk to town, no dog to pet, just the hard, cursing work-a-day life without any of the pleasures and little joys of home.

Bill had quite an interest in cars and mechanics as you have seen and will see more as we go through his letters.

Tell Bob to write and let me know how the **"Dynamiter"** has been performing.

From a letter from Bob, Dated May 15, 1941: Dear Bill, We received your letter this morning, Thursday and we liked it and the picture very much. You should get your oxfords tomorrow, I hope. Well today is the start of a trackmeet and Mother is going this afternoon with Mrs. Karlberer. I will probably won't go except to march in the parade, Friday, as I am going to work for Mr. Rice. Friday and Saturday Greg Rice is going to run. (No relation to the above Mr. Rice). Shep is now in the kitchen watching

Shep waiting for a Cookie

Mother make cookies. I don't think he has realized you are gone but several times he has gone into the bedroom and looked to see if you were in bed. Sure is cute! The other day I got your enlargements at Hollyoaks. There were two of them and they both seemed pretty good. I haven't seen your friends very much, however I did see Bud the other day and told him about your most recent letter (s). He said that he had received one from you.

Last Sunday morning I mowed Walter McLeod's lawn as Paul was ill. That afternoon I drove C. H. up to Florence in his 38 Ford. Walter and Mrs. McLeod had gone up in the morning to Hobblitt's and had gone horse back riding with them. We all ate dinner outside. Mrs. McLeod's little dog was there too, he is awfully cute. Mr. and Mrs. Mcleod couldn't believe that you had left so I told them you had left sooner than you expected. C. H. asked me how I would like to go to Chicago, New York, etc. this summer. You know the old gag. However it would be nice.

At the Merc they put in linoleum on the 2nd floor, by the elevator, but they didn't replace the rug with linoleum as I had hoped. Send Jones a letter sometime.

A few nights ago I was up at Blackie's with Ken and John P. in the **"Dynamiter"**. We met a fellow we knew there who owns a 36 Plymouth. He saw the **"Dynamiter"** and in a cocky manner said he remembered when he had an "A". We told him that we could leave him and he was willing to bet $10.00, we couldn't. Well, needless to say, he was "larned". Next day when he saw Ken, he wondered if that was an ordinary "A"! About all I've done to it is to paint the rear bumper supports and fix the dash by gluing a Ford for 40 sign and a Ford 1903-33 coin over the holes. I also put an aluminum plate over the bottom of each front panel, by the feet. This is where it gets the hardest use. Pretty soon I'm going to fix the brakes, put on shocks and fix the rear spring. All of this takes time and money.

Well I hope you do alright, Bill. P.S. There is an article and advertisement in the latest "Flying and Popular Aviation" about the Cal-Aero Schools.

From a letter home dated May 18, 1941: We're in the hole quite a bit already. We've just received our new uniforms and they look pretty

Primary Flight Training

swell even if they're awfully cheap for what they cost. I got two pairs of pants for $6.50 each, they're worth about $4.50. A jacket that was $4.45 and it's pretty light. The flight hat and three shirts bring the total up to about $25.00. I've also taken out $10,000 worth of Government Insurance. This will take effect on the 1st of June. It runs $6.50 per month, which is more than I can afford. It's a good bargain and the Captain thought we should have it. Once you start it you can't raise the benefit but it can be lowered. I thought for a few months during training that I should have it. If I'm killed in an accident you will receive $12,000, but you know that I'm not figuring on that.

Dress Blues

Haircuts, which are another racket here, need to be had once a week, as we have to wear our hair short. There are four barbers on the post. I had a hair treatment and shampoo and was charged $1.40. We also have to buy our books at the Post Exchange and they run $2.25 each. We also have a $.60 cleaning bill every week. I figure that I will clear about $40.00 this month and will be able to pay some of my other bills.

I was confined to the post for the weekend, because I flunked a Math examination, I only got a 57 in it. It was mostly a lot of questions doing with Algebra. I haven't had this for about six or seven years. We're allowed to flunk a couple of courses in Ground School. I will be done with the Math portion in a couple of weeks.

Ready for Ground School

I've gone to church twice since arriving here. I did this, as it's the only way we can get open post if we're confined. I went to the Methodist Church.

Bob--would you get from my big box in the basement, one group of CPT notes and one air navigation book and send them to me? I will be able to use them here.

From a letter to Bob dated May 31, 1941:
Yesterday was Memorial Day and a holiday for us. We were given open post from 7:00 Thursday evening and then on Friday afternoon we all went down to the beach at Point Hueneme. Spent the afternoon swimming and resting on the beach. My back is quite red today, but not too bad. The beach is five miles from the post but it's easy for

Primary Flight Training

us cadets to hitch a ride. We did ride out with another cadet who has a 39 Ford convertible.

I'm sure looking forward to the day when I can get a car. For me it's terrible to be without one. If I had one at least I could get around and look the country over. Quite a few of the cadets do have their own cars already. The cars range all the way from 29 Chevy sedans to new De Sota coupes. Would you let me know what the speedometer readings on both cars are now? When I left the V-8 had 40,750 miles, and the "**Dynamiter**" had 48,157. Hopefully you've gotten brakes on it by now.

Today was Saturday and payday!! What a mess!! 300 fellows to get paid. This is the way they conduct payday, the officers, with guns on their hips come out with the money, the cadets march up and as their name is called, his money is put before him and then he continues on down the line paying all his bills. When I stepped up to the first table, $144.70 was laid before me, I felt rich for a moment but then it started to go. $6.60 for insurance, $52.00 for board and room, $25.00 for uniforms, cleaning bill was $4.00, $4.00 for haircuts and $3.00 for a Pilot's LogBook. When I was finished I still had $51.00 for myself, which I thought was pretty good. My roommate had about $25.00 from which he owed $15.00 for income tax and $5.00 to me. He ended up with about $2.00 to last him the rest of the month.

There are two little dogs here, which hang around the barracks all the time. They wait for the boys to bring them food from the mess hall. They follow us everywhere we go, marching, flying, or when we exercise. The other day one of them got hit out on the highway and of course we thought he was killed but he got up and ran off and is still alive, however he has been looking might downcast. Today at noon a dogcatcher came to get him because he didn't have a license. When he picked up the dog and started to walk off, all the boys started crowding around objecting. Hardly before a minute had gone by, the fellows had taken up a collection and bought him a license.

The Stearman Cockpit

At the present I have 24 hours and 39 minutes in the air. This is more than anyone else in my flight of 40 fellows. This last Monday I went up for a 20 hour progress check. The instructor or Flight Commander, as I should say, was all smiles. Of course that doesn't mean much except that I'm doing okay, right now anyway. Any day a guy could get kicked out for a thousand different things, but about this, I'm not worried, especially on the flying end.

View from the Back Cocpit

The type of plane we are flying is the Stearman PT-17. It has 220 horsepower and much like the Waco in Missoula but much larger. I now can do Chandelles, Lazy Eight's, etc. These require real flying skill and are far from easy. A chandelle is

Primary Flight Training

a climbing turn which starts in a dive at 110 MPH and ends up going in the other direction, with barely flying speed, 55 MPH, and 250 feet of altitude is gained doing this. The most violent maneuver I've done to date is the Reverse-Power Spin, in which the airplane is stalled in full cruising position, 1750 RPM. A rapid two turn spin one way occurs and then you apply full opposite rudder with the stick held back, Bang! Quick as a flash there's a complete kick over to the other side and the plane does two turns the other way so fast it makes your head swim. We start this at 4,000 feet and end up at 2,000 feet a few seconds later.

Air traffic down here is terrible, we have three fields and it's sure tough trying to land along with 25 other planes. All are buzzing around the pattern at 500 feet and at 1750 RPM. The other day I was cut out four times by a powered glider, a Cub. There's usually bad cross winds, which require you to use a great deal of skill when landing. Several of the boys have ground looped.

Drilling Cadets

Instructor Scott and Cadets

Part of the letter of June 7, 1941 was destroyed: I certainly wish that I could be home for a few days to enjoy a visit with everybody, but in this hard working game the only answer is to hit the ball every day.

I'm an upper-classman now and all the new boys address me as Sir. It's a funny feeling to boss a bunch of men, however it doesn't bother me as much as I thought it would. Tonight for instance, I was the head of one table in the dining room, with seven lower class boys under my direction. When they came to the table they had to stand behind their chairs at perfect attention. If they cracked a smile, I said, "what's so funny Mister?" "Wipe it off". At the command, "seats", we all sat down, then I had to see to it that the boys all used good table manners and that they said please. Other than this, I treated them nicely. They're so timid and scared, I feel sorry for them but I went through it myself, not so long ago. When each man finished his meal, he looked at me and said, "Sir, may I be excused?" If it were all right with me, I'd excuse him, otherwise I would tell him to remain seated.

Thursday and Friday, was spent drilling the men, and I had my share of leading, teaching and commanding. I had a detail of eight men under my command and two other upper-classmen for assistants. We spent two hours drilling and did a pretty fair job of it. However the men still need a lot more drilling.

As to flying, we're really making progress. I have nearly 32 hours now and thus am over half done.

Primary Flight Training

Next week we start aerobatics and we will be doing loops, snap rolls, slow rolls and much more. Sometimes I feel like I'm not doing well but always the instructor gives signs to indicate that I am. My instructor, for the first five weeks has been Mr. Murray, who is also a professional crop duster. He really knows his flying. I've found out I'm going to be transferred to a

Instructor Scott

Mr. Scott as my instructor. Mr. Murray told me that he has had a lot of trouble because he had gotten a bad bunch of students. He told me that I was being transferred to him as I was a good student and this would make it a little easier for him. This of course made me feel like I wasn't doing so badly. Also I was the first man in our flight to go up for an Army check ride. Mr. Murray said that the Flight Commander and he decided to let me do the first ride as I do so well. He said doing this would keep them from beefing as much as they would if the first turned out to be

a poor one. I know that I can't fly anywhere like I should be able to. When I did ride with the Army man, I was lucky in choosing the time to make the best landing I'd ever made. He looked back and said, "Boy, that's what you call really greasing it in".

Believe that I could be doing a lot better in Ground School. This will probably be the hardest thing for me, all the way through training. Some guys learn things without half trying. I will probably end up being a dumb pursuit pilot, who hasn't got enough brains to fly or navigate a bomber. Oh Well! Every man to his own line. When it's Trigonometry, the boy beside me raises his hand to answer. When it's engines, he looks dumb-founded and asks if the piston is "attached to the big end of the connecting rod?" The teacher also thought a Ford V-8 used a master rod and a linking rod, rather than mounting side by side on the crankshaft.

Well seven of us Montana boys came down here, and only four are left. My roommate, Duane Chaffin, flunked out Friday. Wes Hanson also flunked out, as did Al Swingle of Bozeman. I think that the rest of us will make it.

Bill by this time was finally able to leave the post and visited with his relatives and friends around California.

From a letter dated June 19, 1941: Starting Monday at noon, I was the Officer of the Day, for the post. This lasted until noon on Tuesday. The Cadet Officer of the Day is ranking the cadet on the post for that day and has many responsibilities to cope with. A few are, being responsible for all formations, reports, bed checks and demerits. You have a cadet from a lower class acting as your assistant and he does all the typing. It was hard work but I got through it in fine shape.

Since I've changed instructors, my flying has been going downhill. I passed my final Army check ride last week. So maybe I will make it to

Primary Flight Training

the next school all right. This week we are doing slow rolls. This is where you hang upside down on just the safety belt, with nothing between you and the ground, 4,000 feet below. It takes a lot of concentration not to hang on but to just relax and fly. A loop is easy and a lot of fun to do. In one maneuver we dive at 160 MPH, pull up on our back and roll out to normal position, some fun. Well I now have 52 hours and just have 8 to go.

Yesterday, Saturday, Cliff drove down and spent the weekend with me. Today we saw much of the surrounding country that I've wanted to see. We ate dinner in Ventura and later went swimming at the beach. Time went by so fast that I hardly realized that it was time for Cliff to leave. On the 4th, Don and Ed are planning on coming down to visit. We have just learned that we're going to Bakersfield for Basic Training.

The 7 Montana boys, Wes Hanson, Great Falls, Bob Brookings, Livingston, Bob Bixby, Logan, Duane Chaffin, Great Falls, Jack Clapper, Billings, Bill, Al Swingle, Bozeman

From a letter dated July 7, 1941: Well we've just finished a three day holiday and I can't say that I enjoyed it, although I did have a little fun. Went to town with my roommate, Jack Clapper. Of course there was nothing to do for a guy with my outlook on life but I did the best that I could. Had two drinks and then bought a **"Life"** and went home. Jack and I hitchhiked to Santa Barbara, Friday morning and we were lucky enough to get a ride straight through. When we got there we met Don Tomlinson and a friend of Jack's, both are in training at King City, California. We spent until Sunday at noon there. We did everything from swimming at the beach to going to shows and walking around. I haven't walked around that much in my life. A person doesn't realize how nice a car is until they get in my position. A car saves you money on every move. I would rather put my money into something substantial like a car than waste it. The first chance I get I'm going to get one. I may have to wait a couple of months yet but I'm saving to that end. Well anyway, Don and I had a short but interesting visit. Ed was supposed to come but couldn't. This was much to my regret.

I only have 35 more minutes of flying time to do and I'm done with that part of my training. We will probably be leaving here for Bakersfield next Saturday. Might possibly end up being somewhere else.

Certainly wish that Bob would write and let me know how the car is getting along. I sorely miss it. Sometimes I think this is a great life and other times, I wonder if it's all worth doing. A real enjoyment, such as a trip up the Blackfoot for a day would really be nice for me.

From a letter by Bob on July 27, 1941: Lately I've been spending quite a bit on the **"Dynamiter"**. Before the 4th I drove to Cayuse lookout. The **"Dynamiter"** got very hot and spewed water on the whole trip, so I decided to

Primary Flight Training

get a new radiator. It now has 48,753 miles on it. I've only put about 600 miles on it since you left. Dad got a 32 V-8 used radiator from Bell's. He had to solder it and install different necks on it. Had considerable trouble getting it to fit. Did get it installed and painted. Also did a lot of other things to it, such as a new motor mounts, choke, road light, fuel pump and covered the rumble seat with new material. Will be sending you a picture of it soon.

Cadets all ready to fly

Playing Horseshoes at the Cal-Aero Picnic

Out on the taxi-way

Nine in State Are Appointed Flying Cadets

Unusually Large Group at One Time; One Missoula Man Included.

Nine Montana men have received appointments as flying cadets in the U. S. Army air corps, and will start training early next month, it was announced at the headquarters of the Army's Montana recruiting district Saturday.

The nine men, one of the largest single groups called at one time, are William F. Schottelkorb, 315 Blaine street, Missoula; Duane L. Chaffin, Bozeman; George R. Brooking, Livingston; Malcolm H. Haas, Danvers; Carrol J. Ward, Butte; Alfred W. Swingle, Bozeman; Robert H. Bixby, Nye; John W. Hanson, Great Falls, and John W. Clapper, Billings.

Seven of the appointees had reported at the recruiting headquarters here Saturday, and the remaining two were scheduled to arrive Monday to be enlisted. Eight of the men are to go to a private flying school at Oxnard, Cal., and one to Santa Maria, Cal., for preliminary flight and ground training.

All were scheduled to be enlisted and sent to their stations by May 30.

Basic Flight Training

Bill left Oxnard on Saturday, July 12, on his way to Bakersfield, California where he was to continue with his cadet training. He rode into San Jose with some of the other cadets and then visited until Monday with relatives. He met the rest of the group in Oakland, Monday evening at 6:30. He would now be stationed at the Air Corps Detachment, Camp Wasco, Wasco, California for another phase of training.

From a letter dated July 16, 1941: What a mess. It is only under the worst circumstances that I write this so bear with me please.

We left Oxnard, Saturday July 12, at 1:00. I and 3 other cadets went to San Jose via a "32" Nash. We made good time except for two blowouts and arrived in San Jose at 10:00 that night. Well I had already agreed to meet Ed and had no trouble finding him. We visited and looked around town, finally retiring in a hotel at 4:00 AM. Next day we got up late, had breakfast and went to Redwood City. I called up the folks but they weren't home so we went to Frisco and met a friend of Ed's.

We didn't do much of anything, except go out for supper at a nice restaurant. This other kid had gone the way of all cadets and had a new Chevy coupe. We drove out to Redwood City and up to the folk's place. There was a note on the front door saying they had gone away for the weekend. Back to the city and to bed in a hotel. Ed had to leave the next morning so I went out to Redwood again by bus. Pat and the kids came down and picked me up at the depot. They'd been down to Big Sur for a few days. I spent the day there and had a nice visit with Pat. At 4:00, Monday, Pat and I left for Frisco where we met Dinty. They took me out to supper and then over to Oakland where I had to meet the boys at 6:30 PM.

We drove until 2:00 AM to make it to Bakersfield. We were delayed by blowouts, etc. In Bakersfield we stayed at a very nice motor court, upon whose paper I'm writing this letter. All of this, hotels, travel, meals, etc. made me use up all my money $23.00. Ed was broke too, everyone in this game is always broke. So if Bob would be kind enough to lend me a couple of five dollar bills, I can modestly last until the end of the month. Be sure and give my address to everyone at home and tell them I probably won't be able to do much writing for awhile.

Bill on r and cadets in front of their tent

Wasco is twenty five miles from Bakersfield. Hot, God it's hot. We are living in temporary barracks, just tents. We have nice dirt floors, army cots, mosquito netting, dust and terrible odors. We use mess kits and eat out on a tennis court. We have to share a shower that's located in an old corral, however it does have canvas around it for privacy. The toilet conditions are terrible. You don't have to be crazy to be a flying cadet but it sure helps. What I mean by this is that the hardest work that I ever did at home is a drop in the bucket, compared to this. Oh! For a half hour in the big chair at home with a **Time** magazine to read.

From a letter dated July 21, 1941: Have been here just about a week now and am beginning to get the hang of things. The first week was pretty rough. We marched about four hours a day in the blistering heat. We then spent the afternoons in the classroom, listening to lectures on Articles of War, military rules, etc. We were confined to

Basic Flight Training

base last weekend, I don't know why but suppose just to keep us in line. The enlisted men here live like kings and have evenings off, but we're cadets and it's well known that cadets are the lowest things that live.

Wearing raincoats & awaiting physicals

We've all had complete physical examinations again. I just finished taking mine this morning. Despite the terrible conditions, I seem to be in awfully good shape. Blood pressure is okay and in what they call a Scheider Test I scored a 16.

Two cadets won't pass their physicals

Passing is an 8 and perfect is an 18. This test determines what kind of shape you're in. My eyes still seem to be holding out okay, despite the dust and heat. Several of the boys are going to be washed out because they're unable to pass the physical. One fellow came down with the measles and now I suppose we will all be quarantined.

Saturday afternoon they got kind hearted and took us swimming. It was in a channel and certainly felt perfect. Sunday afternoon we all dressed up and went into Bakersfield for a tea dance. What a mess but we're required to go. I'm just now beginning to realize what I got into, when I joined the Air Corps.

The flight line of BT-13s

Today I had my first ride in the new plane, the Vultee BT-13A, and it's really something. It's a low wing monoplane, weighs 5,000 pounds and has a 450 horsepower engine. One look into the cabin and you would think that just one man couldn't possibly handle everything.

Cockpit of the BT-13 "Vultee Vibrator"

Basic Flight Training

After I first got in and adjusted about ten different things we got the engine started. The takeoff is really something, as you get up to about 75 MPH before you lift off the runway.

Bill in BT-13

The propeller is of the high and low pitch type and it must be changed for different conditions, such as landings and takeoffs. There are also flaps to contend with. They must be rolled down 20 degrees for takeoffs and landings. If you don't handle them just right a stall could result. Landing the plane gives you quite a sensation, gliding in at 90 MPH and finally setting down at 70. They are very tricky death traps and a fellow has to keep his wits about him at all times. The plane cruises at 140 MPH. We were up for an hour today and I thought we had only gone a short distance until I found out we had gone 100 miles.

Everything around here is the most sweating, dusty, heat wave, flies, a mess and we just have to grit our teeth and keep plugging along. Not much fun as it's just existing and hoping for something better. It's 8:30 PM and I'm sitting under the one little light bulb in our tent. We don't have to go to bed until 9:30 but the bugs are driving me nuts, so I'm going to put the netting up around my bed and lie under it until I fall off to sleep. All I wear at night is shorts and a sheet over me as it never gets cold.

Instructor and students, Bill 2nd from left

Instructor in front cockpit

From a letter dated July 29, 1941: What do you want me to write about? My first solo in the new ship! Okay. It happened just this morning. My instructor is the cautious, careful type and he made darn sure I could fly the thing before he turned it over to me. A few of the boys soloed in two hours. This morning at 7:00 when the instructor got out of the ship after two times around the field I had five hours. The biggest trouble I have had with these planes is learning to get my thick skull to operate everything at the same time. They move so fast that you cover a long distance just trying to make an adjustment.

I know Mother doesn't care anything about this but maybe Dad, you and Bob would like me to give you a few details as to how they operate. When we first get in the cockpit we check to see that the ship is given clearance for flight. The clearance is written in a booklet, which is kept in the ship at all times. Next we fasten the safety belt and connect the radio headphones. Setting the fuel tank selector to the 17 gallon reserve tank is next and at the same time tell the instructor how much gas is in each tank. Two main tanks hold 120 gallons of 100 octane fuel.

Electrical panel above wing

I turn on the main line switch, which enables all the electrical equipment to function and this starts the radio set to humming. Mixture control, which is used to stop the engine, is moved from lean to full rich. Throttle is then opened about half an inch, controls are unlocked and the stick held back. I check to see that the parking brakes are set, elevator and rudder tabs are moved to the 0 degree position and a quick glance tells me that the carburetor heat is off and also that the oil cooler shudders are open.

Using the heel of my right foot I push the starter energizer, which gradually starts with a steadily increasing whine. Holding the stick back with my knees, I operate the wobble pump with my left hand and the primer with my right. At the right speed I kick forward on the energizer and turn the switch to both magnetos. A heavy roar

Cockpit BT-13

of 450 horses greets the ears and I watch the RPM go to about 600. When the fuel pressure is up to three pounds I move the propeller pitch to low, it's always started in high so that oil won't be taken away from the engine, while it's starting. Now the radio is turned off and radio position is selected along with the correct sending kilos. I pick up the mike and say, "L119 to Wasco Control, go ahead". When they answer I then say, "L119 to Wasco Control, Aviation Cadet Schottelkorb taking off for one hour of dual instruction". They reply with "Roger", which means, OK.

Releasing the brake I taxi down to the runway, carefully checking over things in my mind, as I go. Noting that the fuel selector is still on reserve, I switch it to the right tank, for take-off. Cylinder head temperature is okay, as are all the other things. As I approach the runway, I crank down 20 degrees of flap, the required amount. Setting the brake, I run the engine up to 1,400 RPM and check both magnetos. Now comes the fun. I slowly ease the throttle ahead while holding the stick in the center position. On all the other ships I've flown I've had to push the stick ahead, hard, to get the tail up. It comes up on this plane by it's self. When the tail comes up

Basic Flight Training

I push ahead on the stick to keep the plane on the runway and to gain speed. All this time the rudder is heavily applied to the right to overcome the torque. When the airspeed shows 80 MPH, with a slight backpressure I ease the plane off the runway. Boy, what a good feeling, because the fence was coming at me awfully fast.

Flying in formation

Immediately when the plane leaves the ground, I cut the throttle to 2,100 RPM from 2,300 this relieves the terrific strain on the ship. The horizontal stabilizer is pulled back to maintain a steady 90 MPH climb, then I look back over my shoulder to see that I'm not flying away from the field at an angle. I see I'm heading straight, despite the torque. At 300 feet I make a climbing turn and start around the traffic pattern, leveling off at 600 feet. Next I cut the RPM to 2000 and set the horizontal stabilizer for level flight. In a few seconds I've covered the pattern and am making a 90 degree approach on the south end of the field. Cutting the throttle, I then set the horizontal stabilizer for a 90 MPH glide. As I turn into the field I note that I'm high. This is where the flaps come in. Eight turns of the flap control puts me practically into a dive and gets me down to where I want to be. Correcting the flaps and around 20 feet up, I break the glide and hold off at about a foot. Suddenly the ship is rolling along the ground at 65 MPH. Gradually I apply brakes to keep from running into the fence. At the end of the roll the flaps are rolled up and the horizontal stabilizer is set to neutral, then the canopy is pushed back. Well that constitutes starting, taking off and landing. After another time around the instructor gets out and says, "go ahead". I felt much calmer than when Dick Ogg stepped out of the Piper Cub back in Missoula last fall and said the same thing. It's still exciting.

With the instructor looking on, my first landing was okay, the second a little wheels first and a resultant bounce, on the third one I came down onto the runway with too much flap and leveled off above the field ahead of the runway. Because of this I had to gun it and go around again. With the flaps lowered too much it's hard to pick up speed again, and if you roll them up too fast the plane will drop some. The last time around I did all right and got down okay.

I suppose you heard about a cadet and an instructor getting killed here. I knew them well. The cadet was right near me in rank and I had just had a conversation with him a short time before the accident. That's the game, a few are going to get it regardless. Every day is a crisis and a good nights sleep helps.

From a letter Bill's Dad wrote to him after he received his description of flying: "To Bill the Flying Cadet, We all enjoyed your letters about flying, I believe that I could almost take one of those ships up myself by the description that you wrote. I guess you're having a hard time now, but there are a lot of boys that would like to trade places with you. If you can stick it out and I know you can, you will really have something."

From a letter dated August 11, 1941: I really thought the "**Dynamiter**" looked nice in the picture you sent. Bob must really enjoy it. How does the radiator cool and what does it show on the heat gauge now? Shep looked like the heat had gotten him. It's a funny thing, every place we go there are always a couple of dogs hanging around. We have a cute little pup doing this

Basic Flight Training

now. He's a hairy little devil. A car hit him the other day and generous as we usually are, we got a Doctor for him. First thing we knew we had a $10.00 doctor bill. We all got together and each of us put in a dime and paid it. This morning when I woke up at 4:30 the little guy was in my tent. I called him over and put him on top, with me and we both went back to sleep. At 4:50 AM when the bugle sounded, in the next tent, he jumped up like he'd been shot.

BT-13 off the left wing

My flying is coming along pretty good. Passed my twenty hour check ride in seventeen hours. The Flight Commander said it was the best ride he'd had that day. I seem to do all right most of the time and then at times I think that I'm doing terrible. It's a good feeling to be able to take a plane this size and get it into the air and back down safely. Regardless what happens now I'm all ready fixed for private flying for the rest of my life. The Army really teaches you to fly, and if you can get by here you should be able to get by anywhere.

Just the other day one of the boys was up on a solo flight, practicing spins and somehow he got into one at 8,000 feet and couldn't recover. He rode it down to 3,500 feet and bailed out. The result was $35,000 worth of airplane completely destroyed. The opinion around here is that he just didn't know how to recover from a spin. It was a rough experience for the lad to go through and he ended up with bruises from head to foot to prove it.

At 7:00 this morning I had a solo flight. Early in the morning the air is smooth and good for climbing. I really found out what these ships can do. We take off right beside the highway and I always get a kick out of racing the cars. We pass them up like a dirty shirt and leap into the air and begin climbing at 90 MPH. It hardly took any time to climb to 2,500 feet. I flew over to the Lerdo Field and called for landing instructions and was told to land from south to north. Just had to put the nose down and make large spirals down at 100 MPH. When I reached 600 feet I leveled off and came into the pattern at a 45 degree angle. When I was a quarter of a mile outside the pattern I cut the gun and shifted the prop to low pitch. Then I cut the air speed to just below 120 MPH and put down 20 degrees of flaps, which gives more lift at low speeds. Just a minute later I was down on the runway rolling along at 50 MPH. I give a couple of light pushes on the brakes and I easily stop before the end of the field. I make sure that I roll up my flaps as I taxi by the stage house or I will get two red stars, which would cost me two bits each. Only have one so far and that's enough, because I don't need to pay out any money for making dumb mistakes. Flying, it is wonderful!!

A good place to rest, only shade around

Basic Flight Training

I think we are going to move to Lerdo Field and new barracks at the end of the week. This means that we'll be upper-classmen again.

Breaking camp at Wasco

Everyone doing their part

When we take our forty hour check rides and pass them we are considered definitely okay for the Army and this means no more check rides. However nothing is final until you receive your commission. It's just certain that after passing the forty hour check, that a cadet will get his commission. Then the only thing that will flunk a guy out is disobedience of the rules.

Bill had definite plans to buy himself a car when he finished with Basic Flight Training. He felt like he was tied down without one, as there were many places in California that he wanted to see and be able to visit with his relatives. He did later buy one, after looking around the car lots in Los Angeles.

From a letter dated August 19, 1941: Last night we began night flying and it really was fun. They used smudge pots for the boundary lights and floodlights shone in the landing area. We also used our wing floodlights, which are very powerful. We were sent to various zones at different altitudes so that we wouldn't be running into each other. I was sent to the northwest corner of the field at the 2,000 to 2,500 foot levels. This was zone four upper. At first my instructor flew with me and he made three landings before I took it alone. When the instructor rides with you he's sitting in the back and can't see a thing. When he came in to land he would blunder all over the place and on all three he did a terrible job.

Cadet Bill

My first solo night flight gave me quite a thrill. Lurching over the ground and then into the sky, keeping the canopy open with the cool night air

Basic Flight Training

blowing in my face. The blue exhaust flame on the side is very pleasant also. A blue fluorescent light in the cockpit shows the very important instruments. Once I was up in my zone I flew around in lazy circles. It was beautiful last night at 2,500 feet. The lights of Bakersfield were off to the south about 20 miles but they looked very close. Wasco and Shafter were lighted just below and over to the side were the friendly field lights, which you realize are the most important as they will lead you back to the landing field. Up above there were a million stars and it gave me a beautiful, peaceful feeling that I was alive and able to fly. I was up there for 45 minutes just circling, with my eyes never wandering far from the instruments. Mainly I watched the altimeter, which showed my altitude. Occasionally I would check the needle and ball to see how my eye flying checked with the instrument. You can fly completely blind by using just your instruments. This will come later in my training.

Soon I was alerted by the voice from the Radio Control Ship, below, "Upper Zone Four come in for a landing". I answered, "Schottelkorb in upper zone four, okay". I cut the gun and came down in steep gliding turns. At 600 feet I joined traffic and came in for my first night landing. Around the last turn, I put my base leg where it seemed reasonable. Next I cut the gun and established a 90 MPH glide, turned into the field, snapped on the landing lights and headed in. I leveled off and the voice on the radio says, "easy, hold it off". With a gentle bump I'm down and rolling along at 65 MPH. "Nice landing 129", says a voice in my ear and happily I taxi up to the line and park the ship.

Around the 1st of September, Bill traveled to Los Angeles to look for a car. After looking at several, he settled for a 39 Ford deluxe Tudor Sedan, for $540.00. The car came without any accessories. Finally he had his wheels and would be able to go and do as he chose, when he was able to get passes.

From a letter dated September 8, 1941: Present plans call for us to be finished here the 20th. Unless we get swindled some way the three Montana boys and I will start home about that time. Right now ground school is my biggest worry, as it's tough. I'm trying to learn to receive Morse Code at eight words a minute. We are also doing complicated navigation problems.

Staging house at Wasco

Now I would like to tell you a little about flying. I've now got 160 hours and really making good progress. Last week we did our cross-country flying. The first day we just took a short trip to Corcoran, Lost Hills and back. We got to practice landings on small fields. On the next one we went to Tulare, Coalinga, and back to Lerdo. The last day we took a real trip and I certainly enjoyed it. I took off at 1:09 in the afternoon, following the railroad tracks up to Tulare and since I thought I knew the country, I cut directly west to Hanfor. I tried to spot Mother's, Aunt's place but don't believe that I saw it. Here I headed north and soon was flying high over Fresno. I sat my magnetic course, uncorrected for wind, at 103 degrees and soon sighted Merced. I landed here but only stayed a few minutes. Merced is practically as far north as San Jose. Next I headed south over 95 miles of desert to Avenal. I set my course, climbed to 3,000 feet, unbuckled my seat belt, and put my feet up on the dash. Just flew by the stick alone, and listened to the weather reports from Mojava. It's simply amazing the way these planes can eat

Basic Flight Training

up the miles. At 34 minutes out on this 95 mile stretch I sighted Coalinga. A minute later I called Avenal Radio and asked for landing instructions. After landing and taking off again I headed back to Lerdo. The whole trip only took two and half hours and this included two landings.

A formation flight

Take-off in formation

This week we're learning how to fly in formation, I have three hours of this now. This morning my instructor flew the lead ship and another student and I flew off his wings. It's hard at first but then you get so you can stay right in next to the wing. We start by taxiing out on the runway, in formation, so close that our props are practically taking a piece out of the lead ship's tail. When flying in formation you keep your eyes on the lead ship at all times and do exactly what he does. Take-offs are the most fun, to stay in position the gun, throttle, is kicked off and on violently. We just skid in and out of place. It's hard to stay in position at just 15 feet away in a steep turn, but we can do it. The leader signals for an Echelon, and the number two ship crosses above the other at about 15 feet, then you stack up for a peel off.

This morning my instructor signaled for a Luffberry Circle and for us to peel off at four second intervals. You just don't realize when those planes are gently moving up and down beside you, how fast they're moving. But when they flash, belly up, then down and away you can really notice the speed at which we're moving. I waited four seconds and peeled off to join the rat race, or try to follow my instructor, doing as he did and keeping up with him. Later we reformed our formation and came in for a formation landing. To do this we keep our eyes on the lead ship, leveling off when he does and all landing at the same time. Usually the two ships following bounce more than they should, but that doesn't matter. It's really fun and teaching us flying skills.

Mother, not to neglect you, tonight for supper we had sliced Tomatoes, Potato Salad, Fried Potatoes, Creamed Corn, Carrots, Hot Rolls, Steak and plenty of Milk. This was followed by dessert that consisted of a large bowl of Strawberries, from a can.

From a letter dated September 18, 1941: We don't know anything yet about where we're going next or when. We think that we are supposed to leave here Saturday morning about 11:00. However if they don't have our orders by then, we might have to come back next week to get them. That would just about ruin all my plans for coming home. I'm still hoping to leave Saturday morning and be off until about the first of October. This will give me ample time to get home and back. The only reason I'm expecting any leave at all is that we're finishing up this part of our training early. They just don't give you time off without a reason. I certainly hope we do

Basic Flight Training

because it would give me a chance to relax and clear my mind.

Only have two more hours of ground school left. Both are in Military Law. Yesterday, I finished up my flying and now have a total of 170 hours. The most fun we've had this week was when we engaged in a mass formation. I was top man and it was a beautiful sight to look below and see 14 planes strung out in a diagonal line, all about ten feet apart. The Flight Commander gave the signal to peel off at three second intervals and form a Luffberry Circle. One by one I watched them all fall out and go down. Finally I followed and we had a huge circle, roaring around at 2,000 feet. There was about a half a block between each airplane. Then we flew down into the traffic pattern and in for a landing, each one of us following the same antics as the one before did.

Ready to leave for home

Fire truck and ambulance at Lerdo

Towing Mule at Lerdo

Home on leave

The greatest way to live with honor in this world is to be what we pretend to be.
--Socrates

Advanced Flight Training

Bill did get his leave after finishing Basic Flying Training. Five of his fellow cadets rode home with him. One rode as far as Ogden, Utah then three more rode to Butte, Montana. We catch up to his story on their way back to Luke Field near Phoenix, Arizona.

Bill while home on leave after Basic

From a letter dated October 1st: It took me two hours to drive to Butte, where I met the fellows at the Greyhound Bus Station. We made it to Pocatello, Idaho that night. Got into Ogden, Utah the next day around noon. After we ate lunch Bixby and Brooking went on with an Ogden boy named Bassett. Clapper and I continued on our way together. Seppich had gotten himself a car and left Ogden that morning ahead of us. We spent the night in the car at Cameron, Arizona, as we were about out of gas and everything was closed for the night. Next morning the desert was absolutely beautiful and we enjoyed this as we drove on to Flagstaff. It is a scenic little place sitting among the Pine Trees, I didn't realize that northern Arizona was so nice. The beautiful forestlands are comparable to Montana's.

Phoenix from the air 1941

Pulled into Phoenix at 2:30 in the afternoon, just in time for the dedication of Luke Field. We got to see some nice formation flying. Luke Field has the same aspects as Lerdo, by that I mean it's the same type of field, same buildings, etc. We drove in and shook hands with our buddies from Lerdo.

Luke Field, 1941

Reported in and were assigned companies, barracks and given a bed. There hasn't been any of that old stuff of marching all day like at primary and basic, in fact we have been taking it awfully easy. The only hard thing so far has been the exercises that they have been making us do. We have an officer who delights in seeing if we cadets can take it. He is a perfect physical brute himself. Yesterday we were all called out

Advanced Flight Training

before him and he said, "This is the toughest advanced school in the country and you're going to earn everything you get". Then he said, "We are going to get started now". So down we went and did 25 push-ups, I still don't know how I did the last 5. He never makes us do anything that he doesn't do himself. The upper class-men tell a story about him coming out one day with a sore arm due to several shots he had been given. They were surprised when they went down for push-ups and he did also. They were still more surprised when he did 25 of them with one arm.

Home away from home.

This morning, Wednesday, we got up at 5:40, did ten minutes of rigorous exercises and ate breakfast at 6:00. One hour was all we needed to get our window in shape. We are all in one big room this time, no individual rooms. We filled out a form, which gave them a lot of information about ourselves. This was the last thing we did all morning; I even slept for an hour before lunch. After eating I slept again for a bit. What a life, sleep, eat a perfect lunch and go back to sleep. The best party of this is that we get $75.00 a month for doing it. All good things end and at 2:00 PM we were called back out for 25 more push-ups. There are movies every day.

Movies were one of Bill's favorite pastimes and he went whenever he got the chance. Meals also were one of the things he especially liked and described some in great detail.

I want to tell you about the meals we get here. They were good at basic but here they are perfect. I just don't see how they do it. Milk, cold drinks, ice cream, ham, several kinds of vegetables, service and everything. I wish that you could take on a typical meal here, you would think that it was Christmas.

There sure is a lot of activity taking place here. A water tower is being constructed along with streets, etc. They've just completed a big machine shop with an expensive lathe and all the other equipment that goes in a machine shop.

Control tower at Luke

From a letter dated October 10th: Sometimes I wonder about the efficiency of the Army. We laid around here for two weeks doing nothing, and the flight office didn't even know we were here. Now the Colonel is mad, so we have to fly Saturdays and Sundays for the next three weeks. We haven't had a day or minute of open post since we drove through the gate.

I guess I should have said the other boys will be flying. When we took our physical exams the other day, my blood pressure was too high. That was the first time I've ever had the slightest trouble. Boy, I got mad!! I live cleaner than 90% of these fellows and they pass and I don't. I hope it's just a temporary condition as I had a headache and the hot march over there didn't help either. Tomorrow, Saturday, I go back and try again, meanwhile I have to watch the other boys fly and inwardly wish I could.

Advanced Flight Training

The airplane that the cadets flew at Luke Field was the North American AT-6.

AT-6 Trainer

It takes two or three hours to solo these planes, and get used to the new features. They have a narrow landing gear and are very tricky on the ground. Hope I don't learn the hard way. Just today my friend, Seppich, hit another plane while on the ground. The instructor was along with him and the other plane was parked with a student in it. Result, two ruined wings, cost $3,000.

Various stores from town are showing us uniforms now. We get $150 to get new uniforms when we graduate. Things are terribly expensive, blouse $45, shirts $10 to $12, pants $12 to $19. I'm going to hold off buying anything as long as possible, at least until I see where I'm to be stationed. That will help me to make up my mind on the uniforms that I will need.

From a letter dated October 17th: Well Saturday I went back to the Medical Examiner and had my blood pressure checked. It was still a bit high but the Doctor said I could go back to flying. We have been flying for seven days now and I have gotten in 16 hours. The first few days went pretty slow, as the instructor had to be with us for three hours of dual before we were permitted to solo. The AT-6 is tricky as heck on the ground and you have to be wide-awake or you could ground loop very easily. We've all been used to the basic trainer, which has a nice wide landing gear and very seldom ground looped. I heard that the other half of our class from Sacramento had so many ground loops that all flight work was suspended for a while.

These ships are really a dream and certainly the hottest thing I have flown so far. A very sensitive ship that really has to be flown. The engine is supercharged and has a very high output and consequently has to be handled very carefully, especially at low altitudes. When taking off they have a throttle stop which limits the amount of RPM's. As soon as they lift off the ground the throttle is cut to 30 inches of Mercury Manifold Pressure. Next you adjust the prop pitch to 2,000 RPM, the hydraulic button is pushed and you pull up the landing gear. Once you're leveled off and up at a good altitude a speed of 160 Knots is easily attained. In a dive they go to 250 Knots in a flash.

The country around here is typically barren hills and stretches of desert. It's very interesting to fly over because you can see all the hills and domes so easily. Some of these hill formations are very unusual and provide a temptation for low flying. I had better wait for my share of that, at least until we start machine gun firing down at Gila Bend. When this starts we will dive on ground targets and fire through the prop with a fixed gun.

We are taking team rides now. This is when two cadets fly together, the one in the front seat flies the take-offs and landings while the one in the rear flies under the hood, doing instrument work. While this is happening the boy in the front watches so we don't get into trouble. We always get in a few things for fun like a snap roll, etc. This gives us an idea of how good a flier the other fellow is. It does seem to me that we are all about equal.

Saturday morning we flew for an hour and forty five minutes in close formations. The instructor wants you to get right close to him. He's happy when my wing is two feet from his tail and my

Advanced Flight Training

prop four feet behind his wing. When we think that we have it all down pretty well, he starts acting up, by that I mean doing a Chandelle, steep climbing turn, or a near vertical bank. When flying so close, you have to start your bank at the same time as the lead ship or you could slide right in against him.

In the afternoon I went to town and got a start on getting my uniform ordered. I got the blouse, two pairs of pants and an OD shirt. I'm not getting anything else until I know where I'm being sent. There is a good chance it will be to Foreign Service.

Sunday four of us drove over to Mesa to see the camp where the boys from England are flying. They fly the same plane as we do.

From a letter dated November 3rd: I just have to get something off my mind, I just lost the most perfect opportunity, this afternoon that a young man could ever have. Pan American Airways made a deal with the Army, whereby 88 Aviation Cadets in the Class of 41-1, mine, would be selected to ferry P-40 Pursuit Planes around Africa. They were to be selected from six advanced schools in the country. That meant that only about 15 from each school would be picked. These cadets are to go to a Pursuit School or Tactical Unit like Hamilton Field to take the last two weeks of their cadet training in the P-40 airplane. They would graduate from these units at the same time as their classmates would in their regular schools. After receiving their commissions they wouldn't go on active duty but would be civilians again with a Reserve Commission. Then they would go on the payroll of Pan American. Pan American would give them ten days to settle their affairs, then put them on an airliner for Washington, DC. There they would get their passports and go on to New York and there would get their Commercial License. Of course Pan American would pay for all this and then fly them to Africa on board a regular Boeing Clipper. Also they would receive a generous check for travel pay.

Upon arriving in Africa they will ferry P-40's from Accra, Gold Coast to Kartum, Anglo-Sudan, a distance of 2,600 miles. The trip is divided into eight short hops with all having good facilities. All the flying will take place in the daytime and the return trip will be in a DC-3 transport airline. In fact the Ferry Pilots will act as co-pilots on the return trip and get dual engine experience. Each pilot will make the trip several times by transport before going by himself. The pay will be $350 per month.

They will sign a contract for six months, backed by Pan American and our Army. They will receive two insurance policies, a $10,000 life and $7,000 Workman's Compensation. All living expenses will be paid over the regular pay. They will be furnished modern quarters with individual rooms and baths. After six months the return trip is guaranteed and a bonus of $500 will be paid.

A representative from Pan American was here this afternoon. 100 cadets wanted to take the deal, but only 20 were selected by drawing names from a hat. One of the biggest disappointments of my life was that I wasn't one of those chosen. I would give anything to go. You know there is nothing I can do except take what fate decided!!

Perhaps you heard of the P-40's that were caught in the storm in California. They went through here two days before then. A funny thing about those planes is the way that V-12 Allison Engine runs. You'd never know that there is 1100 Horsepower there. They sounded like a four cylinder Chevy to me. Three Lockheed P-38's passed through here also. Unless a person has seen one of these planes move, he can't possibly realize how fast they are, just **Lightning,** that is all.

Last week we flew at high altitudes to get used to

Advanced Flight Training

an oxygen mask. In an hour and fifteen minutes I went up to 21,000 feet and returned. I took off and climbed 100 feet a minute. Up there it was 20 degrees below zero on the outside of the cockpit. Luke Field, which is a square mile, looked like a postage stamp. The controls were very sloppy at that altitude and the supercharged engine gave out only 15 inches manifold pressure, wide open. It showed 35 inches at take-off. Had no trouble breathing as the oxygen system was turned on. Came down so fast that it hurt my ears and I had to level off every now and then to get used to the different pressure.

Today we had a time and distance problem in cross-country flying. Every student was supposed to meet our instructor at a given altitude, over a certain town at an appointed time. I went to Coolidge and then to Gila Bend where I was supposed to meet up with the instructor at 9:03 AM. As I was approaching Gila Bend, I realized that I was going to be early so I slowed and mushed along at 100 MPH until I figured that I had killed enough time. I then went back to normal speed. You see, I had to be there right on the minute and not early or late. When the instructor passes by he's going past rather quickly at 160 MPH. If I were to be even one minute late or arrived early and circled he wouldn't have given me any credits. I couldn't see him as I flew over Gila Bend at 9:03 AM. I was looking all around for him and the first thing I knew, he and I about collided as he passed by. I joined him and then six of us flew in formation back to Luke Field. On the way we peeled off and went in a Luffberry Circle, which kept tightening up as all the pilots, got on each other's tail. The instructor used to be able to out-fox us and get right on our tail but now we are getting much better as he has to work hard to do it. This must really put the pressure on him, I usually have my glasses and headset pressed off my head by the pressure. This maneuver usually ends up by someone stalling out, or doing a snap roll. This is caused by the propwash of the plane he is following.

Last Friday the upper-classmen graduated with a simple but very nice exercise. Twenty of the instructors put on an air-show and really did some nice formation flying. When they finished they peeled off and came over the field at 20 feet at 200 MPH, one following the other. Many of the cadet's parents were here for the exercises and I was thinking it would be awfully nice if you could attend when I graduate, December 12th. I don't know where I will be stationed but will probably not be able to come home for Christmas.

Don Tomlinson is due in tomorrow and I will be mighty glad to see him. He will be an under-classmen and will graduate four and a half weeks after I do. We have a lot in common. This weekend I drove my car up into the hills and saw a lot of interesting country.

Tomorrow morning I take-off for Yuma on a cross-country, it will be some trip, 303 miles to be exact. Will only take me 123 minutes flying time according to my calculations. Makes you think twice about your navigation, when you start across 150 miles of desert where everything looks the same and there are very few checkpoints. If I can master this here I should be able to do it anywhere.

By the way, I was made a minor officer, a Corporal, at the last choosing of upper-class officers. This was due to my two years of ROTC and the fact that I haven't gotten into any trouble. Not much of an honor but then as we only have 20 officers for 150 cadets it's a privilege anyway.

From a letter dated November 12th: How's the weather up there in Montana? The last few weeks here have been very nice, warm, sunny days and cool nights. However today things changed, this afternoon it clouded up and rained and is still doing it at 7:00 PM. We'll have plenty of mud to contend with tomorrow. We can't kick too much as the weather has really cooperated since we arrived here.

Advanced Flight Training

Will tell you about the cross-country flight to Yuma, nine days ago. It turned out to be a nice easy trip, because we followed the river from Gila Bend to Yuma. Since that one, we have done another that called for more skillful navigation. We went from Phoenix to Kingman, on to Blythe, California and returned to Phoenix. I left at 7:15 AM and arrived in Kingman, 150 miles away airline, in 55 minutes. The route took me over the most desolate country that I have ever seen. At 12,000 feet you couldn't pick out any decent landmarks, just miles and miles of barren mountains. At the time Kingman was suppose to show, there it was straight ahead. Just goes to show that instruments are to be trusted. I landed and refueled, took on 42 gallons. Was such fun landing at the little airport so early in the morning. The fuel truck driver said it takes six hours to drive to Phoenix from there. To me it seemed that I had just left there a few minutes earlier. As I was pulling out onto the makeshift desert runway I notice a large, White Breasted Hawk sitting on the fence. Just for fun I swung my tail around and blasted him off the map. I didn't think he would ever fly but finally the dust got so bad he lifted off and scrammed.

Kingman to Blythe, California was much easier. My route crossed the Colorado River and over Parker Dam and the town of Parker. I almost overran Blythe as I arrived before I had expected. I buzzed the airport to show my numbers so I could prove that I had been there. About 45 minutes to the west, off in the distance I could see the Salton Sea and Los Angeles. The leg back to Phoenix was easy and although I had covered over 400 miles in 3 hours, this included a 15 minute stop, hardly seemed like I had been anywhere.

Don Tomlinson did arrive last Tuesday with his 37 Lincoln Zephyr. Boy did we have a nice visit. The State Fair has been running this week, and yesterday, Armistice Day, we went to the car races there, sure was a lot of fun. The fair is about equal to the Montana State Fair in quality.

Don and his Zephyr

Bill in the desert

Have been doing some night flying lately and it won't be long until we start taking night cross-country trips. Believe that this will be fun and good experience. Next week we will start

Advanced Flight Training

gunnery practice, both ground and air. That's about all there is left except checking out in the P-64 single seat Pursuit Plane. I now have 65

P-64

hours and will probably only get 25 more. I have a month left in which to do this. The ground school finished last week and was I glad.

Monday I signed a statement that I was willing to go on Foreign Service. Won't be too surprised if that's what I get. I did tell my instructor that my first choice would be, becoming an instructor at Basic School. The more I think about flying the old ships and compare it to the AT-6, I don't believe I would like going back and flying in them again.

Well, I'm still asking you to seriously consider coming down for my graduation. Still raining hard outside, so we'll probably be flooded tomorrow. Thursday, well the rain stopped and the sky has cleared so everyone is flying as usual. This is certainly the real country to fly in.

From a letter dated November 17th: So glad to hear that you are coming down for the graduation, that is swell. I don't know much about the schedule except that we are supposed to graduate on the morning of December 12th.

Really don't know how much time that I will have off, hopefully will have enough to show you around some. Still don't know where I'll be going after graduation, probably somewhere in California. The only day that you probably will be allowed on the post will be the day of graduation. That day you will be able to eat in the mess hall with me and the rest of the boys. Well won't be long now.

Just the other day, 18 of us cadets had a nice cross-country trip. We left Luke at 3:30 PM and flew a loose formation to Blythe, California and then on to Palm Springs, a distance of 240 miles airline. We landed in Palm Springs at 5:30 PM. The whole town was there to see us and we had a lot of fun. Their airport is the world's worst, short and just a little path down the middle of a sagebrush field. The third boy that came in, nosed over at the end of the runway and that spoiled our whole day. When it was my turn to land I was determined to get down short. I made a long low approach, used power with full flaps. Came in right over the houses at 100 feet then passed over the cars and people at the end of the runway at 20 feet. I landed short and only used 3/4 of the field. The ground was soft and sandy and it was hard to taxi on. When we finally all got parked there must have been a thousand people ready to look the planes over.

On the way to Palm Springs

Advanced Flight Training

Palm Springs as you know is a famous resort town and there were several movie stars there, and some of the boys talked with them. I have never seen a prettier town from the air. It sits at the foot of a 10,000 foot mountain and is a town of color and beautiful homes. As we flew over we could see swimming pools, which were green in color. We might have gotten to see more of the town if there hadn't been the nose over. The Lieutenant who was in charge was mad at us so we had to wait around until dark, after we all had been refueled. The takeoff at night on that little field was plenty tricky. Was pitch dark when we took off and there were no lights. Was very hard to see until I got the tail up and steered between the two green lights at the end of the runway.

This was our first cross-country flight at night and was certainly different. What looked like barren desert during the day, at night looked like the lights of New York City, everywhere there were lights, miles and miles of them. Palm Springs was even prettier at night than it was during the day, even the swimming pools were lit up. When I was up two or three hundred feet I made a turn directly away from the high peak, and then climbed to 10,000 feet for the trip home. I can see why flyers crack-up against mountains, as you just can't see them at night. The best thing to do is fly higher than anything that is near. It's just as easy to navigate at night as daytime. We merely followed the beacon lights 240 miles back to Phoenix. On the way back, our route lay close to the Salton Sea, and it's quite a sight from the air. It's wonderful being up there all alone at night and seeing lights for miles around, spread out over the desert. Have also flown to Tucson and Blythe again, on night flights. Are going to report to the flight line again tonight so imagine we will be going on another trip.

From a letter dated November 24th: Last Thursday, Thanksgiving, Don Tomlinson and I spent the day together. We spent the morning exploring old roads in the nearby desert, and took a bunch of pictures. Around 2:00 PM we had Thanksgiving dinner in one of the nicer downtown cafes. It consisted of the usual fare for the occasion, Turkey, mashed potatoes, dressing, and French bread. For dessert Don had mince pie and I had a piece of pumpkin.

Saturday afternoon three of us packed up a couple of bedrolls and some blankets. Took my car and went to Prescott. Very nice to be back in

Harold Shook from San Francisco

the woods again and see some Pine Trees. In one place you break out over the mountains and can see for 50 or more miles across the desert back toward Phoenix. Spent the evening in Prescott, bowling and seeing a movie. Cold there at night and I feared my car would freeze up, so covered the hood. Found a nice place back in the hills to camp. I didn't get cold as I slept in the back of the car and had plenty of good warm Army blankets. The two other fellows also slept warm in their bedrolls. It got down to 20 degrees. After breakfast we decided to do a little hunting as I had a 22 rifle and Shipman had his bow and arrows. He's a great lover of this type of hunting and does quite well.

Hiked about 2 or 3 miles and got some shots at rabbits but with all the brush in the way, we missed them. Shipman shot at a hawk with his bow and arrow, it was an impossible shot. Shook and I shot at one also, that was sitting on a bank about 200 feet away. We both shot twice, we

Advanced Flight Training

came close but didn't hit him. If he hadn't decided to fly we would have banged the wretch. Arrived back at Luke around 3:30 PM, in time for dinner. We were tired and hungry but felt like it was a profitable weekend.

Mark Shipman from Fresno, California

Did you hear that Bob Bixby was one of the lucky ones to be chosen to go to Africa for Pan American? Glad one Montana boy was able to get to go. The boys that were chosen leave today for New York to get checked out on the P-40.

We're going to go to Ajo, which is 90 miles southwest of Phoenix, to do our gunnery practice. This will be done out on the desert. All finished now with night cross-country, the last trip was from Luke to Needles, Blythe and back to Luke.

From a letter dated December 1st: Well time is passing rapidly and we are on the last lap now. I've finished my flying as a cadet and have about 270 hours. I certainly have learned a lot here about many things and my flying has improved 100% in this phase of the training. Last week we were having gunnery practice down at Ajo. Takes 30 minutes to fly there from Luke Field. We always flew down in formations and the rest of the day was spent on firing. The AT-6A is equipped with one 30 caliber machine gun that fires through the prop. We shot at both ground and air targets.

The ground targets are arranged as follows, six cadets would use the range at the same time. Each had his own target and always fired on his own. Flying around a pattern at 800 feet we would reduce our speed to 110 MPH and go into a dive with partial power. About 800 feet from the target we would fire a burst and at that time we were about 10 to 20 feet from the ground. Traveling at 160 to 170 MPH we would pull up in a vertical bank and then climb and circle for another shot.

It usually took 10 to 15 trips around to shoot up 100 rounds of ammunition. We each shot 1,300 rounds. The gun sight is a projection type, this works by a light image being reflected onto the windshield. No one did very good at this, as it was difficult to even hit the target. I lucked out and did shoot several very good scores but not consistently. Seppich turned out to be a hotshot and probably better than anyone in our section.

When we did air gunnery we fired at a canvas sleeve, towed by another plane. I only shot 50 rounds during this phase of gunnery. Our poor instructor couldn't hit the broad side of a barn, and most of us cadets outshot him. Of course this was much to his dismay. One day I flew 7 hours and 20 minutes, very tiresome but on the whole I really enjoyed the fun. Ajo is nearly in Mexico and certainly located in lonely country.

What do you know? I'm one of about 28 boys to become instructors tomorrow. In the morning I report to the flight line for Instructors School.

Advanced Flight Training

Looks like I will be stationed right here at Luke.

Invitation to graduation, 41-I

From a letter dated December 3rd: About the matter of formal wear for the graduation occasion. There's to be a formal dinner dance the evening before graduation, however I'm not planning on attending as I don't know any girl that I would like to take and I would just as soon spend the evening with you folks.

I thought the life of a cadet was hard!! Instructor's School, is harder yet. We have to get 25 hours in this school to become instructors. You have to ride observer for the cadets so we fly two hours to get credit for one. I've found out it's a different matter trying to fly one of these planes from the back seat. You have a hard time seeing from back there. If you asked a civilian pilot to fly from the back seat he would think you were crazy, but all in a day's work in the Army. I have been sitting in the front cockpit while the other boys are trying to learn to take-off and land from the back one. Quite an experience sitting there as the plane comes drifting in sideways, with a wing low and bouncing all over the place, not any fun and scary too. The pilot in front is responsible for the plane and that's a lot to ask of him.

A couple of times today it took all the skill and experience I had learned, to take over and keep us from doing a ground loop. Did come very close to losing it once. One thing about it is that the other fellows are going to have to sit in front while I am in back, poor boys. Now I'm getting so that I can land from the back cockpit all right, this took four hours of practice. It's very easy to fly them into the ground from the back seat, this I did a couple of times this morning. This happened at the Phoenix Airport, Sky Harbor. We have been in this school game for two days and I have only logged 6 hours, still 19 to go. Still have night flying, formation, and instrument to finish. I'm not too sharp on instruments and do need a lot more time doing it. Night landings from the back seat!!! That will really be something. Because I'm taking this school, I will have to work hard up to the very last. Hope that I get finished so that I can spend a couple of afternoons with you folks.

Graduation isn't a tremendous thing, but I think you'll enjoy it. However don't expect too much. As I work here every day, doing a bunch of boring stuff, the thing that keeps me going is that you soon will be here.

Don Tomlinson's folks came by yesterday and visited with me briefly. They are on their way to San Diego. Till next week.

My folks did attend Bill's graduation on December 12th. They drove down from Missoula for the occasion. Bill really enjoyed the short time that he was able to spend with them. I didn't attend with them as was too busy at the time with school. Everyone in the United States was on edge at this time because of the bombing of Pearl Harbor and the declaring of war on the axis.

March Field, California

On the 7th of December, 1941, the Japanese attacked Pearl Harbor. This was the start of the war and it changed Bill's plans and the duty that the Army assigned him to do.

From a letter dated December 22, 1941: I'm having a terrible time trying to let you know what has been happening lately. Here is a brief summary of what has gone on with me. After you folks left for home, I moved into town and stayed with a friend at a very nice motor court. This cost us $10.00 per week apiece.

I had started out as an instructor and was assigned to be an assistant to my old instructor. We had a group of 6 new cadets, and I was training 3 of them. I was really enjoying doing this and after 3 hours they were nearly ready to solo. Saturday morning the news came suddenly that we were all to report to March Field near Riverside, California and be there by 7:00 o'clock Sunday evening. Well the rest of Saturday we spent in checking out and clearing our accounts at the post.

That evening at 9:30 I said good bye to Luke Field and drove through Blythe, California and Indio and by 4:00 in the morning I was in Pasadena. I spent some time in Pasadena as I had two flat tires to fix. I went to sleep for awhile and when I woke up I went to a service station and had the flats fixed. Continued on my way to Aunt Rose's and got them out of bed at 11:15 AM. Ate lunch with them and visited with their family and friends. Lynn was working so didn't get to see him. Took me about 3 more hours to drive to March Field. After reporting in we were assigned temporary quarters. I couldn't find a place to sit down and write you so just waited until today.

Last night we went to a free show at the gym. A bunch of movie stars came and put on this show for the men from March Field. They were swell people and very human. They were Betty Grable, Ilona Massey, Basil Rathburn, Charlie McCarthy and Bergen and several other well known stars. In my book they are tops.

This morning I still was in a daze as I reported for duty and checked in at several places. March Field is a huge permanent field and quite the place. Guess I'm stationed with the 14th Pursuit Group and will probably be transferred to Long Beach. They have Lockheed P-38s, Vultee Vanguards, P-40's and other planes here so guess that's probably what I will fly.

Lockeed P-38 Lightning

Curtiss P-40 Warhawk

This all came as a surprise folks and it means that there won't be any presents sent to you this Christmas. Sorry, but you know how the situation is. So all I can do is wish you all a wonderful Christmas and I'll be thinking of you and home on that day. Till later. PS Don't write until you hear more from me.

March Field, California

From a letter dated December 27, 1941: What a Christmas!! Worse one that I have ever had. Couldn't even leave the post so just sat around all day. Didn't even receive a letter to break the monotony and it's all because of the war. They don't want a surprise attack to occur, like the one that happened over in the islands. If we officers were all running around Los Angeles and an air-raid occurred it would just be too bad. Besides people would blame the Army and say it was asleep. Despite the fact that I haven't enjoyed Christmas, I don't mind it as much because there is a reason for it.

I imagine you folks back home hardly realize that there's a war going on, other than what you read in the papers. Well, I certainly do! This post is a mad-house of war preparations. The main buildings are being sandbagged and this is a huge task. All windows are being painted black, both base buildings and homes. The entrances are a series of doorways through canvas flaps until you finally come to the main doors. All cars must be kept off the streets during darkness, so that troops can be moved easily.

At this point Bill stopped writing this letter and finished it later as he was issued a special 6 hour pass.

This was the first chance I've had to get off this base since coming to March Field. John Stege and I took his Chevy coupe and drove to Lancaster, California, a little over 100 miles, to see his folks. Very nice people and they even gave me a Christmas present. We stayed there for 2 hours visiting and had supper. Then back to March Field as we had to be checked in by 9:30 PM. We should only have gone out to a 25 mile limit but we sneaked a little further.

Today is now the 28th and I received orders to report at Long Beach, so here I am. Maybe I will get this letter finished. Boy this is something, we're here at the Long Beach Airport living in tents again. Not too nice as it's all muddy and raining. They are constructing barracks so I can probably stand it for a week or two.

Folks, you ought to see the activity, Army trucks, jeeps, planes, guards, patrols and everything going like mad. I didn't realize until today, while driving through Long Beach, just how important an industrial center this is. Gas, oil, and defense plants of all kinds. This is why we're here, it needs protection.

I'm in a Pursuit Group now and they are really the boys, tough and ready for anything. I love it. Tomorrow I check out on the Vultee Vanguard P-66. Ah!! What a plane.

Vultee P-66 Vanguard

Well this has been a rather unsuccessful letter, but it will give you a rough idea of what's going on down here. We are really awfully poorly prepared as a nation, but we are working fast to make up for lost time.

Today I received the "Reader's Digest", that Bob subscribed to for me, thanks Bob. Also received the candy you sent plus a card from Georgia and George. Continue to write to me at March Field as they will forward it. **Keep this letter to yourselves.**

From a letter dated December 31, 1941: Hardly seems like it's only been six days since Christmas. It feels like it's been months since I was at Luke Field. Been here 3 days now and things are all new and different and haven't

March Field, California

hardly had time to get settled.

Tonight we moved into the third tent we've lived in since arriving here. The first two were staked out in the mud. It's been raining off and on for about a week and the field where the tents are pitched is really a quagmire. Floors of the tents were all covered with water until they put drainage ditches around them. Mud is so deep that even the six-wheel drive trucks were getting stuck part of the time. However the little Ford and Willys jeeps plow right through with the greatest of ease. Tonight they moved some of the officers across the road onto the airport itself. Here at least we have a paved surface for a floor and consequently, it's dry and level. Tents also have a little stove in them, so between it and the stove pipe it keeps the place fairly warm. Have scrap wood to burn in these. For our meals we have to cross the road again back to our tent. Things are pretty crude, but still we are treated like officers. By this I mean our meals are served on plates and we are waited on.

We have been getting up at 6:45 AM, eating at 7:00 and reporting at the flight line at 8:00 o'clock. Lunch is at noon and supper at 5:00 PM. Up until tonight, New Year's Eve, we've been free to go into town until midnight. Until Saturday noon we have to stay close by the flight line or quarters, as it's double duty over the holidays. We Junior Officers are known now as Training Officers and as soon as we have five hours in the new ships we will be become Tactical Officers. All of the Tactical Officers have had to stay pretty close to the base recently.

Seems like I have been living out of my car lately, more than anywhere else. The tents have been so damp that I didn't take any of my things to them. They have issued us a bunch of equipment, and I have that all stored there also. These things are bedrolls, suitcases, parachute bags, mess kits, helmets, oxygen equipment, gas mask, belts, flying boots (wool), jacket and pants which are all wool lined. Got so many things in the back seat that the car is riding low on the springs. Still have all my civilian clothes, but I figure on selling them, if you have any ideas about them let me know. Will send some things home, such as socks, old blue cadet shirts, etc. My sport coat and good clothes are getting all messed up and I probably won't be able to wear them for the duration of the war.

I will try and take some picture soon showing a few items of interest and send them to you. The food here is simple and rough, but very good. Just like out camping!! Boy, I have really been eating since I arrived Sunday night, beans, meat, bread and apple butter, stew, and fruit such as grapes and apples. This makes up most of our main courses.

The biggest laugh in this game is the fact that five of us boys are paying $200.00 a month to live in this tent. How's that for a high rent standard? Four of us are Flying Officers and the fifth one is an Engineering Officer.

Now to talk a little about flying. The airport is located right below Signal Hill in Long Beach. The 14th Pursuit Group, with the 48th, 49th and 50th Squadrons, are the Army units here. Each squadron is now being strengthened by new officers, such as myself, who have arrived recently. I would say that there are 30 men in a squadron. They are flying the Lockheed P-38, Curtiss P-40, and Vultee Vanguard P-66 aircraft. I have only flown the P-66 since arriving here. Bob, you can point out each type of ship to Dad from your magazines? Dad you did get to see the Bell P-39 at Luke Field when you were down for graduation, however they have none of these here. The Vanguard we are flying is equipped with a radial engine, a twin row affair with two superchargers and has 1200 horsepower. It takes off with the engine turning 2700 RPM.

In preparation for flying it we were required to read the Technical Orders on the plane and to sit for two hours in the cock-pit, learning the various

March Field, California

controls. What a fightin' machine I've never seen, it's **dynamite**. It's equipped with two 50 caliber machine guns mounted in the nose, and two 30 caliber guns in each wing. There are six guns in all and they are fired at a fixed point so many yards ahead of the aircraft. I don't believe there's a plane of the fighter type that has more gadgets than this one does.

Among six gun charging handles, a gun selector switch, plus a retractable tail wheel, two speed supercharger control, new type mixture control, third trim tab, retractable hood, oil cooler scoop, retractable hydraulic flaps on the cowling for cylinder head heat control, radio compass, radio directional finder, tail wheel lock, retractable pilot's step and a lot of other things, it was almost a new kind of flying to me. However it still had wings, tail and cockpit.

When I first poured the needle to this baby I knew I really was in something hot and as soon as I was off the ground I knew it twice as well. As there is no room for dual instruction, you have to do it right the first time. It came off the ground before I thought it would and it took me a couple of seconds to get the feel before I could pull up the wheels, I set the prop pitch and the manifold pressure. Climbed up at 145 MPH, 3,000 feet a minute, with the old altimeter spinning around like a taxi-meter. Soon I was up to 10,000 feet, leveled off and throttled back to cruising speed. Even at this altitude you have a sense of speed. The OLE airspeed lays right over at 240, just loafing along. It's got a top speed of 350 MPH at 15,000 feet. A Chandelle from straight and level cruising nets a gain of 3,000 feet. It does handle nice however and flips up into a vertical bank as smooth as silk. Its restricted diving speed is 425 for Army purposes. While in the air it's very important to keep the proper temperatures for the high output engine. To accomplish this the scoop and engine flaps have to be adjusted constantly for the different conditions you have.

Long Beach isn't the best of places to fly around, no room, too many restricted zones, etc. If you should get over the wrong space you are likely to get some anti-aircraft activity stirred up against you. Takes just a minute to be far away from the zones in this ship, P-66. This ship is heavy, it weighs 7,100 lb., and probably the hottest American pursuit plane at this time. It lands faster than a P-38 and has a good wide landing gear, which gives it good ground control. All the weight is supported by a wing, about the same size as that of a Piper Cub weighing 700 pounds. I tried a partial stall and it dropped out at 95 MPH. Next I experimented with the flaps, pulling them up suddenly the plane drops several hundred feet. This means that near the ground they have to be handled with care.

When landing I go through eight operations in preparation to finally touch down, or make contact with the runway. First I check the gas, select the reserve tank, open the canopy, slow down to 150 MPH, select low-blower, check the fuel mixture, adjust heat flaps, then down come the wheels. When they drop down it causes the plane to shudder, like a car which has suddenly had the brakes applied. The flaps are lowered to 15 degrees and then the tail wheel is locked. As you go around the last turn at 140 MPH, you select full low pitch on the prop and lower the flaps to 40 degrees. Establishing a 120 MPH glide you bring it right onto the runway. She settles on the ground and stays there at 105 MPH. A wonderful ship!!

From now on would you send my mail to the address that is on the back of the envelope? I haven't heard from anyone for weeks. I think that all my mail has been delayed in route by sending it to Luke Field and March Field. I did received the candy and cake you sent.

From a letter to Bob dated January 16, 1942:
In your last letter you mentioned the New York trip, well as far as I know we are still going but nothing has been said about it lately. It's just like everything else in this game, subject to change. Probably one of these mornings they'll yank us

March Field, California

out of bed and we'll be on our way. Guess I'll not plan on it or believe it until we're on our way.

Curtiss P-36 Hawk

Now to speak of planes. Evidently I didn't word it right in a former letter when I said that the P-66 is a hot airplane. What I meant to convey is that the P-66 is one of the hottest landing planes of our new pursuit type and that still goes. The P-40, P-36 and the P-38 all come in for landings about 110 MPH and touch down about 90 or 95 MPH. Now the P-66 comes in at 120 MPH, with power on, and touches down about 100 or 105 MPH. The only one that I know of which comes in hotter is the Republic P-47, a 2000 HP job. They say that it's so hot that it comes down at 130 MPH on the final approach. That is mighty fast and requires good judgment to even get it onto a runway at all. You see all of these planes have very high output engines, which have to be handled with care, or else they would heat up or load up.

The last two hours I have had in the P-40 were **combat**. This is where two of us go up and try maneuvers, by trying to get on one another's tail. I really love the 40 although it's not perfect. Some engine trouble and heating have occurred but I believe that if you treat them right they will perform for you pretty well. This morning I went up for combat training for an hour, 9:30 to 10:30. I climbed into the P-40 at 9:20, put on my chute, safety belt, ear headset and **throat mike**. We're now using a throat mike, which is an awfully clever rig, just a little strap around your throat with two tiny buttons that fit on either side of the Adam's Apple. When you want to speak you press a button on the throttle and speak out loud, thus your hands are free for the other things you need them for. Next I started the engine and taxied out for take-off.

Before you take-off you rev the engine up to 1700 RPM and check the mags. This also serves to clear the engine out so that it can take a lot of throttle on the take-off without spitting and sputtering. Next I check the trim tabs, giving a little for right rudder, this compensates for the engine torque and takes the pressure off the right rudder. I put the mixture control full rich and open the cowl flaps full for good cooling on the take-off and climb. The tower operator says 0308 okay for take-off. Answering **roger** I start the take-off roll, this is the real thrill in a 40. The little V-12 engine is very responsive and I have to watch the manifold pressure to see that it doesn't get too high. I've gone over the red line a couple of times without realizing it. It requires a lot of speed to get off the runway and then you have to pull it off. This morning when I pulled it off it was going 130 MPH.

A few minutes later at 12,000 feet we started our dog fighting. Diving, steep turns and all the other things you know of, and still it's pretty hard to lose someone once he's really on your tail. In such a fight, thousands of feet mean nothing; first you're at 7,000 feet and the next thing you know you're at 12,000. It's fun to watch a plane go by you in the opposite direction, it looks like he his going 600 MPH.

Coming down, I like to roll over and make a long power-on glide of about 325 MPH down to 2,000 feet, out about 15 miles from the field. Then I pull up to 5,000 feet using the speed to get me there and go on to the field, calling in and landing. I blacked myself out 3 times this morning in the dogfight. We pull the plane so tight that it makes my feet tingle. I stalled once at 160 MPH, pulling too tight in a turn. The plane just started to shudder, so I dumped the

March Field, California

stick forward and she came right out.

Bob it's really wonderful up there in the sky, sitting in the cockpit of that little **Forty**. Everything is right at your grasp, and ready to go. It gives you a feeling of power and speed, which is amazing. Well I guess I better quit gassing and sign off for now.

Changes were the order of the day at this stage of the war and Bill like everyone else was swept up in them. They never seemed to know where they were going next or what they would be flying. Like all good military men he did what he was ordered. He did have some time off and as he had many friends in the service and in California he was able to visit some of them.

From a letter home on January 23, 1942: Well it's 4:30 Friday afternoon and just time for me to drop you a little note before I get ready for supper. I will shine my shoes, shower and shave and then go over for supper at 6 o'clock. Always is nice to clean up, to go over to the mess hall and eat a nice supper. I look forward to it all day.

Last Sunday at noon I was able to get a 24 hour pass, so I immediately drove to Taft. It was 191 miles from March Field and I drove it in three and a half hours. Arrived there around 5:00 PM. Found Ed right away and he was glad to see me and I him. Spent the evening visiting and didn't do much but eat and go to town. Tried to catch up on things, so did a lot of talking. He certainly has a nice car, hardly a rattle in 9,000 miles. Went to bed at 1:00 AM and back up Monday morning at 6 o'clock. I left at 7:00 AM and was driving through the gate at March Field at 10:00 AM.

Well everything has been changed again. Thirty of our boys have been transferred to bombardment at Muroc, California, 100 miles north of here. They will be flying Martin B-26 bombers, the hottest thing that flies. There are many of them here and they are really something. This leaves about 25 of us here in pursuit. Two boys have been transferred to Foreign Service, I believe it's because of low flying. Now here's the **deal**, three boys and **myself** are awaiting orders to be transferred to **TASK FORCES HEADQUARTERS.** We don't know what it's about or anything and neither does anyone else here. We have turned in our equipment and have cleared ourselves of the post. So now we're just waiting for our orders. They may come in tomorrow morning or maybe not for a week. This is all I can tell you for now, as it's all that I know. Will let you know as soon as I learn anything.

Guess I'm done in pursuit and I really liked it too. Maybe I will get more opportunities and get to fly more varied equipment at the next place, who knows? Then again maybe it won't be so hot. A B-19 was here the other day, it's big all right. Its main tires are taller than a man is. Takes off in one third the distance that a P-40 requires.

From a letter dated January 29, 1942: Last week I received the very nice letter and pictures from Bob. I couldn't believe there could be as much snow there as the pictures show. Here of course there isn't any snow, except on the high mountains which surround March Field and behind San Bernadino. These mountains are very high and there is a lot of snow on the higher peaks.

Right now it is 5:00 PM and outside the hills are a beautiful green. The sun has shinned all day, without a cloud to obscure it's brilliance. With the weather so nice we seldom even wear our leather flight jackets. At this time the P-40s are returning from gunnery practice at Muroc Dry Lake, 100 miles north or 20 minutes flying time.

I also received the "Missoulian" photo section that you sent, it was very good. Also this morning I received the letter from Don Tomlinson, which you had forwarded. He is in the Ferry Command, which is a good flying job.

March Field, California

They ferry the various planes wherever they are needed. He's flying P-40s and P-39 planes to San Antonio, Texas at this time. I wouldn't mind that detail myself.

As for me, I don't know what is going to happen. I wrote you that I was to be transferred, however we are still waiting for orders and not doing a thing. $245 a month to loaf, I've never seen the beat of this. It's getting mighty tiresome and I'm anxious to start doing something. There are four of us awaiting our orders, I hope they haven't forgotten us. Probably nothing will happen for a week or two then they'll decide to put us back in our old group. Don't like this as it means that we will be behind the rest of the boys in flying by this much time. If we don't get some action soon I'm going to go see the Commanding Officer of March Field and see if he can stir up some action one way or another. I do hate to bother anyone, as all have worries and troubles of their own but I will if things don't progress.

B-24 Liberator

I haven't been in a plane for a week now. Guess I mentioned that the other boys are in bombardment now at Muroc. They started at the same time I received orders to standby for a transfer. They are all co-pilots in the four engine B-24 bomber. Time to go to supper. Well as I was telling about the B-24, I would like to get some experience like that also but in the long run I believe I would rather be a pursuit pilot or something where a fellow has a little independence and can do a few things on his own. Those big ships certainly would be a lot of fun, all right. Would be quite a responsibility flying such a big ship, about 25 tons. The crew consists of a couple of pilots, a navigator, radio operator, and the gunners. I've been up inside of them and they sure have plenty of room for bombs. When they land on a concrete runway the tires leave a stream of smoke behind as the tires go from a stand still to 80 MPH at touchdown.

Another trouble with getting into bombers is that it takes more and more study and understudy work before you finally get somewhere. I like to work with something I have already learned and of course learn more as I go along. The boys who went to Muroc are **again** studying code, navigation, etc.. However if they put me into bombers I wouldn't be too unhappy.

Had to take my car to town yesterday to get the generator fixed, the battery keeps getting low. Found out that the brushes were completely shot. Going to cost $2.00 to get them replaced. Have just about licked another month and this means another $250. Gosh! I have a lot of debts coming up, $18 for uniforms, $46 car payment, grub bill, board, car license, income tax, etc. Should do all right however. Well keep writing me, as I want to hear what's going on at home as long as I'm here. PS Bob--Take CPT.

From a letter dated February 2, 1942: I received your last letter and the picture of Bob. He's getting so he looks darn near as good as Dad and I. I think he would if he bought some decent clothes instead of wearing that old suit.

Bob, is it true that you are about to take CPT? Well good, get in there and do it because you will soon be in the Army anyway, for good. If you

March Field, California

take CPT you can still stay in school until the draft gets you, then join the Air Corps as a cadet. Now the requirements are so low that it's almost a farce. You can't make any other plans for the next five years, as we are going to have to take care of this war. There just isn't much use to think of anything else. It's a lot better making $200 a month rather than $21. You'd better get used to the fact that you haven't got many more months at home.

I did take Bill's advice on entering the CPT program at the University of Montana. I entered the service as an Aviation Cadet in the Air Corps and went on to fly heavy bombers, B-24 and B-17, and flew 32 missions out of Debach, England.

As far as the CPT is concerned, put it ahead of work at the store. As far as school, cut down on subjects so that you can do justice to everything. Ground school is very important in CPT, learn everything down pat, because it's 70% of the information that you will need to have in the Army. Get it good once and you'll have it. Remember there is a government final to take for your Private Flyers Certificate. I only wish that I could be **your instructor**. As it is, I will be giving you plenty of advice once you start flying. The biggest thing to learn is getting used to a new idea. Flying is purely mental and it take's awhile for that to soak in.

Bill had a lot of advice for me. Earlier in life and also later I tried to follow in Bill's footsteps and did.

Nothing much is happening here. Still sitting around waiting for orders. The 48th Squadron is going to move to San Diego one of these days. Maybe I will go with them if we don't get some orders soon.

It cost me $3.00 to have the generator fixed on my car. Now I'm going to have to get the front system taken care of, the front wheels start dancing on rough pavement. Will probably have to have it rebushed and get some re-conditioned shock absorbers installed. I'm pretty well pleased with it, as I've gotten 8,000 miles of use from it so far. Guess I can afford to spend a little on it. A car is an awful expense but I don't know what I'd do without one. Could probably manage but it would be a bother. I had to buy the $2.09 government stamp of course and have yet to buy my regular license.

Went down to headquarters this morning to get my paycheck but it wasn't in yet. Will probably come in the afternoon. Some of the boys are getting as high as $275 this month, hope that I do that well too.

Some of the boys here have started flying the Lockheed P-38. I wouldn't mind getting a little experience in that job. At the rate I'm going now I will probably end up flying Cubs in a Grasshopper Squadron.

A funny thing, some of the boys that I went to Oxnard and Bakersfield with, are now flying pursuit at Spokane, Washington, what a break. That's fate for you, only 180 airline miles from home. That could be made in 30 minutes in a P-38. Have you seen any pursuit ships in Missoula lately?

I'm enclosing a couple of terrible prints of the city of Phoenix and of Luke Field. Getting rid of everything that I can but haven't done anything with my clothes yet. Believe it would cost too much to send them home.

Well it's 11:35 AM, so guess I'll take this letter over to the Post Office, walk down to the line and see if I've received any mail and then go eat lunch. Lunch costs me 45 cents and dinner costs a half dollar. Lately I haven't been eating breakfast except when I'm working. I made an exception this morning, however and had coffee and doughnuts at the Post Exchange. It usually costs me about $35 a month to eat.

March Field, California

From a letter dated February 6, 1942: I received your letter in very quick time, only took it about a day in route. I'm afraid your suggestion that I apply for a leave would not work out, the Army just doesn't run that way. This is war and during such a time we just can't get off. This of course isn't reasonable or efficient but that doesn't seem to make much difference. An ordinary business establishment wouldn't last very long if it were run the way the Army is. At times, when it really wants to accomplish something, the Army is efficient. That is because they have the power to enforce a measure by anything up to a death sentence. Recently there have been about five examples shown to me, of the typical Army <u>efficiency</u> or <u>inefficiency</u>, if you care to regard it as such. First there was the proposed ferry trip to New York, that they had us all lined up and ready to go, but as you know we didn't. Nobody knows why or anything else and some say they are still figuring on it. To me they have cried Wolf once to often. Next there was our proposed transfer to **Task Forces** and really we should have kept flying with our squadron until we were called to go but they didn't. Now the powers that be, have agreed we should stay with our squadron until we are wanted. I don't believe we will ever be but we have wasted 14 days finding that out. So now we are kind of like lost-sheep in our own squadron. We missed out on gunnery, so now we are behind the other boys on that score. Guess it's not that all serious, but we do need the flying time to keep from getting stale.

North American BT-14

The other day they were planning to take some P-40s to Hamilton Field, they had 15 boys lined up to take-off within the hour and then it was called off. Why do they do things like that? Yesterday I was going to take another Lieutentant to Long Beach in a BT-14 and return with the another ship. Rushing down to dispatch, I got a clearance and a weather report, and was ready to go. We were all ready to get going and then they called it off as they couldn't find the airplane. An order was issued for 50 officers to move into a certain building, 10 of us obeyed and seven days later they moved us back to the other one. Those that ignored the order were saved the trouble of two useless moves. Oh well! That seems to be how it is all the time, do nothing and accomplish nothing. However if they keep paying us $245 to have a little trouble, I won't kick. A pursuit outfit could be a lot of fun in a good wide awake one, but until I find one, I would rather be an **<u>Advanced Flying Instructor.</u>**

Bill standing by Republic P-43

Now we are supposed to have some straight dope, we are moving to San Diego where we are to fly the Republic P-43. The 49th Squadron is moving to Mills Field, south of San Francisco. I wouldn't have minded going there as it's close to Redwood City, but it's south for me.

Well I'm sinking $22 into my car this month for repairs. It's down at the Ford Garage in Riverside now, have to pick it up around 6:00 PM. It got so I couldn't go over 60 MPH without the front wheels shimmying and shaking the car and me to pieces. They tested the front wheel

March Field, California

balance with a swell little machine, that spins the wheel by an electric motor attached to a roller. It shows statically and dynamically the balance on a gauge. Bell's no doubt have the same thing. Well one wheel was okay and the other would have been except for a small patch I recently had put on the inside of the tire.

I was called away from writing and am now starting again, it's Saturday morning. Well, I got my car with the total cost being $13.32. $8.35 to rebush the front system and the rest to fill and adjust the shocks and clean up the front brakes. They told me my rear brakes were practically making metal to metal contact so that's something else to have fixed. Got a 6-hour pass, so I went into Glendale and visited with Aunt Rose and Julian. Lynn wasn't there as usual. It's a 77 mile drive from their house to March Field. Took me an hour and thirty-five minutes to get back, including city driving. My car is 100% better, smooth throughout the entire range now and rides much better. I don't believe that I told you my car license was $8.00.

I'm not positive but I guess we're going to pull out for San Diego this afternoon. I'll write when we get settled. It's very foggy here this morning, but should clear up in a couple of hours. I won't be sorry to leave March Field as it's been kind of like a prison. Always have to quibble about getting a pass for one thing. Some things I enjoyed, and one was the good show house. Also they put on good shows for us here. The other night, Bob Hope broadcasted from here and a couple of weeks ago George Raft brought out some boxers and we had a good boxing program. Saw Henry Armstrong, Gracia, and even old Jim Jeffries. He's pretty old and bald, but the way he crawled through the ropes showed he's still active and in terrific shape.

How did Bob come out on the CPT physical?

Bill received orders on February 7, 1941 to report to the Naval Air Station at North Island, *San Diego. After all the confusion of the last few weeks things settled down and Bill's attitude changed about the Army Air Corps.*

Douglas B-19, only one made

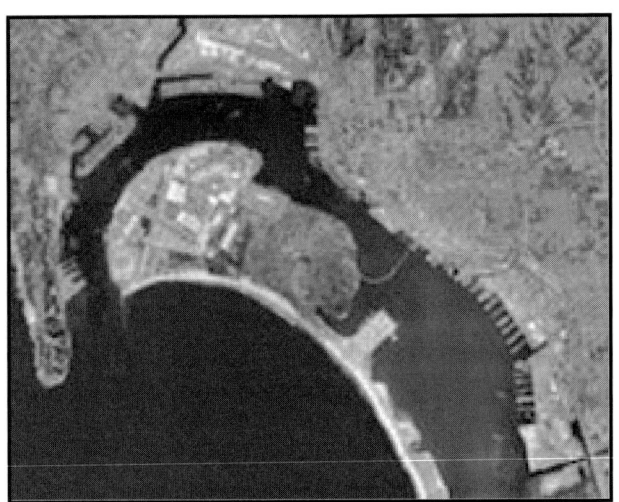
NASA photo of North Island

Naval Air Station, North Island

Bill finally did receive orders and transferred to San Diego. This seemed to put him in a better frame of mind about the Army Air Corps. We pick up his story now.

From a letter dated February 8, 1942: Just a short note to let you know where I am. We received orders at 5:00 PM on Saturday the 7th to report to San Diego. I left March Field around 6:30 PM and drove on into Los Angles by myself. Decided to go to a good movie for a change so I went to United Artist's Showhouse and saw "Louisiana Purchase". Was midnight when it got out and as I hadn't eaten any supper, I was mighty hungry. Went to a cafe and had a hamburger and a cup of coffee. I'm getting so I can find my way around LA pretty good, as I know most of the main routes and can find my way from one section of town to another without much trouble. Found a very nice room for the night for $1.00. I believe there is no use paying anymore.

I was up at 7:30 AM and continued on my way to San Diego. Took me a half-hour to get to Long Beach where I ate breakfast. Two hours later I arrived in San Diego. Of all things! We are located at North Island, the Naval Air Station. You have to ferry across to Coronado and then drive to the station. This airfield is really big and well planned out. They have plenty of room for us and we are living in the same kind of quarters that the Naval Officers are. The quarters are the best I've lived in since being in the Army. We are in a big room with four beds and four large closets. We have four nice chairs, a rug on the floor and a writing desk, what a layout. Also have a nice bathroom with a shower, etc. Adjoining our room there is a reception room, a bar and outside there is even a swimming pool, however there is not any water in it now. They tell us that we only pay $28.87 a month for room and board and that's great.

The Army here is flying the Republic P-43 and it looks mighty nice to me and I hope to be flying one of them soon. The Navy has a bunch of Brewster and Grumman midwing fighters stationed here. Frankly I'm certainly glad to be in the Army. There are so many different kinds of officers, Navy, Marine, etc. here and I don't know one from the other.

**Virgil Smith, John Stege, unknown and Bill
North Island quarters**

The weather was just perfect here today, blue sky and a cool breeze blowing. That's the way summer before last was. Well this hasn't been much of a letter, but I wanted to let you know what the score was.

From a letter dated February 11, 1942: You should see the cute little <u>dog</u> that we have for a mascot. He's just a little fellow about five inches tall. He seems to be always worried as his brow is always wrinkled. The fellows certainly get a

Naval Air Station, North Island

kick out of the way he acts and the things he does.

We've been divided into 3 flights with 10 pilots in each one. We take turns on tours of duty that consist of **alert, readiness** and **unavailable**. While on **alert** you never leave the flight room as you have to be ready to go up in a minute's time, should some hostile ship or plane be sighted. The **readiness** crew conducts flight training throughout the day and remains in the barracks at night, ready for a call if needed. The **unavailable** flight is free for a 24-hour period. While in this flight you are free to go to San Diego or anywhere you want just so you are back within the 24 hours.

Like I said, we are flying the Republic P-43 and it's the best ship that I've flown so far. The controls are handy and everything is smooth and easy to operate. There's as much difference between it and the 66 Vanguard as there is between a car and a truck.

Yesterday we went up on a high altitude formation flight. I was **number two man** on the leader's wing. We take-off right over the bay and bank away from the coast artillery, which lies directly to our west, what fun. I took-off second and banked inside to intercept the leader who was circling wider. Soon I caught him and we climbed steeply to the east. At 10,000 feet I turned on my oxygen and pulled the mask up over my face and nose. Gradually I used more and more throttle, because up there in the rare air the engine needs more oxygen, until the engine was running wide open. Then I got on the **turbo supercharger** lever, this has the effect of a new engine cutting in. It really takes a hold and makes the engine wind up, this is the feature which really makes the "43" an outstanding airplane.

We climbed up to 30,000 feet with ease and still the supercharger is producing more power than our engine can use. The plane flew as well as it had at 10,000 feet and the lack of oxygen had little effect. Outside the air temperature was 40 degrees below zero. By this time we were inland as far as the Salton Sea. After a tight rat race we returned to North Island and landed. What a power plant! It's said that the supercharger will turn as high as 72,000 RPM.

Today I went up on an instrument team-ride and worked on the San Diego beam for an hour. Gosh, the old BT seems so easy to fly and feels very safe after flying pursuit planes.

In the flight room there are tables to write on or read, a Ping-Pong table and lockers for our flying equipment, plus a radio to keep us happy. It's not much of a life but that's the way it is. The enlisted men sleep out in the hangar. Must be a 100 cots out there. They have set up a little Post Exchange where they sell Coke, hamburgers and such. It's hard to realize what a self-sufficient unit this is. Here in the hangar we have an Operations Office, Engineering Office, Supply Room, Parachute Deptartment and even a Medical Office. Quite a little setup, all in all.

There's a complete blackout on the post every night and boy they really makes the place dark. I'm having blackout lights put on my car so that I can drive on the post. They do this by painting the parking bulbs blue and cover all but a quarter inch hole in the taillights.

The other day while I was in San Diego I drove around the bay and up the narrow neck of land to Coronado and then came over to North Island. It's about 20 miles by that route and the cost is about the same, as it cost 25 cents to ride the ferry. Tomorrow I will be the Officer of the Day and will have a lot of administration work to attend to.

I guess Don Tomlinson's folks are still around here and the next time I get a chance I'm going to try and see them. In a couple of weeks I will be in town working on the Interceptor Board for

Naval Air Station, North Island

a couple of days. Write me the news.

From a letter dated February 23, 1942: I don't believe I ever thanked you for the Valentines, which the <u>various</u> Mothers sent. It was a noble idea and please give my thanks to all those charming beings.

So I take it that Bob is all set up for the CPT, this is certainly swell. How is the setup now? I read that there's usually a period of ground school before actual flight-training begins. Is this so? Let me know all of the details.

Yes, I did receive your package with the candy and cookies in it. My roommates and I enjoyed them very much, especially one of them, an older man from Burlingame, California, up near Redwood City. He is 35 years old, married and has two children. He had an insurance business, but was called to active duty as a Second Lieutenant. Another boy is an Engineering Officer who washed out as an Aviation Cadet, but continued to train in a different line. He's from upstate New York and always talks about the woods and rivers of his state. However, he didn't have much to say after I showed him the scenic pictorial from the "Missoulian".

The news that Ed <u>was</u> <u>getting</u> married or already has was news to me. I haven't heard from him for a couple of weeks or so. I knew about the girl and had seen her picture and my opinion is that she is just the type for Ed. Don't know why Mr. Halm should feel bad about it. I believe it's a frequent occurrence among young people between the ages of 20 and 30. Of course he may be worried that she could become a widow.

Heard that Mick Thieme is going to be at Wright Field, Ohio. That is the Air Corps big Experimental Base, Mick should fit in there just perfectly. He's just the type we need for that kind of work.

Now for a little business, when I was a cadet, we had to pay for our own insurance premium for about four months. Then they passed a law that the government would pay for it, so now it's possible to get a refund on the first four months premiums. This will mean about $25.00 coming back to me. In order for me to do this I need my orders as an Aviation Cadet, and the numbers of my first policy, they are with my papers there. I have the second policy here and according to my records I mailed the first one to you on July 11, 1941. Would you please find them and send me the number from the policy, it's about a third of the way down the page, thanks.

Yesterday, I received a letter from Cliff, he told me all of the latest. He said he is doing clerking work and getting along quite well. I don't believe he minds the Army as much as he thought he would. He also said that Kentucky is a pretty nice place.

On my last day off the Shipman's had me over for the evening. I needed a shirt quite badly and only had $5.00 to my name so I took my old black suit to town and sold it for the paltry sum of $2.00, then I bought a shirt for $2.85, a nice one. This happened because all my laundry is lost at March Field. We ate dinner at 7:00 PM and his young wife is a very good cook. We had steak, potatoes, peas, salad and all the trimmings. For dessert she had peaches and whipped cream with cookies. For the rest of the evening we looked at pictures and talked. They have a very nice apartment with a living room, dining room, small kitchen, two bedrooms and a nice bath. Another fellow is planning on getting married soon and moving in with them and this will cut expenses in half. This is what a lot of the fellows are doing as rent is so high, $60.00 to $100.00 a month and this forces them do do this. I left at 10:00 PM as Mark had to get up for the early shift.

There have been a lot of alert calls and patrols lately. We get a call and rush out to our ships and then get off the ground in a real hurry. It's

Naval Air Station, North Island

really important to know your airplane at a time like this. Things are planned out to the second, but there's always a lot of inefficiency despite everything that's planned. The Navy gets disgusted with us as we're having a terrible time. We've been getting more flying time here than at any other place we've been. We're averaging about 2 hours a day. I now have 20 hours in the P-43, and my total flying time is 333 hours. This area is a well-rounded place for training. We have a gunnery range right down near the Mexican border. Our bullets go out in the sea as we dive down on the beach. I find it harder to fire wing guns than the nose guns. The range has to be just right or the slugs cross each other and out they go in different directions. We have been using tracers and that enables us to see where they are going. I've been firing too far back and consequently not getting very good scores.

A couple of days ago two of us went up for practice combat, we were trying to get on one another's tail and stay there. We had just gotten a good start when two Navy attack planes started mixing it up with us. They were about 30 MPH slower than ours and consequently could turn inside of us. We would climb and then dive on them, finally I got on the tail of one, throttled back and managed to stay on his tail. I was just barely staying in, because I was going so slowly, this was really sloppy, but he couldn't shake me. Every little while my plane would shake, stall, and fall out even though the airspeed showed 150 MPH. When this would happen, I would dump the stick and the plane would pick up again. Finally he dumped his flaps and did a wingover, that got me, I just couldn't stay with him any longer. This is how we learn combat procedures and it does give you a good feel of your plane.

Yesterday, I had an instrument check ride with an older officer. Did pretty well considering I've only had 4 hours of instrument flying since graduating from flying school. He passed me even though I missed the cone of silence a little on the radio range. Instrument work is the hardest stuff I've ever done. You would swear that you're making a turn and climbing but **no** the instruments say no. You have to forget how you feel and go against your tendency to automatically correct for it.

If we're not paid promptly I'll have to write for money but hope not. There are women taxi-cab drivers in San Diego now and they are terrible. They just can't handle cars like men. The weather has turned cloudy the last two days and we've had a little rain, however it isn't expected to last long.

From a letter dated March 1, 1942: Sunday morning and this is my situation at this minute. I'm sitting on a leather-covered bench in a room that is forty feet long and twelve feet wide, around it are various doors. To my left and behind me is a door which leads outside. Just to the left of this door is another that opens into the Officer of the Day Control Room. Next to it is one which reads **48th Pursuit Squadron Message Center**. Directly in front of me is still another room which is marked, **Teletype**, two Corporals are in it. One of them is sitting in front of a Teletype Machine and the other is writing a letter, probably home. To the left of the Teletype Room sits a wooden box in which our mascot, a little Dachshund, is desperately trying to get out of. He's feeling pretty blue because the Operations Officer has given him a sound drubbing for mussing the floor. He's a very difficult pup to train. Other doors in the room are marked **Operations**, **Executive Officer** and **Engineering Office**. A group of officers down at one end are throwing darts at a target to amuse themselves. A mailbox with a bin for each officer sits empty before me. On a table is a coffee percolator and cups, we've all just had a cup. On the table also are reports from our Intelligence Officer giving detailed information, and showing pictures of enemy airplanes.

The situation I would like to be in goes like this. A room 1300 miles from here, it's cold outside,

Naval Air Station, North Island

but a comfortable heat fills the room. A man is seated comfortably in an easy chair, reading the paper. A woman is puttering among the breakfast dishes, while a dog groans contentedly on a rug in front of the radio. Oh me! It's not bad to work if you can spend Sundays at home.

I was sent up to the Interception Board in San Diego the other day to see how it operates. There is a table 30 feet long and on it is a huge map of the whole, San Diego area. With push sticks they move all of the forces that they have deployed in the field, subs, planes, etc. These are placed on the map at their exact locations. In another room, is another map manned by a flying officer and clerks to help figure out problems. If a call comes in from the Los Angeles office or from any of the many sentry posts along the coast saying enemy planes are at such and such a position, then immediately a call goes to North Island for 12 planes to scramble. Twelve pilots run to their planes, get into their equipment and get air-borne and form up as quickly as possible. Meanwhile the clerks in the second Interception Room have figured the course necessary for interception. The officer calls the planes by means of secret code words, tells them what course to fly and what altitude. We practice this everyday and usually use some bomber as an imaginary target.

Due to the fact that I've been moving around so much lately, my magazines have been late in reaching me. I'm having them sent home and then you can forward them to me, as you'll know where I am.

Everyday you see scenes here like the one that's on the front of the "Popular Aviation" magazine. We wear life vest like that Navy Pilot and have dogfights with Grumman's just like the one that is pictured. I got a kick out of the article "Check Pilot" on page 55. The plane he was using is the Army BT-14. We have one here which we use for instrument work. It seems so safe and easy to fly compared to the P-43. If I could get out of the Army it would be easy to get a job flying elsewhere. However the Army is okay.

From a letter dated March 5, 1942: Received your letter yesterday and also the one you forwarded from Bud Blanchette. Hadn't heard from him for so long that I figured he must have been transferred, but he's still in California at Camp Roberts.

Thanks for looking up the policy number for me, now I can go ahead and attempt to get the refund. I will mail the second policy to you soon. I received a nice long letter from Ed and he told me all about their marriage.

Consolidated PBY Catalina

You spoke of the Santa Barbara sub-incident. That night I was just ready to go to bed when they called us out to the line on an **alert**. We stood by waiting to go at the slightest opportunity. Out on the bay the Navy PBY patrol bombers were taking off loaded with bombs. They are capable of staying out for 24 hours without refueling.

A couple of days ago there was an impressive sight as an alert was called because of a submarine that was reported out at sea. Across the field came the Navy amphibian bombers followed by the Navy Brewster and Grumman fighters. Next came the Army P-43s in perfect four-plane formations. Off the ground they went wheels up and climbed swiftly at 160 MPH.

Naval Air Station, North Island

More groups took off and soon the air was a mass of fighter craft, but of course no enemy showed up. Probably one of these times we will get a little action.

US Navy Brewster Buffalo

This week we have been concentrating on ground gunnery. I fired the fifty-caliber guns for the first time. They fire much slower than the thirty-caliber, and you can almost count them as they pass through the prop blades. When two of them fire the cockpit fills with burned power and things shake quite a bit.

Lockheed C-36 Electra

Now we're checking out in a C-36, a twin engine Lockheed 12. This is a small transport, which will hold about 8 besides the pilot and co-pilot. I've been waiting for this, as two-engine stuff is good experience for anyone. Mainly the reason we are getting checked out in this plane is to get us accustomed to handling two engines. The rumor is that we're going to get P-38s for the squadron. Boy, the famed Lockheed P-38, this is the one I've always wanted to fly and now it looks like I will get my chance. The Lockheed may have some disadvantages but it certainly has speed. That's no lie. I could be home to Missoula in 3 hours flying time in one.

Here lately, the weather has been perfect, warm and sunny. Cool breezes blow in from the bay, it's perfect. Got my check yesterday. They claimed they overpaid me for quarters to the extent of $40 for last month, so it was held back. This cuts me short so I won't send as much home this time, hopefully I can do better next month. Going to get my picture taken soon.

Some of the boys from the squadron have just arrived back from a ferry trip. They flew P-40s from San Antonio, Texas to Spokane, Washington. They flew along the coast instead of going via Salt Lake, Utah and Missoula. Hopefully some day I'll get to make a trip, which will include Missoula.

Had a swell letter from Bud Blanchette, as I said, and he is always the humorous type. This is what he said about you **Mothers**. "It seems strange that our oldsters have taken up **BRAWLING** yet with so many mutual interests it's at the same time inevitable that they should." This is what he had to say about Ed. "News of the week, it appears, is made by our confirmed bachelor friend of some years, Joe Edward Halm, who has taken for himself an awful wedded wife." (Funny, but keep it to yourself.)

Have received a card, which shows I have an Instrument Rating. It says, "This is to certify that Schottelkorb, W. F., 2nd Lieutenant A.C. of the Air Corps Reserve of the Army of the United States has passed the test in instrument flying prescribed by W.D.A.C. Circular 50-1. Then it's signed by a Captain at Hamilton Field.

From a letter dated March 10, 1942: Yesterday I received a very nice letter from Ed and Jean. They are settled in Maricopa, California, which is only a few miles from Taft, as you know. A

Naval Air Station, North Island

funny thing, their street address is 431 Madera, same number he lived at on Mount Ave. They want me to come see them as soon as I can but I don't know when that will be as haven't been getting any days off lately and that makes it bad. Ed spoke about the classes that he is training and one of them will be **42-G**, he was in **41-G**. You can see how fast the classes are going through, they're training thousands of cadets now and the standards are much lower. Jean says they have a nice piano and that Ed is vainly trying to become proficient in its use.

Finally I've gotten my income tax filed. Had to pay on a total of $796.40 and the tax came to $2:00, not half bad. We're fortunate in having an Adjutant here who takes care of these kinds of things for us. Just took him about 10 minutes to type mine out. While he was at it he fixed me up with an Emergency Blackout Driving Permit, so that if I get caught in one I can drive.

From noon on the 8th until noon the 9th I was Officer of the Day again. It's not a bad job as it mostly consists of filing flight plans for outgoing ships. All the planes must be identified or they could be shot down.

On the 22nd of March, I'm to work on the Interception Board in San Diego. Have to work there for a week and won't be getting any flying time during this time. I could get a room at a hotel but think I will just walk back and forth and ride the ferry. It's a good long walk but it cost 25 cents to cross on the ferry with the car and that would come to 50 cents a day, too much, I will walk. Car is still on the blink anyway and probably I'm going to have to buy a new battery. Yipe!

Last letter I told you we were going to be checked out in the C-36, Lockheed Transport. Well we've been and now the squadron has received four Lockheed P-38s. I took one up for my first hour a couple of days ago. Boy this is some boat. It's really nice for it's purpose, which is to intercept bombers. It can't turn nearly as short as the P-43, in fact the thing goes so fast that it takes from San Diego the Mexican border to get it turned around. That guy that said, that a light-plane pilot with 200 or 300 hours and with thorough ground coaching could probably fly it around the pattern and land is crazy. It's a lot of airplane to handle and I'm glad I've had as much experience as I've had before I took it up.

It weighs 13,500 pounds, or more than 4 Fords. 2300 horsepower is available for take-off at 2800 RPM. The changes, mainly, that I had to become used to were, the twin engines and their synchronization, the wheel control instead of the stick and the nose wheel. It really handles nice on take-offs, rolls straight down the runway. This is because there isn't any torque due to the engines turning in opposite directions. One of the main things you have to watch is to watch that both engines are showing the same manifold pressure. At 100 MPH it will lift right off the runway. It has two of everything in it, as there are two engines. There are a lot of instruments to watch. It's very nice in the air and easy to fly. It's fast all right, just how fast I'm not at liberty to reveal, but it will equal the magazines figures at a certain altitude.

Landing it is a matter of a good straight approach and come in with power on, as they don't glide. Without the engines running they would just sink like a rock, so we fly them in, power on, at 100 MPH, which is very slow. You sit down on the main landing wheels then ease it forward onto the nose-wheel. It really rolls straight down the runway. About the hardest thing to do is slow it down to 175 MPH so the wheels can be lowered. Maybe some day I will have one with my name on it as the pilot. They're really armed and the cannon in the nose is big enough to blow a house apart.

Did I write you about our squadron insignia? Walt Disney produced it for us, it's a Firefly diving away from a very streamlined Cat, and it's very good. We're flying night missions at the present time and this gives the searchlights crews a chance to spot planes. So far they haven't been doing very well and we've been able to dodge them easily. Once they find us we are blinded and have to switch over to flying on instruments.

48TH FIGHTER SQUADRON

My friends flying the B-24s up at March Field are having lots of fun. One of them just got back from North Dakota, they flew all the way up there non-stop. Bye now.

PS He- "Do you shrink from kissing"? She- "Goodness no, if I did, I'd be nothing but skin and bones".

From a letter dated March 19, 1942: Dear Mother, Dad and Georgia, Perhaps I'm a little late with this letter, but here it is. So you have found a use for my old place at the table. It must be nice having Georgia home again. Wish I could be there to see her.

On my last day off I did a lot of shopping. Hadn't done any for a long time so I was short on supplies. The first thing I did was have my picture taken, as you wanted. So soon I will send them home to you. Had a shop that does good work take them for me. I decided to get a nice mounting so is costing me $9.40 for 6 pictures. I'm only getting that many for a starter but if you think I should have more, just say so. I can't afford to give one to everyone I know but I really should I suppose. I'll leave this up to you, figuring who should have them. I'm going to give one to Ed. The proofs will be ready Friday, so I'll choose the one that I think is the best then.

Tonight three of us, Stege, Seppich and I are invited over to the Shipman and Sorenson's place. Sorenson is a nice fellow from La Grande, Oregon. His father is a preacher and recently came down with his, Wally's, girl-friend, and then married them over in Yuma, Arizona. They are living with the Shipman's. The four of them invited us over for dinner at 7:00 PM. I know that I'll enjoy a home cooked meal. We will have to leave their name and number with the Officer of the Day so we can be contacted in case we're needed.

If all goes well and we get from noon Friday until Saturday noon off, John Stege and I are going to drive his 41 Chevy coupe to Bakersfield. It's about 240 miles from here and will take us about five hours of driving to get there. I will go on to Maricopa and he will stay in Bakersfield to see a girl-friend. I'll spend the evening with Ed and his wife. We will of course have to leave early the next morning, making it a very short visit. However this is the way things are done during war times. I hope nothing comes up to prevent us from going.

Next week I have to go to the Interception Board, uptown and that means no flying, Curse! I like to fly every day. I also like to appear eager all times, even if it does get a little tiring at times. I just want more time in the P-38. We had four planes to begin with but various bad landings have reduced the number to one. We've just received 2 new ones from Frisco but the older boys get most of the flying with them. We're

Naval Air Station, North Island

suppose to get in 23 more new ones from there also. I will more than likely get to go up to Hamilton Field, North of Frisco, to pick one up soon. Took the two new ones less than two hours to fly here from Frisco.

A call came in from Hamilton Field for a list of pilots with 60 hours of time in the P-40. Looks like some of the older boys might be going over the water soon. I only have 10 hours in one.

Yesterday as I was taking off in my P-43, the left rear section of the canopy blew out. I heard something go **swish** but didn't have time to look, as we were making a formation take-off. After I got up I looked and the glass was gone and the brace was sticking straight out into the prop blast, at 200 MPH. I had to come back and land.

The other day an older pilot and I flew to Long Beach and back on instruments. I got under the hood as soon as we left the Long Beach Airport and flew on the beam all the way to North Island. Quite a feeling to fly 100 miles without any outside contact at all. Does give you a lot of confidence for flying in bad weather.

Now that the cost of living has gone up still more, we realize what a good deal we have here, $25.50 a month for room and board, you can't beat that, especially now that milk is 17 cents a quart. Had a nice letter from Pat a couple of days ago, guess I'll have to write her again soon.

From a letter dated March 22, 1942: Yesterday, the 21st, I received your letter. You didn't mention anything about the proofs I sent. I just imagine that by the time you wrote you hadn't received them. Do hope that I get them back in the mail today.

Yesterday I started my week's duty at the Filter Center, Interception Board, uptown. My shift is from 4:00 PM until midnight. My job consists in establishing radio contact with our planes and directing them, so that they will intercept the enemy or whoever they are sent after.

Los Angeles has a master plotting board and we have a smaller one of the San Diego area, this extends about 100 miles around us. All over the country-side are located civilian air-raid spotters and Army D-Racks. The D-Racks pick up an airplane and figures it's approximate altitude, speed and location. This information is relayed to our board and immediately a symbol, with certain markings, is shoved onto our board at the right location. A check is made to see if any of our aircraft or boats are in that vicinity, if so the target is termed friendly and if not is termed enemy. If it's identified enemy, Los Angeles calls me and tells me to scramble 12 planes. I put in a call to North Island, from one of my many phones, and call a scramble. After this my helpers, three girls, get busy and calculate on our map, with the world's best navigation equipment, just what the course our planes will have to take to intercept the unidentified target. As soon as the flight leader is in the air, he calls saying that they are airborne. I give him their heading, altitude and time by means of secret coding words.

Another part of my job is to establish and maintain radio contact with the planes doing the night flying. Two planes go up and fly on certain courses so that the searchlights crews can practice spotting them. Last night I went into the Search Light Room to do my part, I didn't know what to expect but soon found out. It was another plotting board that shows all the lights and a bunch of stuff that was all Greek to me. I took my place beside a Major Banes, who communicates with the crews manning the lights. Takes about 10 enlisted men and a First Lieutenant to work the plotting board. Also in the room is another Major and even a General. There I was, mystified as to what my job was but after we started it wasn't too bad. I established contact with my two planes and kept them informed as to what they were supposed to be doing. When the lights reported them out of their course, the Major told me and I relayed the information to the pilots. What a riot, here I was a green 2nd Louie and the General was asking me all about the planes and what they could do. Yes, it's swell to be a **flying** officer.

Gradually more P-38s are arriving and soon we'll be flying them entirely. I like them quite a bit but they have a lot of disadvantages. Too much stuff to handle and to get out of order. The P-43 is remarkable for service and dependability, but those Allisons are a headache for trouble. Time will tell.

I'm sending some pictures. By the way the 4 of us boys had a wonderful time at the Shipman's the other night. Elaine can really turn out a meal, just as good as if she'd been doing it for 20 years. Things were real swell.

USS Hornet

The other day, the aircraft carrier Hornet and some destroyers steamed into port, so now the Town has more sailors than ever. We knew they were coming and flew out to watch them arrive. My flight was sent out to sea for 80 miles that morning. The weather was perfect as we started out to sea, climbing steeply as usual. The 43 climbs at practically a 40 degree angle, so steep that when you are in the back of the formation looking at the planes ahead, you would swear they are going to stall and slide back on top of you. However when you glance at the airspeed and see it's 150 MPH, you know that all is well. We leveled off at 12,000 feet and far below could see the aircraft carrier with the protecting destroyers hovering close around. The white wake that the ships left extended for miles behind them. We circled the barren waste of San Clemente Island and then started our trip home. We made it a long power decent passing over North Island at 2,000 feet indicating 300 MPH, then landed.

From a letter to Bob dated March 27, 1942: By the time you receive this letter you'll probably have had your first lesson in a Cub. I've wanted to talk to you about flying for a long time, but there wasn't much use telling you anything until you've had at least one ride. Now you will be able to see the problems you're going to have to cope with. After one ride, there will probably be 100 questions, which you will want answered. Your instructor probably won't quite be able to satisfy you with his answers. Before I speak, for speak I shall, about flying itself, or the way it's done, I would like to impress a few **points upon you**.

First, you've gotten yourself into something, if you intended to or not. They have you now and the only way out would be doing something pretty awful. This would make you lose your self-respect. Until we win this war, your life, my life, and Dad's life will not be our own. To win this war the government is drafting skills as well as men. If you can fly, you are valuable, and consequently will be used where needed. Dad is a skilled mechanic and if they ran short on manpower, the Army could take him for truck repairing, aircraft work, or even factory machine work. Down here, the Consolidated Plant has 40,000 workers earning good money. Thousands of these workers are girls and women. The factories simply can't find the men to do the jobs, that's just how serious the shortage of manpower is becoming. Many of these workers in skilled jobs wouldn't be permitted to quit even if they wanted to. Your job, my job is the same way. That's a blundering democracy for you.

Naval Air Station, North Island

Do you have any idea how poorly prepared we are to win this war? First we don't really have any decent equipment. Speaking for my game, what have we got? A few Pursuit Planes that really should be classed as advanced trainers. They are heavy, undergunned and slow. Just name one Pursuit Plane this country has that's really tops, you can't. The P-40 is way too slow, and climbs very slowly. The P-39 is a dream except for one thing, a typical American trouble, too much weight due to necessary armor plate, etc. The P-43 is too heavy and slow and under gunned. The P-51 Mustang is probably as good as any except that it'll take a year to get them built. The P-47 is probably the going thing but again no quantity. It's more of an interceptor, because it, like the P-38 weighs in the 13,000 pound class. With this weight it cuts it's dog fighting and quick turning ability in half. The Germans however make a light plane with the barest equipment. They put up a plane of 4200 pounds against ours of 6600 pounds with approximately the same power and ours wouldn't come out too well with theirs, despite our quality.

Anyway we're really poorly prepared. We're turning out pilots fast, yes, but it takes 6 months to a year to get a pilot really trained, in any other line other than instructing, this is time after flying school. So that's the setup, you're going to be a pilot so put everything you have into it. Be good at it and it will always pay you. You can get by, taking it easy and joy riding but someday when you are mid-plane in a seven-ship echelon, 4 feet from the next plane's wing you will be glad that you worked hard on Crossroad Eights way back in CPT. So learn everything you can and remember it, it will pay 100% later on. Let there be no mysteries about flying, for that breeds fear and a lacking of confidence, which will hold up your progress.
The first take-off will be a big thrill to you but it is old stuff to the boy up front. He knows airplanes will work and he also knows why. So get that idea quickly and you'll do fine. Accept your new concept of transportation as natural, because it has proven safe and natural by thousands of pilots before you.

A couple of other points, however you will do these anyway, I know. Let me impress these upon you so you'll never fail. When you are suppose to be at the airport at 1:00, boy you be there before then, with your equipment ready and waiting for the instructor. Never let him wait for you. Always appear eager and no matter how tired you are, always jump at the chance to get in more flying time. This will make you get along twice as good as the guy who doesn't. This is true even if the other guy is a better pilot than you are. Enough preaching, let's talk about flying.

Probably one of the things which causes the most damage to aircraft is taxiing accidents. Many times pilots have gone through years of careful flying only to knock off a wing tip on a hangar, or taxi into another ship and chew it's tail up. Of course things like this are never excusable so if you want to have trouble, have a good honest to goodness ground loop and really do it up right.

There'll be several things entirely new to you, of which you need to get the hang of right away. One is the trim tab or adjustable horizontal stabilizer. It's purpose is to take the load off the stick, forward and backward. For instance, flying straight and level, if you find that you must hold heavy backpressure to maintain your altitude, then move the lever backward to take the load off. This is true also if you have to hold forward pressure to maintain the altitude, except you have to push the tab lever forward. It will take practice, but don't hesitate to use it, because you will be using it a great deal later.

Now there's the Magnetos, Dad can tell you what a mag is on a twin-ignition system. The engine in the Cub will run well on one but does a lot better with both operating. Before you take off

Naval Air Station, North Island

the engine is revved up to 1500 RPM, turn the Mag Switch over to one mag, observe the drop in RPM, then switch back to both and allow the RPM to pick up to normal. Then it's time to test the other mag. In a Cub, one mag operation will probably only cause a drop of 50 RPM. Now your instructor will give you this dope, so do it his way. I'm just trying to give you a few tips on what can be done without getting the plane into trouble.

While good coordination makes for good flying, don't get the idea that if you move the rudder more than the stick, you're going to spin or cause any other trouble, other than perhaps minor skidding or slipping. The Cub can be handled pretty roughly and sloppy before anything is going to happen which will cause you trouble. When you practice your first stall, you'll see that you practically have to stand it on the tail before it'll stall. Just keep a normal climb and a normal glide and you will never stall.

Let's go through a take-off. First make sure you're clear to go. Check against that hill for planes coming in low and also remember to look up high also. Line up on the runway and advance the throttle slowly to wide open. As soon as you're rolling push the stick all the way forward and hold it in the center. Stay on those rudders and keep it straight no matter if it feels like you're bouncing all over the place. When the tail comes up, come back on the stick and ride about level. It'll fly or bounce itself off the ground. Around 10 to 20 feet level off and gain speed before establishing your climb. Now here's a real tip. On takeoff you'll be traveling at low speed yet the engine is turning at a high speed. The engine turns the prop one way, left, and that tends to turn the plane to the left, torque. So that the plane will stay straight at **cruising speed** the wings and rudder stabilizer have been set to balance this tendency. However at less than cruising speed you're going to go left unless you hold a slight amount of right rudder or dip your right wing slightly. That's why on the first take-offs you started out on the right side when you passed the border.

Now a few words about landings. Get the idea that the ground is your friend when you come in, don't shy away from it. Come down slow in a normal glide, break it gradually about 20 feet up so that you end up about 2 feet just skimming along. When your lift is gone come back on the stick and you will settle in on three points. You'll know that your lift is gone when you start sinking. It's all easy when you know how. They'll tell you that if you hit wheels first you'll go up again. Well you will if you yank back on the stick at the same time you touch the ground. If you just hold the stick you'll just roll along on the wheels until the tail drops. That's the kind of landings we make with the AT-6 and the P-40. Well, I guess you're thoroughly bored by now.

From a letter dated April 3, 1942: When you sent the proofs back to me you said you wanted one that faced toward the front. Well numbers 2, 3, and 4 all did that, so I picked number 4 and went hog wild and ordered 6 of it. Now you want number 3, in a small frame, so as soon as I get to town I'll order it. The others will be ready on the 7th.

I finished my week with the Interception Board last Saturday night at midnight. Got time off so decided to go to Maricopa. Left here at 8:00 AM Sunday and arrived there at about 1:00 that afternoon. Family man Ed greeted me from his front porch and invited me in to meet the Mrs. Jean is very nice and perfectly suited to Ed. They have a nice house, with plenty of rooms, and nicely furnished.

We drove up in the hills to see the little ranch house where Ed lived with two other fellows before he was married. The garden was coming along pretty well except the part that the rabbits had eaten. They were only paying $10 a month rent on it but they lived like kings. Later on we went to a show in Taft and then spent the rest of

Naval Air Station, North Island

the evening just talking. They have a gas range and Jean fixed us a nice little supper. They've certainly received a lot of nice gifts and she showed them to us, towels, tablecloths, silverware and an electric iron from me. Ed is so restless usually, and I was surprised to see how settled down and contented he seems to be.

Had trouble with my car going there and when I got ready to leave Monday morning, it wouldn't start and had a flat tire. Finally I got it started and I limped over the hill to Los Angeles and home. Think it's the fuel pump but haven't had time to work on it yet.

There were a couple of days with poor weather but now it seems to be getting better. There has been small patches of mist about 1,000 feet in the mornings. We went up above it this morning and the sun was shining beautifully. I went up in the BT as observer for John Stege, who was going to do some instrument training. We flew through patchy clouds at 1,000 feet and came out on top at 1,500. At that time he was under the hood and ready to begin. I gave him the controls and called San Diego Radio telling them that Army Q-1214 was entering the Radio Range at 6,000 feet, preparing to work a problem on the east leg. Then I just sat back and took it easy, making sure that we didn't run into another airplane, or get into any dangerous attitude. I also kept an eye on the gas supply and engine instruments. The BT runs like a Model A and we had a very nice ride. When he was finished I took over and landed the crate.

After about a half-hours rest, Flight Commander Bing told John and I to go up for an hour and practice combat in the P-38s. Oh joy!! That's what I wanted to do in the first place. We took all our equipment out to our planes and got ready to go. You need about 5 hands to get them started, as there's so many things to work. Soon both engines were running and we were ready to go. I'm getting so that I can taxi them now, at first they felt awfully clumsy. We use the engines and brakes for steering when we taxi. If you want to turn right, stand on the right brake and blast the left engine. It's a riot to see a 38 come up to the line with it's engines alternately blasting and the ship sinking and rising on the nose wheel shock absorber. Soon John and I were out on the take-off point, here I checked and double-checked everything to make sure that both engines would keep running on the take-off. We decided not to make a formation take-off as we've only had about four hours in them and didn't want to push our luck. I left first, pushing my throttles to 35 inches manifold, and then waiting for the speed to pick up. The pick up is terrifically fast and at 110 MPH it lifted. Wheels up, Prop RPM reduced to 2,500 and a climb of 160 MPH established. One turn and the altimeter reads 3,000 feet and the hand was going around faster than a clock hand being turned by hand. Now I had time to check everything over, even manifold pressure and RPM, oil cooler shutters half-closed, coolant shutters half-closed. The gas-selectors on the main tanks, generators charging OK, fuel pressure even, mixture automatic rich, oil pressure and temperature normal, radio on correct frequency, everything was OK. On the radio I could only get music from Mexico.

Now I was at 10,000 feet, below Johnnie, flashed by going in the opposite direction. My fuel pressure started to drop so I turned on the electric boost pumps. Oil temperature went up so I closed the shutters to prevent congealing, same principle as a car radiator freezing up. At 12,000 feet I put my oxygen mask on and set the flow for 20,000 feet. When I reached 16,000 I leveled off and waited for Stege. We made several passes at each other, taking about 20 miles to every turn. These planes weigh as much as a Ford Tri-Motor and they won't turn sharp like a P-43. We next tried some formation-flying. Nuts! First I would start to go by so I'd cut back on the throttles, then when I gave it the gun one turbo would catch first and send the manifold pressure on that engine way up. This caused

Naval Air Station, North Island

unequal pulling. It's going to be a job learning how to do this. Stege got on my wing and we started down. We made a big circle and passed over the field at 1,500 feet indicating 350 MPH. You have to see this to appreciate how much speed a couple of 38s can show. After we got down, I felt sleepy and exhausted. The high altitude flying takes something out of you and then too, the 38 is quite a bit of ship to horse around at any altitude. Oh! But I enjoyed that ride. Up there at 16,000 feet the 38 is the greatest sky-eating baby I've ever seen. Thousands of feet mean absolutely nothing to it. A 38 at 2,000 feet doing 350 MPH could pull up from the town of Lolo at a 45 degree angle and go right over the top of the mountain, Lolo Peak, Great!

Well! Pleasant surprise, I have just received a cake and a box of shaving soap and lotion. I wonder who has been so good hearted as to send me all these things? Thanks a lot both of you. Stege and I are spending the night here on the flight line, so we'll eat some of the cake this evening. Our hours are really long now that the days are longer. Get up at 5:00 AM and have to be down here to the line by 5:45, then we are here until 7:15 PM. Makes for a pretty full day.

Have you heard that we in the Army can now mail letters free? Seems funny, putting a letter in the box without a stamp, I'm still doubtful.

According to the latest letter from Don Tomlinson he's going to make a good-will tour of South America in a P-40. He also mentioned that he would probably be promoted to a First Lieutenant before too long. Several of our boys have been promoted to First Lieutenant, so I imagine it won't be too many months before we of class 41-I get our silver bars.

How's Bob getting along with the CPT?
From a letter dated April 8, 1942: It starts: Hello Peaceful Valley, This morning I tried to get the pictures but the place is mobbed with orders so it'll be a little time yet. Will send them as soon as I can.

Yesterday was our day off, so several of us boys went down to the beach and had a nice swim. We took a volleyball along and got a lot of exercise throwing it around besides the swimming and running that we did. The water was a little cold at first but soon it felt good. This is the first real exercise I've had for a long time. Today I'm stiff and sore.

Our schedule for each month includes, four hours each of combat, air gunnery, ground gunnery, instrument flying, high altitude flying and link trainer. All this besides our regular patrols and alerts. This should give us about 50 hours of flying a month if the weather cooperates. Lately it hasn't been up to the usual San Diego standard but hopefully it will improve.

Now I know more about the P-38, so I'm better able to judge them. A few days ago we went on a high-altitude formation flight in them. At the low altitudes I could keep in pretty well but as we got higher I had more trouble, due to the supercharger lag. Not that the 38 isn't a high altitude ship, because it definitely is, but I would start to over run the leader. I would have to cut the throttles back and then get on them again and this would cause lag and I would drop back. When the turbos did kick in, one would be ahead of the other and one engine would start pulling ahead of the other. Well it turned out to be a good work out and I certainly learned a lot. We went up to 22.000 feet and I about froze my hands and feet before I found the heater control. Coming down was much easier, because we didn't use much power and we stayed together in formation. They are awfully heavy and so it's something like trying to fly formation with a Douglas Transport.

Some of the guys don't like the 38 much, consequently there are a good many pros and cons as to it's merits. Some of the guys have tangled, after a fashion, with some of the Navy fighters and reported that they didn't fare very well. So when Major Keith, our recently promoted Commanding Officer, decided to take B Flight up in six 38s to jump anything that they could find, we of C flight decided to give them a little surprise with our group of P-43s. The Los Angeles Controller gave us an alert call, this was so that the 38s wouldn't suspect us. We took off first and started climbing fast for altitude. We started up the coast and circled back to pounce on the 38s. We came back over the field at 13,000 feet looking for the 38s that were supposed to be at 10,000 feet. Boy, were we fooled, they taken off 5 minutes later than we did and now were sitting at 16,000, about 3000 feet above us. However they were gentlemen and didn't attack us then. Of course, we learned all of this later. We went on looking for them and finally spotted two of them playing around 3,000 feet below us. Oh! I thought we would surely get them now as we would dive on them and they just wouldn't be able to dodge us. Down we started, screaming, our blunt nosed 43s along at better than 300 MPH. We were spotted and the 38s started a slight dive. Instead of bearing down on them we got down to their level and trailed out behind. We gave our 43s the supercharger and tried to catch them. I was pulling 45 inches of mercury, cruising is 30 and takeoff is 41, so we were really beating them but it was hopeless. The 38s now far out of range started their gentle easy climb and just ran circles around us. Soon they were above us 2,000 feet and started their dive at us. That was the most hopeless feeling I have ever had, to be going wide open in a superb little plane but seemingly standing still to the graceful 38. They were specks in the distance when they started their dive but a fraction of a second later they loomed large as they flashed past my tail. They could have shot down the whole bunch of us. Then with their terrific speed they pulled up, did a wing over and came down again from behind. I was indicating nearly 300 MPH, when those 38s went by me like I was standing still. As they circled in front of us, our leader vainly tried to Chandelle up to get a shot but the 38 appeared to be going a third faster. Then the 43s went on in to land hopelessly defeated.

It was the most pathetic demonstration I have ever seen. No pilot here, now doubts the 38, of course the 38 is really not a fighter, it's an interceptor. Its job is to go out and shoot down bombers. It can't turn with a fighter, but it doesn't have to fight as it can outrun anything I've heard of.

This morning we again took a little altitude hop, just up to 20,000 feet. The 38 just begins to come in to it's own at that altitude, in fact it flies much better there than a low altitude. On our way down at 13,000 we ran into a Navy Brewster Fighter who was in a playful mood. We peeled off and started after him, he surprised me before I was ready and got a good pass at me. I started to climb with him on my tail,I then gave it 35 inches, 2700 RPM and left him flat. Did a wing over and back down and drilled him dead. Meanwhile the other three 38s were making passes at him also. The poor guy tried everything in the book, slow rolls, split "S"s, he literally stood that thing on it's tail trying to climb up to a 38, but the 38 was in it's element and we drilled him time and again. I've never seen anything like it. The Brewster is really a honey of a ship, in fact, I think it could give a 43 a good run. After an hour and a half of horsing that baby around I really felt like I had done a day's work.

This afternoon we had 10 more P-38s to bring back from Long Beach. Right after dinner they took us up to Long Beach in a Lockheed Transport. Long Beach is now the headquarters for the Ferry Command and there are hundreds of pilots and planes there. We attended to the red tape and signed for the ships and took our equipment out to the planes. These are new P-38Es and plenty nice. My generator burned out as soon as I took off, so I cut all unnecessary electrical equipment and decided my battery would last for 25 minutes, the time it takes to get back to San Diego. We made it with all 10 planes and no mishaps, so now we have 25 planes. Major Keith said we will each have a 38 of our own now, I certainly hope so. This way we will fly our own plane and be responsible for it. We will learn it's characteristics and know just how it has been treated. I think we will respect a plane more and give it better care under this setup. Well I've talked enough about things here. What about home? Has Bob reached the solo stage yet?

From a letter dated April 18, 1942: No doubt by now you've received the pictures of me. What do you think of them? They're much better than I had hoped for, of course they touched them up a little. They're what's known as a Gold Tone Picture and there's a little art work done on the them. When I get the two small ones I will send them along, should be within the week. Sometime ago I told you that several of us had gone to Shipman's for supper, well with this letter, I'm enclosing three pictures taken that evening.

A week ago Major Keith led 16 of us to Long Beach in our P-43s. We thern turned them all over to the Ferry Command at the Municipal Airport. They have been a wonderful little ship and we gained a lot of valuable experience in them. I had nearly 60 hours in one, which was more than most of the fellows had. From there we were taken to Los Angeles in an Army Ferry Command bus and after eating we departed for San Diego on the train. This was an interesting little trip and somewhat different from the everyday run of things. Now we are flying Lockheed P-38s exclusively.

Had to have the rear brakes relined on my car and also the drums turned. I didn't like spending the money but this was a pretty necessary item. I need to keep it in good running shape. It cost me $10.70, which wasn't too bad and now the little boat is running pretty good. The engine is working well, in fact I only added one quart of oil in 1,300 miles and that included the trip to Maricopa, where I drove pretty fast.

Seppich took the fatal plunge the other day and was married in Yuma, Arizona. He married a girl from his hometown, that he has known for years. They found a house in Coronado with the rent running $100.00 a month. Coronado is a beautiful place but there is such a demand from Army and Navy people for houses, that rent is sky high.

Perhaps you saw the pictures in **Life** magazine of the B-17E, it's crew and the maintenance workers. Well here we have the same setup. My plane is crewed by four men and two others take care of the guns. That makes six all together. Some of the time they have nothing to do and other times have more than they can handle. They do have to work long hours and also have to work out in the weather, plus putting up with the dirt from the prop blast. My Crew Chief is a twenty year old Corporal, who has been through an intensive mechanical course to get his rating. He enlisted in the Army when he was 18, after he completed high school. The Gun Chief has been in the Army 12 years. He started out in the Coast Artillery and then went to school and received his rating as an Airplane Machine Gun and Cannon Mechanic. Frequently when I have nothing to do I go out to the line and talk to the crews about the plane. They are all very nice to me and are always willing to show me how things work. Before my gunnery mission the other day, the Gun Chief explained the machine guns complete operation to me, so I had a good working knowledge before firing them.

The 38 is a dream on gunnery. There is no torque in the dive, so the guns fire right where they are pointed. Also I shot the cannon and it's the clear rig. It doesn't kick much more than the machine guns, and really puts out a good-sized slug.

Naval Air Station, North Island

A few nights ago, I flew the 38 on a search-light mission. The take-off was from a runway that's pointed out to sea and due to the blackout there were no lights for reference. This was the first instrument take-off I've made. Rolling along the ground at 50 MPH, I simply couldn't see a thing, so I just got down on the instruments and went to work. At 110 MPH, off the ground she came and I established a climb. At 1,000 feet I looked back and saw the lights of town and then had a horizon to go by. When the search-lights spotted me there was such a glare that again I had to depend on my instruments. The lights look blue when looking down on them and boy are they bright. I was sent on several different courses about 25 miles out over the ocean and then would return, thus giving them practice on picking up an airplane. Talk about a dark and lonely world, this is the way it is when you fly out over the ocean at night. There is <u>nothing</u> out there but inky blackness.

From a letter dated April 26, 1942: Mother, you started your last letter out with, "Wondering how you are". Well I wasn't, as when your letter arrived I was sick in bed with a cold. Had to spend 3 days in bed and didn't help much as I still don't feel very sharp. Twas just a plain old cold but as usual I have a rough time with one. Today I decided I had better get up, as I was just getting weak from lying in bed. A cold in any form, especially a head cold means that there is no flying of any kind. This can cause inner ear infection and real trouble. Looked like I wouldn't be doing any flying for a week. Bill Hanes was about to take his turn as Intercept Officer, so I decided I could do that and recover my health at the same time.

So here I am on the late shift, for another week, in this bleary outfit. Ordinarily I wouldn't have had to come up here for couple of weeks but this way I won't miss another week of flying later on. It's now 2:15 AM and consequently I still have five hours and forty-five minutes before I get to bed. I don't feel sleepy but I certainly will be by the time my shift is over.

Bob congratulations on making it aloft with heavier-than-air machinery. Write me the details and I will soon write you on the subject. I heartily enjoyed your last volume.

The insignia on my shoulder is a blue airplane spinner on a bright orange disk. It means that I'm a member of a combat, fighting, force and this distinguishes me from a training, observation, and other units. The Walt Disney squadron insignia is now available to put on our leather flight jackets. These insignias are not put on the planes in time of war and the planes are camouflaged.

You said Bud was in town on a furlough. I suppose you mean Bud Blanchette. The lucky guy! If only I could get a few days off.

B-17

Not too long ago, we were lucky enough to hear a talk given by an Air Corps Captain who had just returned from Australia. He'd been in the same outfit as Colin Kelly and was a Pilot of a B-17E. I won't mention any figures but it was astounding how little equipment we had over in the islands, so little, that our group of 20 P-43s would have been a major increase.

Naval Air Station, North Island

The first days of bombing just about spoiled everything. The Japs destroyed over half of our B-17 and P-40 planes. A terrible blow, as they were destroyed on the ground, before they could even get into the air. From then on it was just a question of being run out of one place and then another. We had no help from the English but the Dutch were great help and well prepared. Our boys didn't have any fields to operate from and consequently, eventually had to move to Australia.

As to the merits of our planes against the Japs the Captain said this: "Our pursuit planes won't turn with the Jap fighters nor will they climb with them, the P-40 that is. However they are far superior in all other respects. The Jap pursuit plane is a lightly made crate and it only takes a few bullets to blow it to bits. A P-40 pilot dived to an indicated 325 MPH, with a Jap on his tail, he pulled up sharply and when the Jap tried to follow, his wings gave way and came off. As to speed we know our P-38s has 60 MPH on a Jap fighter. In one case a B-17 took all the lead that 18 Jap Fighters could give it and it didn't go down. Yes, we have the goods, so all we need is plenty of it and good bases that have continuous supply lines.

Well our outfit is to be broken up, soon we hear. Evidently there will be two squadrons formed out of this one and each will receive some new 2nd Looies to train. We 41-I boys are getting to be old pursuit hands now and probably will play a large part in training any new-comers. As of now I'm thoroughly in love with pursuit and wouldn't want to be anywhere else. I would rather fly the P-38 than any plane I know of. It's a lot to handle but once you can do it you feel tops, as it out performs most other planes by a wide margin. Getting so that we can hit the sleeve in aerial gunnery now too. A week ago I got 9 hits out of 60 rounds, not a high percentage but considering Major Keith was the only one to hit it at all a few weeks ago.

With the squadrons divided we will probably get Foreign Service within two to four months. It's all right with me! I'd just as soon get the war over with and get back to the farm. All of us pilots are working steady now, no days off. We get up at 5:00 AM, leave the flight line at 7:15 PM and are in bed by 9:00 PM. Plus every few days we have night flying also. This gets awfully old and we could really all go for a week's rest. Three of the boys just came back from another ferry trip, San Antonio, Denver, Salt Lake, Boise and Spokane, that's pretty close to home.

From a letter dated May 13, 1942: I know you've been waiting for some time to get a letter from me, so here it is. I took a second week on the Interception Board as I told you before, then went back to flying. Although I'm not in the best of shape, my cold is over, and now I feel like I need a good rest and some exercise. However, I'm afraid that I'm not going to be able to do either. Things here are in a big turmoil and I need all the strength I've got just to make the daily grade.

A week ago I bought a new battery for my car and I figured I had it in good shape for as long as I would need it. But that was before I let a friend borrow it to go over to Coronado for the evening. The streets over there are in bad shape and also have deep drains ditches at the intersections and you really have to slow down to cross them or throw everyone out through the roof. Well he hit one about 35 MPH and he certainly fixed my car. Went through the springs, bent the front axle so that the wheels are out of line, the hood won't fit, and the grille is twisted. Besides all of this the rubber bumpers on the frame were knocked off, and the shock absorber links are gone, plus a hubcap was lost. Oh me! I drive it 11,000 miles without a dent and then he wrecks it in one evening, a mile from the post. I haven't had a chance to get it fixed yet and it will cost around $25.00. He's going to pay for it so I won't turn it in to the insurance company.

Naval Air Station, North Island

Well a good many things have happened here lately. The 14th Pursuit Group has divided and formed two separate groups. This means that each squadron had to divide also. Our squadron divided and formed the 48th and the 82nd. I'm still with the 48th and I consider this a lucky break. Major Keith sent everyone to the new squadron who'd had any trouble. Luckily, I've never caused any damage to any plane I've used, or any other on the ground. Some guys have wrecked as many as four planes. Of the 14 older pilots that are left in the 48th, I don't know of one that I would call less than good and some are exceptionally good. Now each squadron will be getting 20 new pilots. They'll all be fresh out of flying school and it's going to be a big job checking them out in the **38**.

I spent all of yesterday checking a group of three new men, out in the cockpit, and letting them taxi the ship. Boy they are really green and I talked so much I became hoarse. Before they will be allowed to fly the 38, they must spend five hours in the cockpit, and 3 hours reading and learning the operation instructions. They have to fly two hours as co-pilot in a Lockheed C-40 transport, plus one hour of taxi time. Then they're ready to explain all they have learned to the satisfaction of the Flight Leader. We're hoping to check them all off without any accidents but I know this won't happen, as some just don't have the judgment to handle this much airplane.

Despite the fact that I've been in pursuit for five months, I'm one of the old boys now. **C** flight, my flight, is composed of the Flight Leader, a 1st Lieutenant with 14 months of pursuit experience, a 1st Lieutenant with 9 months, two of us 41-I boys with 5 months and 6 new boys without any experience. Now I'm an Element Leader in formation instead of a Wingman.

The recommendation has been sent to Washington to have us boys of 41-I promoted to 1st Lieutenant. Now it might come through in a month and it might not come through for 3 months or never. I'm hoping it won't be long, because those silver bars on the shoulder of a flying 1st Lieutenant means that he's earning $310 a month. This would be a good deal.

According to the latest talk, which seems to be very accurate, it will be only a month before we take-off for foreign duty. We're suppose to give the new boys intensive training so that they will have at least 60 hours flying time in by then.

Things are really in a big mess, as there is not any place for the new plane crews to live or eat. We can't get parts for the planes but most of all there is poor coordination between various units. Everyone is trying and putting in longer hours than they ever have before. We practically live on the job, as there are no more days off. Because the new pilots aren't trained, we older ones have to carry on the work. This was almost too much when we had double the number of experienced pilots. Yesterday it was from 5:30 AM, on the line, until 11:00 PM when we finished flying 2 hours on a search-light mission. This morning the Dawn Patrol started at 5:45 AM, and to top this off the Navy still has banker's hours.

What do you know? Chuck Luedke came down to San Diego for 3 days and I managed to visit with him for two evenings and showed him around the field the morning he left. He stayed with Jimmy Gamble and his wife. Jim is now working for the Highway Patrol in San Diego. I don't know if Jim will get in the Army or not. They have a baby boy, 8 months old, and they're mighty proud.

Sunday, seven of us went up to Mines Field, by Los Angeles, to ferry back some new 38s. They flew us up in a Douglas DC-3 transport. They're like a regular airliner except the interior is stripped bare. I used to think they were quite a plane but when I flew it a couple of minutes as a co-pilot, I found out that it was just another airplane. They don't have anymore equipment than a 38. The 27th Squadron was at Mines and

Naval Air Station, North Island

is getting ready to leave right away for Foreign Service. Their new 38s are equipped with streamlined belly tanks, which look like bombs. Every couple of minutes they would buzz the field, coming right down to 25 feet. Well, we delivered our ships all right and it seemed like it took only a few minutes to get from Los Angeles to San Diego.

Douglas C-47

Every week we get in about 3 hours of practice in a Link Trainer. This gives us instrument practice and it's a good way to keep in touch with it. You've probably seen them in the "Aviation" magazine. They don't fly quite like an airplane but they will do almost anything that a real airplane can do. The other day I went into a spin in one doing a climbing turn because I'd let my airspeed drop too much.

Well if we're going to leave the country soon I will make every effort to get home but right now it looks hopeless. I pray that something will turn up so that I can get a few days off, I hope so.

From a letter dated May 22, 1942: Well the days flee by and I hardly realize the passage of time. I live each day for that day, because I have very little time to dream of the past or speculate on the future. Each day brings me a new experience in handling men and situations.

This evening at 8:10, after dinner, as I was leaving the Officer's Club, three of our enlisted men came to me with the news that the Mother of one of our men, Corporal Clayton, had just died in San Antonio, Texas. As 1st Lieutenant Bing and 1st Lieutenant Johnson were both off the post that left me as Commanding Officer for our unit, the 48th, here at March Field. The poor boy was pretty well broken up so I wanted to get action as soon as possible. I went to Operations and called long distance to Major Keith, an official call, in regard to what authority I could use. According to regulations at March Field, we would have to check back to the home of the boy and confirm his Mother's death but that would have entailed hours. Major Keith said to forget this procedure and make out a leave form and sign my name as Commanding Officer. He needed money and as I had spent my extra money on my car, his friends raised $50.00 amongst themselves in just 5 minutes. Now that's real spirit. Then as luck would have it, we were able to get him a ride in a Douglas transport to somewhere in New Mexico. This helped him a great deal. All of this happened within a space of about 20 minutes. Yes, the responsibility is great. Seems there is always someone running up with a problem saying, "Lieutenant Schottelkorb can I do this or that?" It's turning us young men into older more mature men.

To work backward from the time I left the Club. My supper cost me 80 cents and it consisted of pork with dressing, potatoes, a lettuce, tomato and avocado salad, and to top it all off an ice cream sundae. Before supper I spent a half-hour in the officer's swimming pool. It was 108 degrees yesterday in Riverside, so I simply have to get myself in shape. A Pursuit Pilot must be physically fit.

Our work is progressing fairly satisfactorily. We've checked out 24 pilots without one serious accident and we attribute that to careful training on our part. All of the new pilots have around 6 hours in the 38 now.

Naval Air Station, North Island

As for myself, I've been doing a lot of ferry work. I took a P-43 over to Long Beach and turned it over to the Ferry Command. It seemed strange to get in a conventional pursuit plane again after the **38**. Also have made 6 round-trips to North Island in the 38. It's somewhat over 100 miles and takes 25 minutes, counting take-offs and landings. Just seems unbelievable to cover two such widely separated points in just a few minutes.

One day I made 3 trips to North Island and back. On the last trip, I drove my car back, as it had been repaired. The return trip by car took three and a half-hours of hard driving on a windy highway 395. On these trips I usually fly at 6,000 feet as my flight plan indicates. However for one stretch of about 30 miles in the hills, I come right down on the ground and skim the gullies and flat meadows at 50 to 100 feet. I'm doing this at 300 MPH and in a slight dive the scenery reels by at an ungodly rate and occasionally I see a sheepherder, who's wondering at the follies of man, as he watches my sleek bullet shoot by. Lookout towers, lakes, roads, fire protection paths are all clearly visible as I sit relaxed in my little enclosure. I spend much of my time in these flights looking at the scenery, however my eyes never wander far from the oil pressure, temperature, coolant temperature, gas, and ampere gauges. Yesterday on the return trip I encountered bad weather, so I followed the coastline for 50 miles. I Was forced to fly as low as 400 feet to keep out of drifting fog. Weather reports gave March Field as clear so I finally pulled up through 1,000 feet of fog, on instruments and could see the field.

On another trip I tested my guns. Back in the hills I found a clay cliff with a spike sticking up that was about 10 feet high and 5 feet across. Diving I opened fire with 4 fifty-caliber guns and that spike just crumpled in a cloud of dust.

It cost me $34.00 to get my car fixed and now I have to get that from the boy who wrecked it. Most of the cost was in straightening one corner of the frame. It's not quite as good as it was but seems okay.

George Rose, a friend of mine, is a 1st Pilot on a B-24 here at March. We attended flying school together. Today he showed me through the boat and soon I'm going to make a hop with him. The only way the 24 differs much from the 38, as far as controls goes, is that it has 4 throttles and the 38 has only two. I believe in 10 hours that I could handle one. George on the other hand would like to check out in the P-38. He would have no trouble as less weight, 7 tons, and his bomber weighs 30 tons.

March Field frequently plays host to famous people. A few days ago Andy Devine ate at the Officer's Mess. He's the same homely, squeaky voiced boy that he is in the movies.

Next month I'm going to have to buy some clothes as the Group Commander, Colonel Olds, has specified that we need certain clothes, so there goes another fortune. Evidently I'll have to get a military coat and they cost a lot. Also need another pair of pants.

Was good to hear your voices when you called, I only wish that we could have talked longer. PS Got a letter from Don Tomlinson from Brazil.

From a letter dated May 30, 1942: Right now I'm back at North Island again. Training at March Field went very good at first and then we ran into a bunch of trouble which prevented the boys from getting in many flying hours. Most of this was encountered in trying to keep the airplanes running. The mechanics would no more get one running when something would happen to two others. We only had six planes in which to train 24 pilots and we couldn't keep more than two or three running at one time. One quit us when we first got back there as the exhaust pipe clamp came loose on one engine and burned the outside metal clear through, besides the damage to other items. Took two weeks to get that plane back in commission. Other planes were down for 50-hour inspections, nose wheel replacements and millions of other things. We weren't able to get parts and disorganization of one kind or another was always present. Nevertheless I learned more about organization and administration during this time than I had ever dreamed of before.

Bill along the coast at San Diego

Being there was somewhat like a vacation in it's self, as we only worked from 7:00 AM until 6:00 PM. Occasionally I was able to get in a swim in the afternoon or a game of handball. Evenings we were free, so we could go to the post show house and see a first run movie for 20 cents. Did some sitting around the Officer's Club and read all of the latest magazines. I usually went to bed around 9:00 PM, because I have felt really worn down. There are so many places to go to during the day that I hiked nearly 20 miles every day. It was much more expensive to stay there. We ate our meals at the Officer's Club and they ran 40 cents for breakfast, 50 cents for lunch and supper ran from 80 cents to $1.35. The room ran 75 cents a day, so you see I got rid of a good pile of money in the two weeks I was there.

Four of the new pilots and I were called back to North Island. Back here things are again in a big mess. Now we're up at 4:15 AM, report to the flight line at 4:45 and can finally leave at eight in the evening. We get 45 minutes at 6:30 to eat breakfast and have the same amount of time for lunch at 11:30. We eat supper after 8:00 PM. It's certainly getting old but I'm sure it's not going to last for long. At first we had a hard time finding a place to sleep but now we're located in a swell house right here on the post. We share it with 2 Naval Officers and 1 Marine. It's completely furnished and has a fireplace, a nice kitchen with a GE refrigerator and stove. Very nice but of course I'm not there very much so doesn't do me much good.

I forgot to mention that while we were at March Field we got one Sunday off. It was a reward for our good start in the training program. That Sunday I was able to take a P-38 to Taft. I thought that Ed might be gone to Montana but I wanted to take a cross-country anyway and thought I better while I had the chance. Taft is 150 miles airline from March Field. It took me 35 minutes flying at 11,000 feet to get there. It was a beautiful sight seeing all the lakes, roads and forest fire paths below. When I dropped down into the valley, I circled the field a couple of times to make sure my depth perception had adjusted from the high altitude to the low altitude. Coming in on a green light, I landed easily on the short runway. Ed wasn't there, so I filed another flight plan and returned to March Field. On the way back I followed the radio beam for practice. In an hour and fifteen minutes I had been over 300 miles, into an entirely different part of the country and in a different atmosphere. This all happened so fast that I could hardly realize it.

They now have balloons with cables over the Consolidated Plant here and also in Los Angeles. These are something else to look out for, when flying. I'm writing this letter down on the flight line so consequently it's a mess but I know you want to hear from me even though such is the case.

B-25 Mitchell

A lot of the fellows seem to be having good luck getting chances to go home. It looks worse than ever for me now. Might be a slight chance as soon as the new boys get a month or so of training behind them but until then I can't even think of it.

Stationed at the field now are B-25, B-17 and B-24 bombers. I've been playing around with some P-39s and have come to the conclusion that we have the best ship in the P-38.

PS Being as I'm starting to talk about planes again, I might tell you about something that happened at March Field. A bunch of boys came through with their B-25 bombers. These planes are plenty fast and as we got shooting the breeze with the pilots, they claimed that our 38s couldn't make more than one pass at them from a superior altitude. They would admit that the 38 was the fastest but said it wasn't enough faster to be able to fly from side to side making passes. Of course, we told them that we thought we could do this. They invited us to try the next morning when they left the field, if we thought we could.

I had forgotten all about this conversation when I came in to land the next morning, until I saw two groups of three each, B-25s, leaving in formation at 6,000 feet. I decided to make a pass at them and was able to, so continued making passes as long as I pleased. I would start on one side, 1,000 feet above, dive down getting all three in my sights, then passing them behind and below. My excess speed would carry me up 1,000 feet on the other side where I could wheel around and start again. I made about 10 passes and then came down and flew in formation with them. I then put on full military power, 2,900 RPM and 41 inches of Mercury to each engine and walked out in front of them, then pulled straight up to 1,000 feet above them. I dipped my wings in a salute and returned to March. I think they will have a little more respect for the P-38 now.

From a letter to Bob, dated June 6, 1942: Twelve years ago, this time of year, I was working on an Arithmetic final and dreaming of flying. Today I'm working on flying and dreaming of the final. It's a condition out here in the west. That's the trouble, we're on the coast whereas if we were inland we would have a little fun occasionally.

Naval Air Station, North Island

My squadron, the 48th, has moved back up to March Field with the Headquarters, all equipment and such are there also. However there are 9 of us still down here at North Island on Detached Service with the 82nd. We'll be on this status until the 20 new boys from the 82nd are considered able to take over regular alert flights. There are about 8 of them now although some of them haven't checked off at night yet. We'll be glad to get back to March Field, because this place is getting to be a regular slave-driving place. We get up at four and quit at 8:30 at night. I haven't been in town for three weeks and am just about fed up. I've a lot of business to take care of, on the outside and it doesn't look like I'll be able to get at it very soon either. When I left March I had to leave my car and a bunch of laundry and so am just about out of clean clothes.

We always kid the Navy boys about coming to work at 8:00 and getting to quit at 4:00. We tell them that they don't know there is a war going on. It does seem kind of unfair at times but guess I wouldn't trade places with them for anything.

They have sent a few extra squadrons to this coast from Louisiana to help out during this time of extra alert. They are flying the P-39. Many of the pilots are old friends of mine whom I haven't seen since we left Bakersfield at the end of Basic. Bob Brookings is now in San Diego with one of these squadrons. He started out from Montana with me when we went to Oxnard.

I suppose you saw the pictures in "Life" of the P-39 firing the 37MM cannon. At March they had a contest between a 39 and a P-51 Mustang. They came over the field at 1,000 feet, wide open, side by side and started their climb to 20,000 feet. At first the 39 pulled ahead and left the Mustang, however at 14,000 feet the Mustang took the lead and beat the 39 to the given altitude by 15 seconds. Both are good ships. We think maybe we will get a chance to check out in the 51, later on, at March Field.

Around here we easily whip the 39. Several times we have fought them and it's the same old story. In a 38 you can set your own style of battle and if you use the 38s advantages the 39 can't touch you. All we have to do is a shallow dive and a shallow climb, then turn and dive on them. It's absolutely unbelievable how a 38 will climb after the speed you pick up from a dive. These things will really zoom and not lose speed. Trying it out the other day I found that with 2250 RPM cruising, 24 inches of Manifold Pressure, much less than cruising and going 400 MPH, you climb practically straight up for 4,000 feet before the speed will drop off to 150 MPH. The Rate of Climb needle goes to 6,000 feet a minute and stays there. You're used to the Altimeter needle gradually moving up in a cub, well in a 38 it moves like someone moving the hands of a watch in preparation to setting it.

Lately we've had quite a bit of bad weather and often we've been flying over the water at less than 500 feet, while out on our patrols. Last week we were about 40 miles out, playing around with a Navy Convoy. With all of us in a string we would go right down beside the ships, 10 feet off the water, and then pull up to 500 feet and then come down on the other side. Fun seeing strange ships that we could investigate, most of these were carrying lumber cargoes on their decks. Another time we went out to sea for gunnery practice. The leader dropped an aluminum filled paint can on the water and the contents formed a white spot on the water and this was our target. We did this until the spot was all broken up.

They have issued us a jungle kit and it contains a hunting knife, match container, fishing tackle, first-aid kit and other equipment. Well drop a line and let me what's going on. I haven't felt much like writing lately but once we get back to March we should be working decent hours again, so I will try to do better.

California to England

There is a period of 20 days that there were no letters home from Bill. He evidently finished the training of the new pilots at North Island and then reported back to March Field. Bill did call his parents to let them know that he was leaving for Windsor Locks, Connecticut. As we pick up his story they have left March Field and are on their way to the East Coast.

From a letter dated June 27, 1942: I'm just writing a short letter to let you know a few of the details of what we've been doing. We left March Field Sunday morning with a great deal of turmoil trying to get started. However things went better than I thought they would. Two ships were delayed, one of them Shipman's, when a malfunction caused a belly tank to drop, before taking off.

I'm in the Third Flight leading the Second Element. We got started at 10:30 AM and in about 10 minutes all 23 planes were in the air circling. I'd expected a longer take-off run because of carrying 300 gallons of additional gasoline, but the 38 handled the extra 1,800 pounds with ease. After the entire squadron had formed up we started over the mountains. It was beautiful, this Sunday morning, flying at 1,000 feet over those blue California lakes, high in the mountains, with my 38 purring perfectly.

Right here I will mention a few words about our new 38s. This is fairly confidential stuff so don't tell this to anyone. What I mean this isn't stuff the newspapers or anyone like that are supposed to have. Of course the Halm's or our other friends don't care anyway.

To the layman the ordinary 38 cockpit is a mite out of hand but the new ones are something to make a military airman shake his head at, in amazement. On the take-off each engine develops 1,325 horsepower. They're the latest Allison engines in production. The tail section has been changed for better dive recovery and they are **red lined** at 100 MPH faster than the older ones. Two belly tanks, which are perfectly streamlined, each holding 150 gallons, are slung underneath. The radio equipment is entirely new and of English design. It's the ultra high-frequency type and can't even be used to connect with the ground in this country. It's a push button type and also has devices for friendly plane identification and position location. Now we will be able to find our way home and won't be shot at by our forces, plus it has many other devices that make it the most advanced radio there is. It's so secret that it contains a bomb, which we can detonate, and blow it up, should we think it would fall into enemy hands.

We are equipped with identification lights and such to signal to boats. The oxygen equipment is new and works swell. Four of us went up to 38,000 feet in the new ships above Los Angeles to test the oxygen equipment. It's a different world up there and the equipment worked perfectly.

To continue with the trip. It took us three and half-hours to get to Amarillo, Texas. From there we flew to Kansas City and St. Louis. Covered a lot of distance over beautiful rolling green hills. Two hours away from St. Louis and we were in Dayton, Ohio. We have been here 4 days now because of the weather and doing minor work on the ships.

British Spitfire

While here I've seen a lot of new stuff. Mick Thieme showed me all around Wright Field. Got to see the Spitfire, B-19, B-47 and many other planes. It's all wonderful but I'm certainly glad to be flying a P-38. Mick and I have been having a grand visit. Ohio has a lot of green rolling hills and quite civilized. Tomorrow we should make our last hop into Connecticut.

As you recall Mick was a buddy of Bill's from Missoula, and was a Test Pilot at Wright Field in Dayton, Ohio.

From a letter dated July 1, 1942: 48th Fighter Squadron, Bradley Field, Windsor Locks, Connecticut. Your letter was waiting for me when we arrived the afternoon of June 29th. Note the change of address and also that the squadron is now a **Fighter** and not a **Pursuit**, as it formerly was.

Now to carry on with things that happened at Dayton. We stayed at Patterson Field for five days having our radios worked on and waiting for the weather to clear. It was a good rest for me, going to bed at a decent hour and getting up at 8:00 AM. Helped me recover from the long hours at San Diego and March that I had put in. The towns and transportation systems there were very crowded so we stayed on the field, in sort of a pilot's hotel.

On the 28th we thought we were all ready to go, had 6 planes in the air, when they called us back because of the weather. This meant that the 6 planes had to land with full belly tanks. They all landed OK, but 3 of them came back to the line with smoking brakes, because they had to get on them hard to stop at the end of the field. Next day we all got off even though the weather was a little murky, and we got along all right.

First we went up to Cleveland, Ohio and then followed the shore of Lake Erie to Buffalo, New York, to Utica, then over Springfield, Massachusetts and on into Windsor Locks, Connecticut. We spent three hours in the cockpit making this trip. The countryside was much the same on this leg of the journey, green rolling hills, groves of trees and heavy vegetation. Totally we've spent 12 hours to fly the entire distance. That is pretty quick considering the indirect route and the slow cruising speed that we've had to maintain to keep all the planes together. Usually the Airspeed Indicator was at 230 MPH, which is slightly less than cruising. It certainly seems like a small country now, and it's hard to realize that I'm now on the east coast instead of the west. My airplane went the entire distance without having trouble of any kind. Neither engine failed to start on the first try the entire trip. Some of the boys had troubles of various kinds but we did manage to get all 25 planes here without serious mishap.

Now the field here is the real thing, it's had a scientific retouching, to make it practically invisible from the air. Runways are painted in spots with greens and browns, which causes them to blend in with the grass. The hangars are hidden by trees and all buildings out in the open look like houses and barns. It was a good idea and seems to really work. In fact it's practically like camping out. Our headquarters is located right in the woods, a block from the runway.

The big problem back here is transportation. We've only got a Ford, one and a half-ton stake truck, and a carryall. The carryall is a Dodge Panel that has been issued to the squadron. With all the men on the line and a thousand other things to do, it's hardly enough wheels. Everything is so far apart on the post that a car is practically a necessity for any business which has a time element connected to it.

The gas rationing makes it tough on the outside also. There are very few cars on the road now and it looks like people are beginning to feel the effects of all these things that are in short supply. How about sugar back home? Some places we go, we get it and at some we don't.

Windsor Locks isn't really much of a place. I went to Hartford a few nights ago and saw a typical eastern city, small narrow streets and a different atmosphere. The people, too, seem to be somewhat different, a little less friendly.

California to England

At this time all of our planes are undergoing inspections in preparation for further training, of a type which I'm not permitted to disclose. They've been giving us heck about giving out information so I guess I'd better try to keep quiet. I could get into serious trouble if you should happen to give out the wrong information. Now we know what we're going to do and how, but I can't talk about it. We'll probably be here for three or four more weeks and then **X**. I will say that what a young man did in a Ryan Monoplane back in 27, won't have anything over what we're going to do, if you get what I mean.

Spirit of St Louis

Could certainly use the old **"Dynamiter"** now, if I could get gas to run it. Tell Bob to forget about a trip this summer, such things just don't exist at such a time. Shipman has sent for his wife, as have several of the other boys. Many plan on buying an old car to get around in.

From a letter dated July 6, 1942: A little note to let you know the happenings of the last few days. I'm expecting a letter from you shortly, but so far have received only the one, which was here when I arrived.

My clothes and most of my other things are still at Patterson Field. I've sent a letter to Mick to see if he can locate them and send them to me. Certainly hope that I get them soon, as it's hard to live with the few items I have. Most of my laundry is here so I have two tan shirts and two tan pants, also a good pink shirt and pair of pants, so able to get along. Really have to time my laundry just right.

Did you receive the suitcase and bag that I sent? I bought the bag for 50 cents just for the purpose of getting my things home. I hated to wad my coat and pants in like that, but it was about the best I could do. The cadet clothes are really pretty good and I believe Dad could wear them to work in, if they were cleaned and pressed. All the note books and papers I would like to have saved, as they contain a lot of valuable information.

Well, we've been here for 6 days now and are pretty well settled in. I have a room all to myself in a barracks, it's rough but it's fun to keep it clean. It's very adequate even though it's not worth $40.00 a month. We have a small Officers Mess, and the cost is $1.10 a day to eat there. The food is pretty good but they are a little short on waiters.

We got $51.00 travel pay for coming across the country, but it did take quite a little to stay in hotels, although not that much. I was waiting before submitting my papers for regular pay as I didn't have a **Termination of Quarters**, from March Field. I will have to pay out $40.00 for the month of June. Can't get this done until my stuff catches up with me, as the necessary papers are in the baggage. I spent $28.00 for a third interest in a 1933 Plymouth Tudor. Not a bad little car and serves the purpose of getting us around. Cars are certainly cheap back here. There are 3 in the squadron, and not a one cost $100.00. When we pull out we'll sell it for what we can get for it, and I doubt we'll lose $10.00. Now I don't have to bum a ride to town.

I thought a lot about you folks on the 4th, and the following Sunday. It's times like that when I wish that I could be home, but we worked as usual. The night of the fourth, six of us drove over to Springfield, Massachusetts, about 20 miles and had a lovely dinner, at the Hyland Hotel. The meal was really nice and it should have been as it cost $1.79. Seems nice to work regular hours again. It's everyday of course, we start at 8:00 AM and are off at 5:00 PM. Pretty soft compared to the San Diego alert days.

C-61 Fairchild 24

Douglas A-20

As far as flying goes here, we've got a lot of different planes to fly if we want. There's a Fairchild 24, four-place monoplane, like Johnson's, available. I mean to take it up some time. Also a PT-13 and an AT-6 are available for instrument time. One of the best things that has happened was that they checked 5 of us 41-I boys, in the squadron, out in the **A-20C**, Douglas Attack Plane. I've been waiting a long time to get my hands on that baby. 10 minutes of cockpit time then I took it up. The engines are 1,650 HP each. The plane holds 4 people easily, 1 in the nose, the pilot, and 2 in the rear. However I went alone, as it was my first time up. Once a fellow gets a good cockpit procedure, the rest is easy, for in every plane you've got to check the same things at the same time. I flew it for an hour and made a darn good landing. It lands easier than a 38 and glides better too. The 38 needs the engine to glide, but the A-20 will actually glide on the wings alone. Not much slower than the 38 either, about 20 MPH is all. It weighs around 20,000 pounds.

Today I went up in a B-17. Stege and I watched the pilot take it off and then we went all through it from the nose to the tail. Then the pilot stepped down and we each were able to get about 15 minutes flying it. What a truck, it takes two men and a boy to push rudder on it. It's a nice plane but I'm glad to be flying what I am.

We've been flying formation with them, four 38s and one 17, two 38s on each wing. They're about 60 or so miles an hour slower than we are so we have to run about half-power. You don't have to think very hard to realize why we are flying with them. Well that's the news.

From a partial letter with the Postmark reading July 14, 1942: The first thing that happened was the confining of all officers and men to the post. This was done to keep any news of our movement and progress from leaking out. **Now** very soon we'll be moving out. It might be two days or it might be two weeks, I don't know. The thing is, our time is nearly here. We're not to make any long distant phone calls to anyone.

I will continue to write as long as I possibly can, I can't promise anything beyond this letter. **If you don't hear from me over a long period of time, 2 months even, you're not to worry as it's going to be perfectly natural.** That's the instructions from the War Department. We have been warned and warned about the secrecy of all the things that we know anything of, and if anything leaks out it's likely to bring

Again a part of the letter was missing. The next part of the letter was instructions to his folks about his financial affairs. He also made arrangements with them to have his car, that still was in California, sold.

Now the biggest worry is that my luggage is still missing. Mick says they are tracing it and that it has left Patterson Field. Something is wrong somewhere. Gradually however I've been laying in supplies. Did buy a raincoat today for $24.00, it has a detachable liner so is really an overcoat too. Socks and other things I have plenty of. You wanted a set of wings, well they are in my luggage. If I can't get them sent soon, have Ed get you a pair. They only cost around $1.50 or two. With my luggage is also my log-book with over 500 hours carefully recorded, sometime they will show up. This letter has been mostly business, but I will write soon and you do the same.

I've seen a lot of the country lately. We've made trips to Boston, New York and all over locally. New York is beautiful from the air, and while flying over I dipped my wings at the Statue of Liberty. Those tall buildings seem to come out of the depths and reach out to you in the sky. Today Mark Shipman and I flew a C-61, Fairchild 24 to New York City and back. It's the first light plane I've been in since leaving home. Felt funny, but easy to fly, just crept along at 100 MPH instead of 250.

From a letter dated July 20, 1942: I finally got my luggage, thanks to Mick. Boy I'm certainly thankful for that. Consequently I was able to send you my car papers and such stuff.

We're still here, but I think it'll only be a matter of a couple of days now. I guess I just can't realize that I'm about to leave the United States. In this game you just harden in to certain things and nothing much of anything bothers you. So, I repeat if you don't hear from me for 3, 4, 6 weeks or longer, don't worry. I'll be enroute and absolutely unable to contact you. However you can write me and I'll have mail upon my arrival. The address is:
    Lt. William F. Schottelkorb
    0-431164
    48th Fighter Squadron
    14th Fighter Group
    A.P.O. #1255
    C/O Postmaster
    New York, New York

Better copy this down in several places. This is the last place I'll be able to mail letters from while in the United States.

Well what to talk about-------today. I spent a good deal of time packing my plane with my personal belongings. In the very nose there is a small camera door which opens and reveals considerable space, in which I put my heavy flying boots, shoes, rubbers, 10 bars of soap, ink, toilet articles of all kinds, sweater, etc. In the lower part of the gun trays I put my heavy flying coat and pants, and also another pair of shoes. I got two new pairs of shoes, one a service pair, from the Quartermaster for $3.80 and a good pair in town for $6.60.

In the cockpit I have two oxygen masks, first aid kit, canteen, 45 automatic, jungle kit, fishing line and hooks, flashlight and batteries, match container, and a hunting knife. In the back of my parachute there's another jungle kit with a huge long knife, etc. In the left boom I put my handgrip with a change of clothes and a few other things. All this combined with two 900 pound belly tanks really gives me a load. The rest of my stuff, parachute bag, tin helmet, new style, gas mask, etc. won't go in my plane.

As a Formation Element Leader I have what is called a **Wingman.** He flies on my wing in all formations. He's a little fellow, cute as the devil, and smaller than the rest of us. His name is Paul Ziegler and he's a 2nd Lieutenant from Los Angeles, California. We've been doing a lot of flying together lately and he's really a good pilot.

Flying on a 1,000 mile cross-country with a B-17 the other day we ran into a solid overcast. I was on the left wing of the bomber and Paul was on my wing. On the right bomber wing was Captain Bing and his wingman. We were out over the ocean about 50 miles and suddenly this overcast was upon us. I closed in on the B-17 as close as I dared and then we were into the overcast, taking my altitude off the bomber while he was on instruments and Paul taking his off me. I was 8 to 10 feet from the bomber, and could just barely see him. Boy how to keep from getting old! Here I was between two airplanes, in pea soup fog and clouds, with everything depending on my keeping sight of the bomber and holding steady so Paul could keep me in his sight. If I had of made a jerky move, Paul would have run into me or lost me in an instant. If either of us lost the B-17 we would be lost in the fog without any directions, as we had been too busy to navigate, and besides that was the bombers navigator's job. Somehow I felt calmer than I had many time before on practice flights, probably because this was the real thing. This time we had to do it or else. Ask a civilian pilot how he would like to do this and he would recommend you for the nut house.

Suddenly we broke out on top at 3,500 ft. into a beautiful sunny sky. Paul and I were right there on the bomber's wing and everyone waved to us from the bomber. The captain and his wingman from the right side lost the bomber and ended up lost themselves. Finally by use of the radio we found them 5 miles west of us. Everywhere we looked, all we could see was this sea of white without an opening anywhere. After 15 minutes and still no opening, the bomber pilot decided to try his luck below the stuff. Down we went again, Paul and I right in there. Captain Bing had enough of this, so he stayed up on top. We broke out at 50 feet above the water and looking straight ahead the overcast seemed to touch the water. The Bomber Pilot called Captain Bing and told him, below overcast, altitude 50 ft, airspeed 200, and course 30 degrees. Captain Bing answered and asked are you coming back up? Back up we went and broke out on top again. Shortly after 1:00 PM we spotted Maine's forestlands as the overcast finally broke up. It was contact flying back to Windsor Locks. Yup, it's great.

Some boys are always having trouble with their planes, but most of them don't know a thing about engines. All you've got to do is have an understanding of things and it's easy..

This next stage of Bill's life starts with his departure from Windsor Locks, Connecticut. The notes are from Bill's diary and are written as they appear in it. Bill knew they were close to departing but when he wrote the last letter home on the 20th of July didn't know the exact date. This diary was returned to Bill's folks after he was reported missing in action.

From Bill's notebook: This notebook is the property of:
    0-431164
    1st Lt. William F. Schottelkorb
    48th Army Fighter Squadron
    14th Army Fighter Group
    USA
In case of Accident send to:
    Mrs. W. J. Schottelkorb
    315 Blaine Street
    Missoula, Montana
    USA

Dated July 25, 1942: Well today was the start of the real thing. All the boys got up at 6:00 AM and ate their final breakfast at Bradley Field, Windsor Locks, Connecticut. I really enjoyed my three weeks there, probably because it was the first time I had been back east, and things were different from what I was used to in the west.

We took off at 11:00 AM for Westover Field, I had to return to fasten down a gas cap which came off on the takeoff, and was causing me to lose a lot of gas. So I landed at Westover alone, and had the plane filled with 606 gallons of gas. By this time I was ready to eat, but they decided to get us started right away, so no meal.

Lieutenant Holman in B-17-5A took the lead and Captain Bing, Lieutenant Ayres, Lieutenant Ziegler, and myself were on his wings. We encountered some fairly bad weather in Northern Maine, but it was broken in spots, so we continued easterly at about 5,000 feet. The air was very rough, just below the clouds.

California to England

Northern Maine is really beautiful. Very heavy forests with few roads or signs of habitation. One mountain range, about 5,000 feet, was encountered, but the rest of the country could only be considered hilly. After two hours we landed at Presque Isle, Maine.

On the B-17 wing

Because of the weather Johnson's flight landed at Augusta, Maine, on a 3,000 foot. runway, with full belly tanks. Thomas ran passed the end and was slightly hurt. His plane was completely burned. So we lost a plane and a man before we had hardly gotten started.

Presque Isle is very nice, with small farms around it. The town itself, is about 700 population, I was told, we were too busy to go into town.

After dinner and signing in at the barracks, we went back to the hangar for the briefing. A Ferry Command Captain went over the entire route with us and made every effort to help us out. The Weather Officer then told us what kind of weather we could expect, and where we might encounter each type. This briefing took two hours and it was a tired bunch, that hit the hay that evening.

Dated July 26, 1942: We were lucky and had good weather today and consequently we got an early start. Holman took off at 8:00 AM and we four in the P-38s were in the air by 8:10. We gathered in a **V** of three B-17s with four fighters on the wings of the 17s.

Again we passed over rolling hills, and dense forestland. After 35 minutes we hit the Baie de Chaleur, meaning the Bay of Chaleur, and saw the small town of Dalhousie, New Brunswick it looked to be of about 200 population. Shortly after this the B-17 took a double drift and announced our ETA (estimated time of arrival) as 1610 GMT. We now have set our watches ahead four hours, as we will now be going entirely by Greenwich time.

Now the country is becoming rougher and lakes are more frequently seen. At 1305 patch, military time, scattered clouds drifted by below at 5,000 feet, and five minutes later I sighted the St. Lawrence River. The weather was turning out exactly as predicted and it was perfect for visibility.

At 1322 we reached the shoreline, and to the right I could see Petite Anse, Quebec, which seemed to be a small, lumber shipping, community. The river was beautiful, calm, blue and inspiring. Inland from the town a small waterfall comes down to the river for about 500 feet. Downstream, I could say, (it's really as large as an ocean), there were a group of fishing boats huddled closely together.

At 1340 we were just off of West Point, Anticost Island. There were a few dirt roads running among a few small communities, but other than that there didn't seem to be much population. At this point we were 280 miles from Presque Isle, Maine. In ten more minutes we were across the St Lawrence River and starting inland toward Goose Bay, Labrador. Now the country became very rugged, heavily timbered and infested with more of the most beautiful lakes I have ever seen. A small river ran inland for perhaps 40 miles, that I could trace, and joined those deep blue lakes. What a paradise for a canoe. There is no kidding about it being wild country as there's absolutely nothing but lakes, forest, and hills for hundreds of miles.

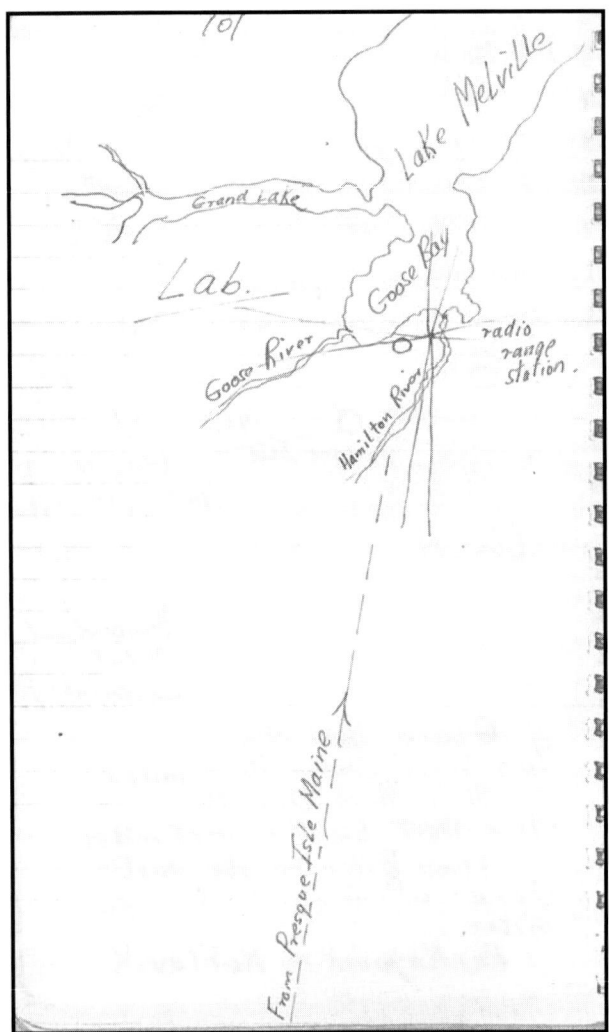
Map by Bill of trip to Goose Bay

At 1400 we ran into heavy broken clouds and the 17's climbed over them to 9,000 feet. I closed my cockpit cold air vent and turned on the heater, as it was becoming cold. Soon we let down through a hole, and to the left and about twenty miles ahead we saw Goose Bay Airport. Now the country was simply perfect. Small lakes, with heavy forests of Spruce Trees surrounding them. Sure looked like good Moose country.

We picked out our runway and peeled off. It was a gravel runway, but plenty long and a 25 MPH crosswind caused me to crab plenty and I had to hold the wing down while on the ground.

Once out of the plane, in the sunshine and snappy air I really felt good. We walked over to Operations through the woods. I would have like to have stayed for some time, but Major Clark gave us a short briefing while we ate, and we were off again.

Lieutenant Holman took right off, and we followed with our three 38s, as Captain Bing's plane had an oil leak. Starting uphill on the runway with full belly tanks was quite a task. We couldn't run the engines up at a standstill, as the rocks would damage the props. I tried to lift off at 100 MPH and 35 inches, but it took 40 inches to do it.

P-38s off Bill's left wing

Taking off and heading for the coast the country is more barren. There are a few large lakes, but mostly small streams and potholes. I guess you would call it an Arctic Wasteland, with a few patches of snow still visible.

At 1900 I could see open water over Cape Harrison, and soon we were out over it, looking at the hundreds of icebergs. One in particular interested me. It had three perfect cone towers on it, and an open space in the center that was about water level. At first over water flying is interesting, but it soon becomes tiresome and the pilot wishes that land could be sighted soon.

California to England

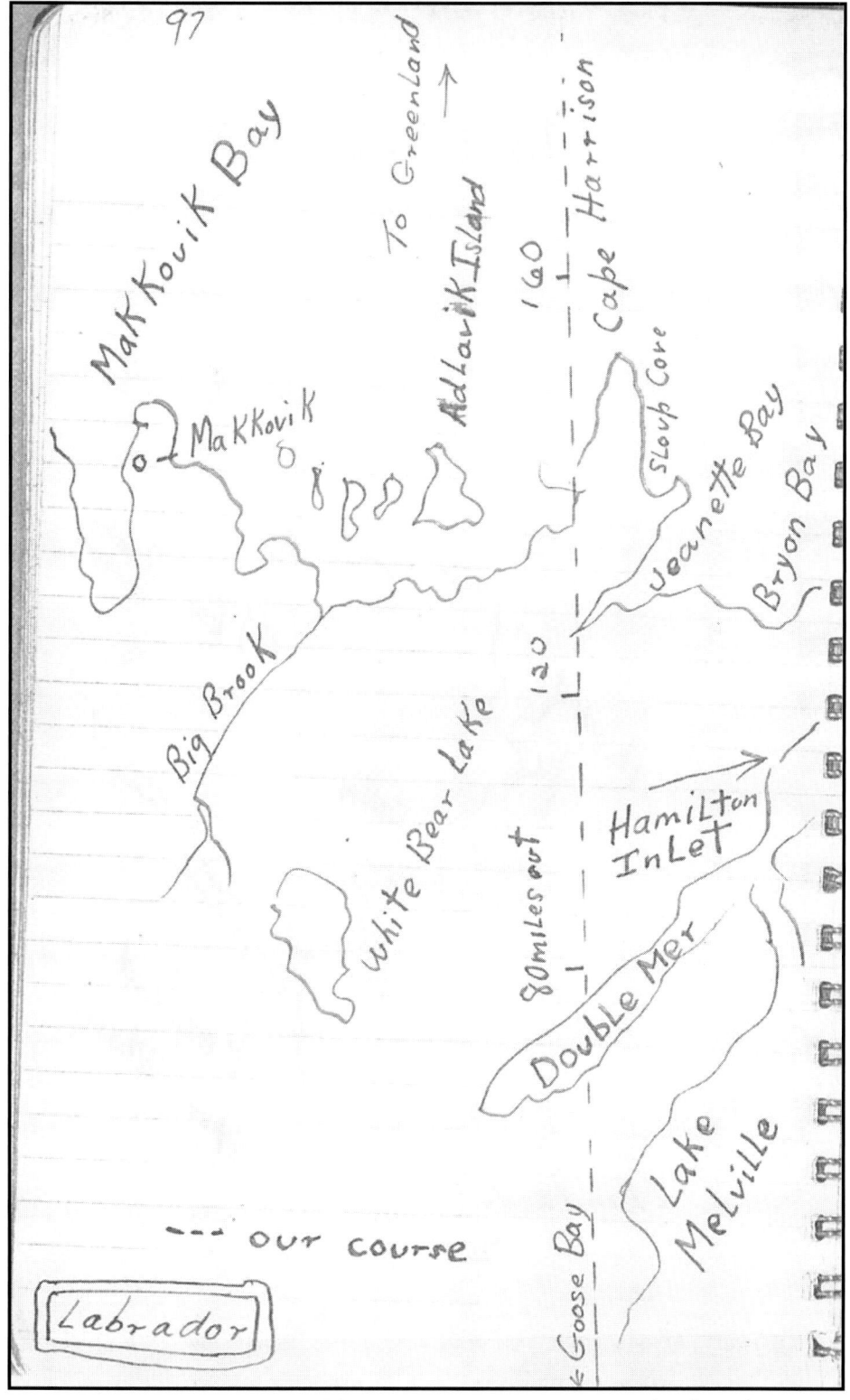

Map by Bill

At 2,000 feet the B-17s took a double drift. At 2050 we started over a mass of low-lying clouds, and at 2142 we sighted the mountains of Greenland, probably 80 miles away. It took quite a while, it seemed, to finally reach land. We let down and entered Tunugdljarfik Fjord then went toward Bluie West One, (Narsarssuak). It was a beautiful sight, the bay was full of icebergs and the mountains were very rugged. I was able to take several pictures before we closed in for close landing formation.

We flew over the runway, peeled off and came in. I was deceived by the mountains, which made the whole airport seem small, so I drug it in with power over the icecaps and cut the gun to land on the end of the steel mat runway. It was a good landing, but the mat made an awful racket as the 38 rolled over it. I was the first of the 48th to land.

Food at BW-1 was rough stuff and most of the boys couldn't go it very well. Our quarters were long buildings, cheaply constructed and housed probably 25 men. The trouble was it was dark only for about two hours and we never knew when to go to bed or when to get up. We stayed here two days and while we were waiting for the weather to clear. We did various things for entertainment. We examined an iceberg that had washed ashore from the Fjord, took many pictures and hiked all over the place.

There were many civilian workers from the states who were earning big money running shovels, and driving trucks. Naturally the price of certain items ran very high, and some of the boys who had whiskey in their planes, sold it for $20.00 a quart. It was a lonely spot. The only other settlement was across the Fjord where a few Eskimos had a settlement, however this was forbidden ground to the Army. There were quite a number of "Husky" dogs running around and they weren't the least bit friendly. I tried to pet several but they wouldn't even look at me.

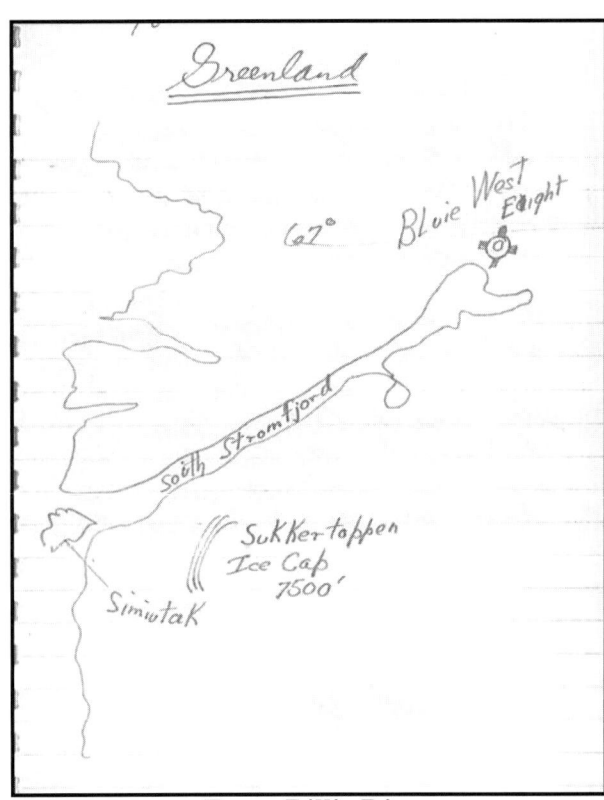

From Bill's Diary

The Coast Guard kept two fairly good-sized boats in the water, and there were two barges for unloading and a speedboat for running back and forth. The Army had an AT-6, in which some Hot Pilot kept doing steep turns close to the ground. The Navy had about 10 PBY's here for patrol and rescue work.

The 1st Pursuit Group was caught in bad weather and two B-17s and 6 P-38's sat down on the ice cap, and had to be rescued. They stayed there eight days and didn't have to suffer as radio communication was maintained and food was soon brought to them. I guess they had quite a self-sufficient little community set up before they finally walked to the coast and were rescued.

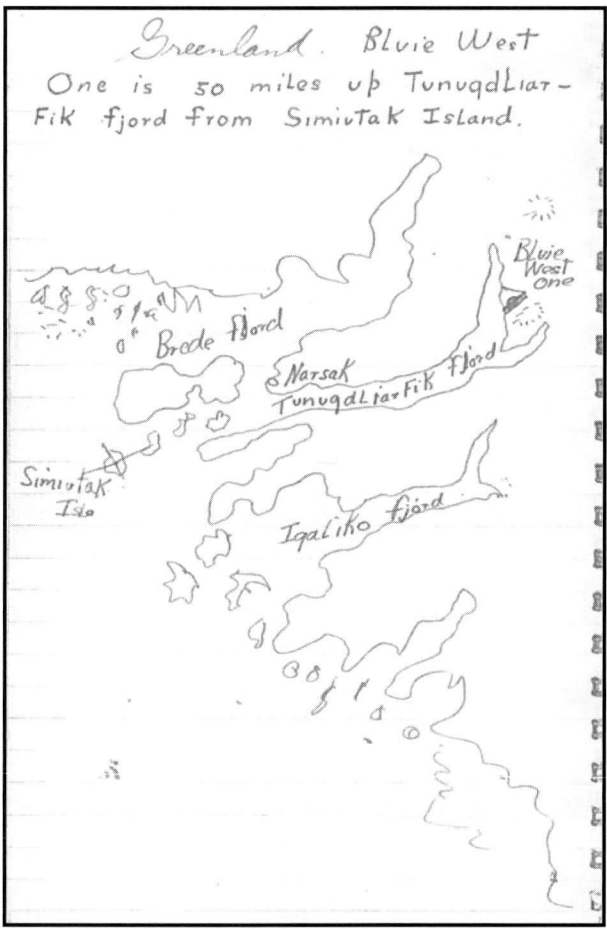

Another map of Greenland

On the 29th the weather cleared and we took-off for Reykjavik, Iceland. The trip over the ice cap I shall always remember clearly for the rest of my life. Three bombers took off on the steel mat first so that they would have time to gain altitude for the trip over the ice field, at 10,000 feet. I was the third fighter to leave and I noticed that the mat was very rough on the take-off. I climbed and kept climbing at 35 inches of Mercury. It seemed good to clear the engines out and give the plane a good workout after the slow flying we had been doing with the bombers.

Out over the bay and up toward the glacier flow, we saw a wonderful sight, glacier lakes, rivers, waterfalls, and rocky mountains with small lakes in natural pockets. One circle and we were on our way. The glacier came down from the ice cap, a great rugged, dirty mass of ice between the rocky mountains on either side. Nearer the top the smooth white ice cap started and extended as far as we could see. Toward the south near the shore line were some of the most rugged rocky peaks that I have ever seen, but inland the ice cap was a perfect white expanse for miles, broken only by an occasional rift, crack, or stray peak.

The Icecap on Greenland

We flew at 11,000 feet and I imagine that the cap was from seven to ten thousand feet. From BW-1 to the east shore of Greenland is 120 miles. Easy in an airplane, but what a dreary expanse if one were on foot.

This was the ice cap where the planes that Bill had written about previously had been forced to land. At this time he tells more about them.

On July 15, 1942 two B-17s and six P-38s of the first outfit that had flown this way were caught in bad weather and had to made forced landings on the cap. The first 38 to land did so with wheels down, and flipped over on his back. All of the rest sat down with wheels up, and everything turned out all right. They lived for eight days on the cap and had a regular community set up. They dug the ice from under the prop on one engine of one of the B-17s, ran the engine, which furnished them heat and power and they were able to use the radio. A SOS was put through, and a plane was dispatched to drop them all of the supplies they needed. Finally directions were dropped and they hiked 17 miles to the east coast where a Coast Guard Cutter picked them up. So there is over a million dollars worth of airplanes on the Greenland ice cap for someone to salvage.

The east coast was the same as the west, rough rocky peaks, and glaciers running into the sea. Several large Fjords were filled with great icebergs. The trip to Iceland was routine except for the last half-hour. We ran into dark clouds and detoured below and around them. It started to rain just about the time we hit the coast. We were flying at 400 to 500 feet and could see small farms right along the waters edge, and there were dirt roads running into the interior.

We passed over Patterson Field and then over Reykjavik. By the time we peeled off to land it was raining so hard the forward visibility was entirely limited. I had a terrible pattern and approach. First I lost the man in front and with a quarter flaps down I was mushing along at 130 MPH. Then I lost the runway and was down to 200 feet before I picked it up and came in for a hard landing. The strip was only 3,000 feet long on that particular runway and we all used our brakes plenty. Some of the boys landed at Patterson. 10 minutes after we all had landed the rain stopped and the sky cleared.

Our quarters in Reykjavik were tin huts holding 10 cots each. Warm and comfortable and especially suited to the climate, which was cold, and subject to frequent strong winds. The people of the town were rather cold toward us, and on one occasion we were called "Dirty Americans" by a girl that we passed on the sidewalk. However, one old gentleman spoke to us with a very friendly attitude. He told us the history of the island, and many other interesting things. The population of Reykjavik is 38,000, while the entire island is about 138,000.

Car traffic was left-handed and I always looked the wrong way before crossing roads. They say you soon get used to it. We went into one little shop for coffee and cake, and the frosting on the cake was made out of some kind of sour cream, but it was good. There seemed to be many natives having their afternoon cake. We ate one good dinner in town. That was at the Borg Hotel and cost eight Krona or about one dollar. Afterwards there was a dance and they played American music.

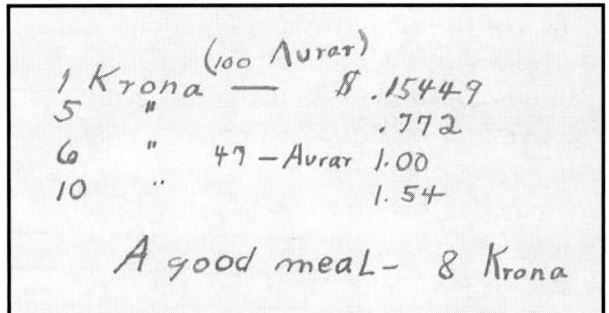

Bill converts the Krona

On the 31st of July we made an attempt to leave Iceland, but had to return because of weather when we were half way along the Atlantic route. Finally on the 3rd of August we did get a chance to again try. Everything was going good for the first half-hour. I enjoyed the trip by the coast of Iceland. The first jog took us over the mountain range to the east of Reykjavik and flying low I could see that it was mostly volcanic ash, and we had been told this. Then past the low plain on which the airport of Kaldadarnes is situated and directly over three small islands where there was located quite a sizable little community.

About this time I started having plane trouble. My generator had been showing very little charge for some time, so I decided to check it by inducing a heavy electrical load which I hoped would cause a great enough drain on the battery to cause the generator to kick up the charging rate. This would happen if the generator was working properly, and that's what I wanted to find out. I turned on the electric fuel boost pumps, the gunsight, compass light, cockpit lights and soon the generator charging rate jumped to 30 amps.

Now I was satisfied that my battery was in good shape I settled down and enjoyed the trip. Five minutes later I noticed my fuel gauges were flickering and that the inverter on number one was flashing the warning light. Switching to number two inverter didn't ease the situation, and I was very much puzzled. Then I noticed that I couldn't increase or decrease the RPM in automatic setting, and also that my drop tank fuse warning lights were becoming dim. If the battery was weak why didn't the generator charge more? So I made the entire journey without instruments and in manual prop control with a dead radio.

Another item that gave me worry and caused me not to enjoy the trip, was the fact that we were flying over a solid overcast at 3500 feet. After hours of flying by feel and ear, and of trying not to overrun the B-17, and trying not to lag in manual pitch, the bomber gave the close up signal as we were to start through the overcast. What a mess. I had everything I could do to stay with that bomber down through those clouds in manual, and I'm afraid that I made it rather rough for Ziegler, who was on my wing. We broke out of the clouds at about 1500 feet into rough rainy country and directly ahead was the Stornaway Airport, Isle of Lewis. We made a circle around the field and landed.

We had tea and sandwiches and were briefed for our trip to Ayre, Scotland. In the meantime my dead battery was replaced, and although I was convinced there was something more wrong, I decided to fly with the rest of them to the next stop. The weather was very bad in spots and we flew as low as four hundred feet to get below some of it, while in other spots the sun was shining and everything was perfect. This we were to learn was typical English weather.

The parts of land which we did fly over on this leg were of a rough, rocky, hilly nature. Patches of green pasture were tucked on the hillsides and small villages of red brick houses were frequently seen. Once we saw an old castle tucked away on the side of a hill and another time we swooped over a lighthouse at 400 feet.

We had been warned to stay clear of all shipping, but that was hard to do, when we turned away from one boat we would be sure to pass close to another. But the right people must have been warned, for we weren't fired at.

After an hour and thirty minutes the weather looked very very dark ahead, and seemed to extend right down to the ground. But suddenly out of the haze we were at Ayre, Scotland. It sits on the shore of the North Sea. We made a circle in preparation for landing. Just as we were on the straight approach ready to peel off, my props ran away. So I put them into manual and made a normal approach. When I was down to twenty feet I encountered violent prop wash from the ship ahead and a wing went down, bad, just before I touched down. I tried to pull it up with rudder and engine, but didn't have much success because it just wouldn't take in manual pitch control. I just came back hard on the control column and dropped in hard from about five feet. It was a poorly controlled landing, and I felt as though the plane were flying me instead of me flying it.

To top off everything, there was a nit-wit on the runway with a bike who wanted me to turn off on a taxi strip as the first two ships had done. However, I had landed longer and still had too much speed to make the turn. I hit the brakes hard once but saw that it was no use. I nearly ran the poor boy down before he realized I was going straight on.

Here at Ayre, we learned the setup of the English Airdrome. They have a well concealed field with a few necessary hangars and control buildings along the edge, as do American Fields. The sleeping quarters and other buildings are blocks away from the actual landing fields. They consist of small groups of inconspicuous buildings, grouped in the corners of odd fields and resemble farms. They are reached by walking down small one way dirt roads. Transportation as we knew it at home just does not exist.

The Fighting 48th was given a building to itself and as we were all completely done in we retired early. That is all except Hank Ayres, who decided to have a few beers with the RAF boys. Just as we were becoming well settled and things were becoming still, we heard heavy sounds in the distance. We thought a city was being bombed and all rushed to the windows to have a look. However it was too far away to see anything so we all returned to bed, realizing each to himself, that at last we were in a war zone. Incidentally the beds were very hard and the so-called wool blankets were not very warm, but so what, this is a war my son!

We had all enjoyed a peaceful slumber of about an hour when we heard a bunch of drunken voices in the room. Hank Ayres had returned, plastered and had induced about ten of the RAF boys to come and have a drink with the Fightin' 48th. He was in a jolly mood, but the most of us hadn't had enough sleep to be very patient. So while Hank was trying to get Wing Commander Morgan introduced to Captain Walles, we were all trying, by threats, to get him in bed. The RAF boys took the hint and left and finally Hank, thoroughly disgruntled was settled in for the night.

Next morning we put in our Flight Plan for Atcham Field and took off following a RAF Beaufighter, who was to lead us. My plane took a turn for the better and with generator charging

California to England

50 amps, I was able to have all the normal plane equipment in operation. We followed the RAF plane, which cruised at 210 MPH. This was only 24 inches of Mercury for me. We flew south over green rolling hills to the Strait of Dover, then to the Isle of Man, and on inland 50 miles to the town of Shrewsbury, where our base is located. We entered the left-hand traffic circle at 2,000 feet and came in for a landing. One very good idea is in use here, instead of the tower flashing a green light at the pilot here at Atcham Field there is a green blinking light at the end of the runway. This way the pilot doesn't have to concentrate on landing and watching the tower for a light at the same time.

**The gang on Greenland in front of their living quarters. While there they found that the mosquitos were abundant and some wore mosquito netting over their heads.
L to R, Carroll, Yates, Sorensen, Ziegler, Cole, Smith C.W., Stege, Bill, Eubank, Singleton, and Ayres**

Combat Training in England

This portion of Bill's diary takes place in England. With the trip across the Atlantic over, they settle into more of a routine schedule.

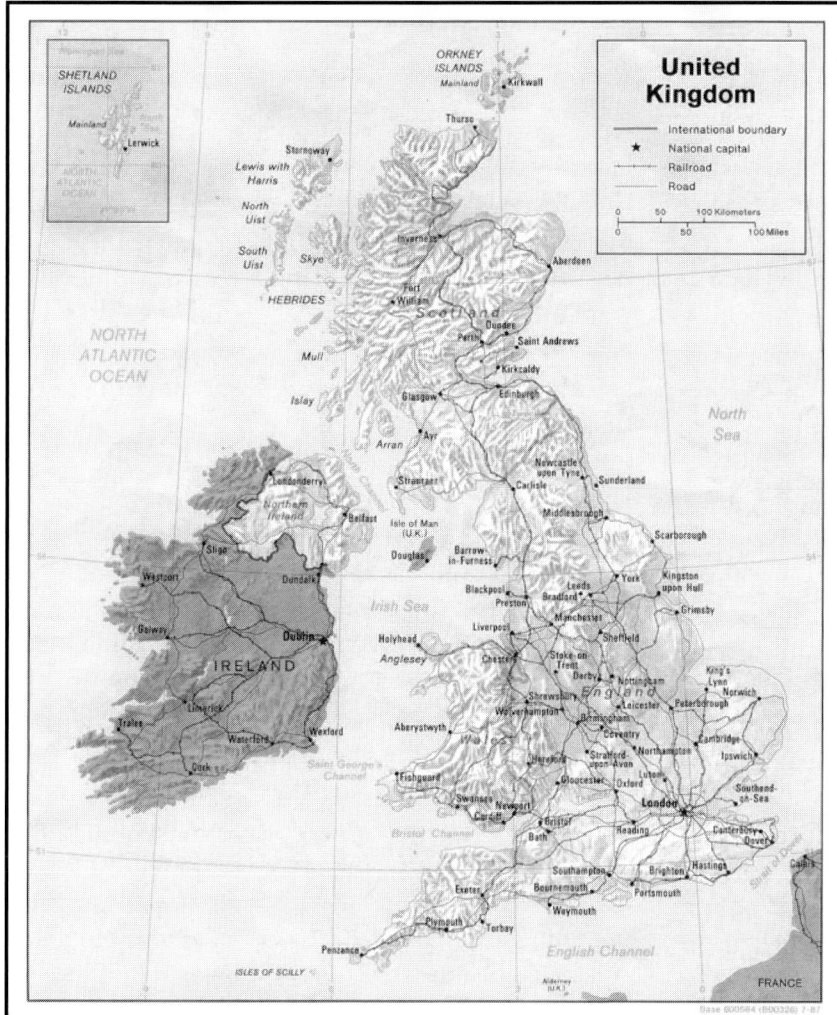

We soon settled into our quarters and they proved to be very nice little rooms. I'm sharing a room with Wally Sorensen. The room is about eight feet wide, and fifteen feet long. The beds are located at each end and we have a writing table, chest of drawers and wash basin for each of us. We also have a small stove, but the coal is so bad that it'll hardly burn, so we haven't had much luck with a fire as of yet.

Atcham Field is a beautiful job of concealment. The runways are surfaced with ground rubber and that is suppose to take more readily the coloring used in concealment. The planes are dispersed around the edges of the field, and parked near trees. The rest of the field is green grass, with a few necessary building, such as the Control Tower, located at good points. Our barracks are in the wooded land that belongs to some Lord, and in the evening his deer come down to feed where we can see them.

The second evening we were here we went to town in an Army truck and just walked through the streets, noting things that are different. Everything is old, the streets are narrow, and due to gas rationing, everybody was walking and staring at us. At one place we saw a game of Cricket being played, and an old fellow explained it to us. It's an easy man's game, it seemed to us, because one man was doing all the work and the rest were just standing around. Later on we went to a show. We saw an American feature and one English feature. At the English one we learned a great deal. One thing is that the English have an entirely different sense of humor than we do. What's funny to them is absolutely simple to us.

As our airplanes are in poor shape and also we haven't any ground crews, there was nothing for us to do for several days. We were given a two day leave, so we made a trip to London. The round trip ticket cost about $8.00. One way distance was 125 miles. Well the whole 48th arrived at the railway station in their shiny uniforms, and it must have been quite a sight, judging by the way people stared at us. We pulled out at 4:30 PM, and enjoyed daylight all the way. The English countryside was nice, I must say that.

Combat Training in England

Everything was green, there were small hills and clumps of trees and nearly every bit of land seemed to be serving some purpose. This was for a pasture, a garden, or as a storage place for some piece of war machinery.

Ziegler on Bill's wing on way to England

Birmingham was the largest city we passed through, and what a mess it was. Slums, warehouses, back alleys, rusted machinery and bombed out brick buildings. Right there I decided that if Americans only knew how lucky they are. Here the people seem to be so cramped. There was a couple spending the evening, on their balcony, watching the train go by. More people were tending their gardens behind a high board fence. I wondered what they could do on a Sunday that would compare to our motor trip to the Powell Country at home. Yet I know that they have their enjoyments and get just as much kick out of them as we do. This is their home and that's what they're used to.

The train was OK but very slow and it stopped frequently. However like most things in wartime England, it wasn't clean. There's not any manpower to waste on things that are not vital. Upon reaching the station we took a cab to the American Officers Club where we had a very tasty little supper. The rooms were all filled but we managed to get a room at the American Eagle Club, 16 Princess Garden.

After we had cleaned up, we started out to enjoy some of the nightspots. We were due for a rude surprise on that score. First, we found that in order to go into most clubs, one had to be a member, so naturally this let us out. Furthermore everything closed at 11:00 PM for the night, so we finally had to give up.

Next morning we set out on a walking tour. First it was Hyde Park, where we saw some of the very fine statues that are located there. Then we found our way to Buckingham Palace and managed to be in time to see the Changing of the Guard. It was a very military process, and one that was typically British. One of the guards explained to us, how one lone Jerry had come down between the balloons and dropped two bombs. One landed in the street and one on the grounds of the estate itself.

Next we went to Westminster Cathedral, and up to the top of the tower. There we had a wonderful view of the whole city of London and of the many ruins nearby. Westminster Abbey was not far distant, and there we saw where the famous people of English history were buried. One of the most important was Neville Chamberlain. In the Abbey there were people visiting from all nations. A group of about twenty-five Hindu soldiers were being shown through while American soldiers rubbed shoulders with those of New Zealand, Australia, South Africa and Canada.

Farther on, the Houses of Parliament stood on the bank of the river, Big Ben and all. They are beautiful buildings, but at present they're also dirty, and again there's just no one to take care of them. Next we took the underground railroad to another section of the city where the Tower of London is located. We went on a conducted tour, which was lead by a very interesting old man in a costume and he certainly knew his history. Around the tower is an old moat, that at present is drained, for sanitary reasons, and of course there was the drawbridge, which let down from the tower and formed the road to the inside. The whole structure is made of old rock and plaster.

Combat Training in England

Inside the guide pointed out the various building where different things had taken place. These were things like where this certain queen had died or where so and so had lost their heads. One of the towers was named "The Bloody Tower", and another one was where Sir Walter Raleigh had been kept prisoner. In the courtyard there was a spot where all the be-headings had taken place. The guide explained how sometimes the axeman didn't make a clean stroke, and therefore would have to keep hacking away until the bloody head fell off.

We also went through the small church on the grounds. Services are still held here although the date of the buildings runs back to the 13 hundreds. On the walls are inscribed the names of many famous people, who were connected with the church. One, which made an impression on me, was that of Sir Thomas Moore, whom I remember well from my history lessons.

Another building, the old Feasting Hall, dated back to Norman Times, and that of William the Conqueror. That as I remember was about 1066, when the Battle of Hastings happened. In that hall, we also saw displayed suits of armor, old swords and an old type, early attempt, of a machine gun. Also located in the building was a chapel, where many of the Nobility are married. Also the King and Queen come here for special ceremonies on Christmas Day. Bombs have hit a few of the newer buildings, but on the whole the place is in very good shape.

That evening we ate at a very nice place and had wine and all the trimmings. A beautiful blond girl waited on us, and we learned she was a refugee from Holland, her name is Nick-O-Let.

The next day we hired a cab and were driven to all of the most interesting spots in London that we hadn't already seen. St. Paul's Cathedral was perhaps the most inspiring thing I saw in the whole city. It brought to mind all of the studying I had done in Humanities, and I tried to recall all I could of domes, nave arenas, flying buttresses, etc. But the most beautiful thing of all was looking upward at the dome from the bottom floor. Later we went to the roof and surveyed the great damage that bombs had done nearby. This area was the most heavily hit at the time London was bombed so badly. One bomb hit St. Paul's but not much damage was done. Also saw where the Great Fire of London had started and also London Bridge, etc.

In the afternoon we went to an American movie, "Holiday Inn". While waiting in line, we were entertained by an old fellow who performed stunts such as standing on his head, on a bottle. Also an old woman that sang with the most god-awful voice I have ever heard. Each of these characters earned vast fees when they passed the hat.

Twelve o'clock that night we departed by train for Shrewsbury, and arrived there at six in the morning. Six hours to go 125 miles!! Then we had to walk the five miles back to the base. We were pretty well shot when we got back.

It's been a big change for us, but I believe we've done very well in adapting ourselves to the way of life over here. We're used to cars of our own back home and over here very few people are allowed to run their cars. The cars, which are in service are small hacks, which are not even as good as our Willys. I have seen few cars as good as my 39' Ford that I had back in the states. Nobody here could buy gas or pay taxes on such a car. All of us use bikes for our transportation and we are so wild that everyday somebody is being skinned up from taking a spill.

One day a Lord, a high ranking Marshall in the RAF stopped in to visit us. He was a humorous old fellow who had served in the last war, who I'm afraid wasn't too well up on the tactics of modern air warfare. He impressed us with the idea of how well the British could take it. "No matter how long the war will go on", he said, "the British can take it a week more than the Hun."

Combat Training in England

Yes, we have learned a great deal about the English people. Basically they are quite nice, but I'm afraid they're terribly impractical. War or no war, busy or not, they must have their tea at a certain time of the day. It's humorous to see a group of workmen suddenly throw down the picks and shovels that they're leaning on and sit down to drink tea and eat cakes. And they do this several times a day.

A group of mechanics came in from the First Pursuit Group and started getting our planes in shape after the trip they made over the water. In this way our training gradually got under way.

One of the planes in Greenland

Dated August 18, 1942: There are many things that we must learn in the next six weeks so that we can readily fit into the British way of flying. First we must learn traffic control of airdromes, radio procedure and code, so that the channels will flow smoothly during emergencies. Also we must learn homing so that we will be able to find our home airdrome.

To accomplish these ends we've been having a series of lectures on aircraft recognition, radio, combat tactics, etc. We have seen many movie reels of combat and ship strafing. We were assigned our own Operations Building, and it has proven very adequate. It has a room for all the various departments, that we have.

Finally on the 17th I took my first ride, in my plane, to look the nearby country over. My 38 felt very light with the belly tanks off and I had a good ride. For something to do and something to gain experience, I feathered one prop, and buzzed the field at 250 MPH at 150 feet.

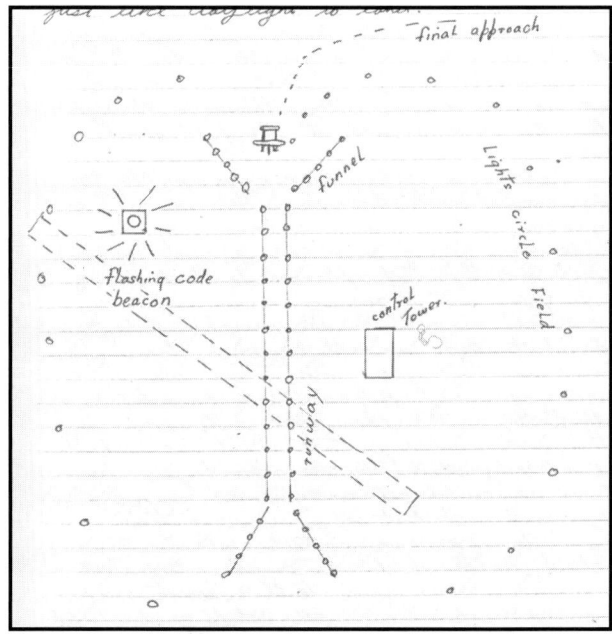

Traffic pattern and approach

Now we're trying to organize the flights so that everyone will be happy. Right now I'm in Shipman's flight and that's where I hope I remain as I know I can do good work there. Today, the 18th of August, I received a pleasant surprise, the entire Ground Echelon of our squadron arrived and that gives us many needed men that will rush forward on the work here. Many of these men we haven't seen since leaving March Field.

The officers told us that they came over in a convoy that carried 90,000 men. Some of the ships carried as many as 9,000 men, and thus things were too crowded for comfort. The rest of our men are slowly arriving by Air Transport on the DC-3s. Lieutenant. Haln, our AR Officer, and Lieutenant Dees, Communication Officer, have also arrived. At this time our Operations Department is in full swing and we are operating as we did at Bradley Field. Most of us are getting in one or two hours of flying a day. Captain Watson is leading us in tactical formation. We

Combat Training in England

have three flights of four ships and fly in this manner:

This formation spreads us out into a search formation that provides good visibility for all the pilots. When any one of the pilots spots an enemy aircraft he immediately peels up and around 180 degrees. This movement catches the eyes of the other pilots, and they do the same. Thus the formation is quickly formed in the opposite direction, and offensive measures can be taken. We're also practicing homing procedures and learning the English method of speech over the radio. There's plenty for us to learn, and it will be some time before we are proficient.

Captain Fulmer, of Group Operations, gave us a talk on tests that were conducted by the RAF on the four leading pursuit planes in the world. The German FW-190, P-38F, Spitfire 9, and the North American Mustang P-51 are the best. At very low altitude, 2,000 feet all the planes, except the P-38, ran about the same. They all will indicate about 360 MPH and the P-38F about 350 MPH. The tests were conducted up to 23,000 feet, and at this altitude the P-38 was faster than the FW190. It was also said the **190** could out climb the 38 and also out dive it. The rest of the airplanes were somewhat equal with variations at different altitudes. However a Major who flew the P-38 said, "the British underrated it probably because of the fact that they declared the machine to be of little value as a combat machine". They did this some time ago. Our plane, the P-38, will undoubtedly be superior at altitude.

August 22, 1942: We started some low level navigation work. Lieutenant Skinner and Lieutenant Ayres left Atchan on a two-course route to a town in the Northern Midlands, Rubin is its name. I left on a direct route for the same town with Lieutenant Warren on my wing. Course was 339 degrees, airspeed 210 MPH, time 11 minutes. The weather was stinky with low mist and fog. I was tempted to turn back several times, mainly because of my wingman's inexperience, but decided that we would get conditions much worse than this in actual combat. Well, the hills and checkpoints go by mighty fast under such conditions, but when our ETA was up we spotted the other two ships and our objective. We took up 2nd element on their wing and came on back to base.

August 23, 1942: We arranged a controlled interception with the English who were flying four Spitfires. Sorensen took off leading and I was with the 2nd Element. The controller gave us a vector, and soon we saw the Spitfires behind and 2,000 feet above us. We turned and climbed toward them and this greatly spoiled the effectiveness of their attack. Lesson number one, don't be taken by surprise. Then the controller gave each of the flights a vector and gave us a chance to have interception with the Spitfires. It took three attempts to hit them, mainly due to the fact that we were above the clouds and the "Spits" were below. The controller fixed our position by the contactor method and by voice.

Tonight we were entertained by a group of traveling actors. They put on a very humorous show and everybody enjoyed it and had a good time.

From a letter dated August 23, 1942, from somewhere in England: This is the first letter that I've written since our arrival here, although we've been here for some time. First a few questions. What about my car? Did you receive all the papers, wings, etc. that I sent from my last station? Did you learn my address and distribute it among my friends? AirMail only should be used, and it will still take 10 to 15 days one way.

Combat Training in England

Now that I'm here I find that I can't write letters in the way that I would like to, censorship is the reason for this. As officers we are allowed to censor our own mail, so naturally I'll have to speak in general terms. I ache to tell you what really has happened to us since we've left the states. I won't be able to mention any towns, times, or anything of our operations.

Just before I started writing this note I received my first letter, and certainly did enjoy it. I see it was mailed the 6th of August and so it made pretty good time. I'm amazed at what goes on back home. For instance, Bob taking a trip during times like these. Boy, as a 1st Lieutenant over here, all I have is a bike, and was darned lucky to get it. Only the Commanding Officer is allowed a car and that's only a puny little hack. It seems to me that you would have the cars stored in the garage and only use them when necessary. I hear that there's going to be gasoline rationing in California very soon, so maybe this will make the people a little more conscious of what's really going on. You can hardly expect people to be any different until they've seen just how destructive a bomb really is.

You mentioned that Ed is at Blythe, California but I didn't understand the address that you gave me. Would you please repeat it more clearly another time?

Now to attempt to give you a little light on our situation. We're at a RAF airfield somewhere in England, I can't say where. Our field is five miles from the nearest town, which is larger than Missoula. We can get there by an occasional Army bus, by our bikes, or by walking. That I have done just once. We live in small low buildings, two to a room. They're very comfortable, with desks, chairs, small stove, chest of drawers, and a wash basin. Every night of course, we have a blackout, and the curtains must be drawn. Everywhere over here it's the same thing.

Our food is getting better, but was simply terrible at first. We will soon be on American rations. Never the less I haven't had a glass of milk for over two months, and steak is unheard of. Each restaurant is given only so much food and if you don't get there early, you might just as well forget about getting anything to eat. It's the same way with any item, which you may wish to purchase and you also need a ration card.

I have the money system well in hand now. A Pound is worth about $4.10. There's 20 shillings in a Pound and 12 Pennies or Pence in a Shilling. Of course there are various small coins, ranging from a Farthing, which is half a Penney, and a Half Crown and it's two and one half Shillings. It keeps you thinking at first but soon you get the hang of it. For instance if they want to charge you one Shilling and three Pennies for something, they merely say **one and three**.

Soon after our arrival we were granted two days leave, and so we all went to London by train. We visited all the famous sites. One of the first places we visited, was Buckingham Palace. Here we watched them change the Guard, it's a very impressive ceremony. The English Soldier is much more military than the American one and they take their duty very seriously. We went also to Westminster Cathedral, and Westminster Abbey. In the Abbey were people of all nations, a group of Hindu Soldiers were sight seeing right along side those of New Zealand, Canada, Poland Australia, and of course the United States. I'll write more about this visit later.

Right now I just want to let you know that everything is all right, and that probably any worrying you might be doing as to our safety is absolutely unfounded. Being in a war isn't half-bad. It's very rarely that there's any real danger. Life goes on over here just like anywhere, and I believe the people on the west coast of the United States are much more jumpy than people over here. Rain or shine, 4:00 in the afternoon,

Combat Training in England

everyone takes time off for tea. Write often.

August 24, 1942: Today we did very little flying due to weather conditions and they were very bad. However we had plenty to do as there was the Link Trainer, and I took an hour in it, practicing the ZZ Blind Landing Approach, with a ceiling of 300 feet. For the complete Blind Landing Approach, with 50 to 100 feet ceiling the beam is used. The English Link is much different than the American one. It has a stick control, which is stiffer than our American wheel control column. It has a Pioneer Compass that must be reset after each turn. The thing that gets me is the turn and bank, instead of our needle and ball, they use two needles. Boy, I really had a time trying to get everything adjusted and keep my headings and letdowns right. Anyway, it was a very profitable hour and I gained much knowledge in radio procedure and technical knowledge.

In our flight, each pilot has been assigned an enemy aircraft, on which to research information and explain all the vital features to the rest of us. We each have to give a talk to accomplish this.

The Lockheed man gave a talk on P-38s and explained a great deal about the Turbo Superchargers. It seems our main trouble is keeping the carburetor air temperature low. If we had better intercoolers that would boost up the power rating.

August 25, 1942: This morning we watched three movies reels on the use of oxygen in flying. It was quite humorous in spots, but I did gain several good tips, which I was able to use this afternoon. Shipman, Sorensen, Ziegler and I took off on a high altitude mission. I checked over everything on the ground and got my oxygen mask on before take off. Leading the Second Element, I took off too closely behind Shipman and experienced the worse prop wash I've ever had in my flying career. At about 50 feet it caught the right wing, and brought it up until I felt as though I was going to be twisted right into the ground. I certainly had very little control of the airplane. I made it all right and climbed fast. We passed 8,000 feet climbing fast, pulling 35 inches of Mercury, steady, with airspeed of 190 MPH. Only took us about 15 minutes to reach 28,000 feet. The plane performed perfectly in all respects, and kept much cooler than other planes I had taken to this altitude. So I was very well pleased, especially in

Squadron in England, back row, left to right:
Singleton, Bill, Stege, Johnson, Skinner, Ethell, Williams, Gobel, Ziegler Carroll, Cole, Smith C. W., Smith V. H., Yates
Front row:
Segraves, Watson, Sorensen, Eubank, Bing, Walles and Tollen

Combat Training in England

that my carburetor, air temperature remained about +20 degrees C.

Ziegler got sick up there and threw up into his oxygen mask. He dove straight down and came out at about 8,000 ft. He had partially passed out for most of the way down, due to the lack of Oxygen.

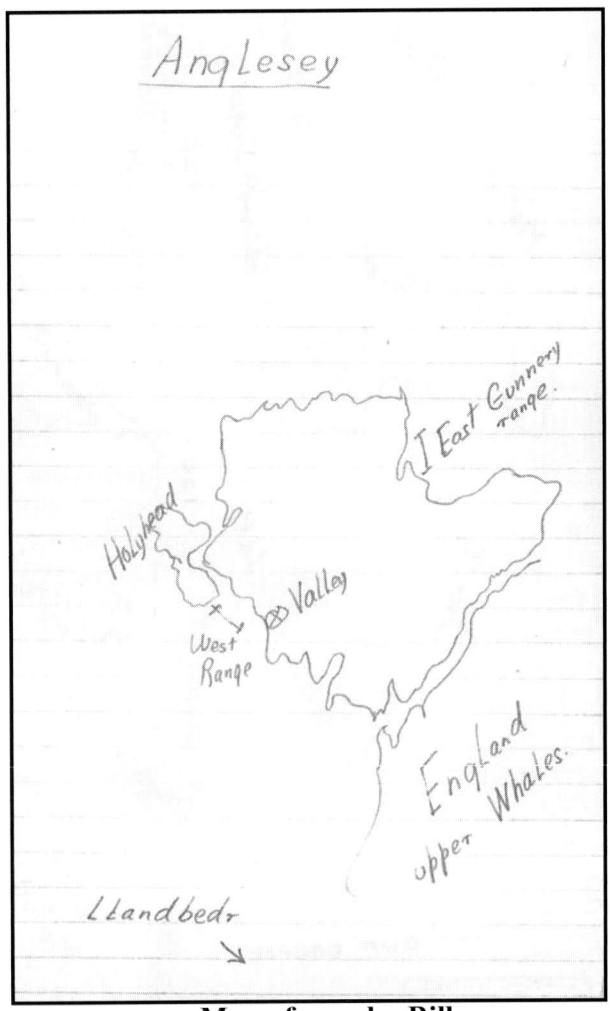
Map of area by Bill

Mark, Wally and I played around up there for some time. We slow rolled, did Split S's, and generally tried out the aspects of the airplane. I hit 370 MPH in a dive at 20,000 feet, and did experience some tail buffeting when I pulled it out. Finally we got down to 2,000 feet and found that we didn't know at all where we were. Everything looks the same all over this bloody country and the weather is always so bad that you can't find any land marks even if you happened to know where they are. Mark tried to get a homing but failed as his mask had blown off in a dive. Sorensen's radio had been out the entire trip. So I took the lead and contacted our Station Lawton on C channel. They came in loud and clear and directed me to change to A channel. This I did, but was unable to contact Violia.

The territory was strange to us and we saw that we were over strange factories and towns, so we kept a very good lookout for balloons and cables. After four or five unsuccessful attempts to contact on A channel, I turned back to D channel and again contacted Lawton, and told him my situation. He acknowledged and after my transmission, gave me a course of 240 degrees to steer. Corrected on my card to 233 degrees, we flew for 40 miles and ended up just slightly to the east of the field. A wonderful navigation aid to have when you are lost in the country.

We three had just landed, and had started back on the track when we saw Lieutenant Warren coming in on one engine. He was doing a nice job, making a good approach, when the signalman at the end of the runway shot a red flare off in his face. Warren gave it the gun with his one engine, and decided that he couldn't make it, so he set it down. By this time he was over half way down number two runway, which is downhill, and there was no wind. He hit the brakes immediately after landing, and had the wheels locked up for over half the remaining distance. He went through the fence and tipped up on the nose. Although not too badly damaged, the plane will require a good amount of work before it will be in commission again.

August 28, 1942: Today none of us flew because the planes were all grounded. It seems that the First Pursuit Group is now moving to their operational area, and as none of their planes were equipped with the rear view mirror, it was decided that they should have ours. In the exchange quite a blunder was made. They took all the canopies

Combat Training in England

from our planes, shipping them 125 miles to their new base, and then took the mirrors off and shipped the canopies back. It would have been much simpler to have just removed the mirrors right at Atcham.

The Commanding Officer of our group arrived today, Colonel Thayer F. Olds, a West Point Man. In his quiet, but definite manner he went about the business of setting a more definite policy concerning every phase of our training. Every morning now we report at Operations, ready for duty, and we have to stay there come what may. This means that we are not to be seen running all over the post, doing, apparently, nothing.

This evening we had a very informative talk given by a RAF Intelligence Officer. His job is to gain information from captured prisoners of war. He told us there are four things we must give to the enemy if we're captured, name, rank, serial number, age, these and nothing more. Our manner should be one of polite attentiveness, but any attempt to gain information should be treated with a quiet, polite, "I'm sorry but I'm not able to tell you that". This will be more effective than anything else, and may gain an earlier release.

August 29, 1942: This morning the Colonel inspected Operations, and was very displeased with it's state of uncleanliness. Consequently we're now trying to keep the place cleaner. The unsanitary toilets are not to be used, they are merely a can set in the rest room, and must be emptied daily. The Parachute Room is trying to build some shelves, because that department is very crowded.

Finally about 10:00 AM, we were able to get the eight planes in C flight in good enough shape to start a few days of aerial gunnery up at Valley in Anglesey. My ship was just brought up from the hangar where an entire new nose strut had been installed. The old one was leaking hydraulic fluid and couldn't be fixed with the tools at hand.

We took off in two, four ship flights with Shipman leading the first, with him were Cole, Ethell and Gobell. I led the second with Tollen, Sorensen and Ziegler. We all got off in good shape except for Ziegler, of all things, he had a prop feather on him. That was as ticklish a thing as could happen to a pilot on take off. He staggered along on one engine at 100 MPH and made it back around and landed.

The rest of us set out on a heading of 300 degrees and had a very nice flight. Just before entering Anglesey, we went over a fairly high range of mountains. There's a few mountains in England, which could be climbed. We skimmed the ridges at 50 feet and the grazing sheep ran wild. Then we made a power let down into Valley and made a good landing.

Here we're working with the RAF, Flight Lieutenant Crab, a very pleasant young officer, was in charge. He was formerly in a Night Fighting Squadron and is now taking his rest, which he earned by having 200 hours of combat duty. They're pulling the socks or sleeves by Lysanders, a strange old high winged affair that flies at about 120 MPH. The English Officers here at Valley seem less friendly than they do at most posts. We're here to work and consequently don't dress too well, as it's hard to carry clothes around with us.

I feel rather guilty when we file into the mess in our sloppy suntans and the English Officers are well dressed. As a whole our officers seem to be younger for their age than the English. Probably because they've never had to take the responsibility or have had the hard knocks of the British. The mess is very pleasant, and here I learn, still more about English customs. In the mess each man is assigned a napkin which he deposits in a hole with a number.

There's much construction work going on at the field and we've had an opportunity to observe the so-called low-class English worker. They have a funny habit of taking tea morning and afternoon, a habit of which we Americans like to scoff at. But I don't know it might be a pretty nice habit at that. What do people live for? At certain points around the post, these tea trucks from the YMCA arrive. They're manned by two women and they sell chocolate, tea, cakes, etc. The mechanics use these, but the civilian workers have small fires out in the fields around which they huddle at teatime.

I forgot to mention another feature of the mess. After the dinner is over and everyone retires to the recreation room, there's a coffee stand, where everyone has himself a cup of the brew, rather nice.

August 30, 1942: Today I'm 24 years old. Am getting a good start on getting bald and daily trying to do better.

The weather was very bad, and we didn't fly at all today. Instead we studied deflection shooting and combat films. This seems to be the idea.

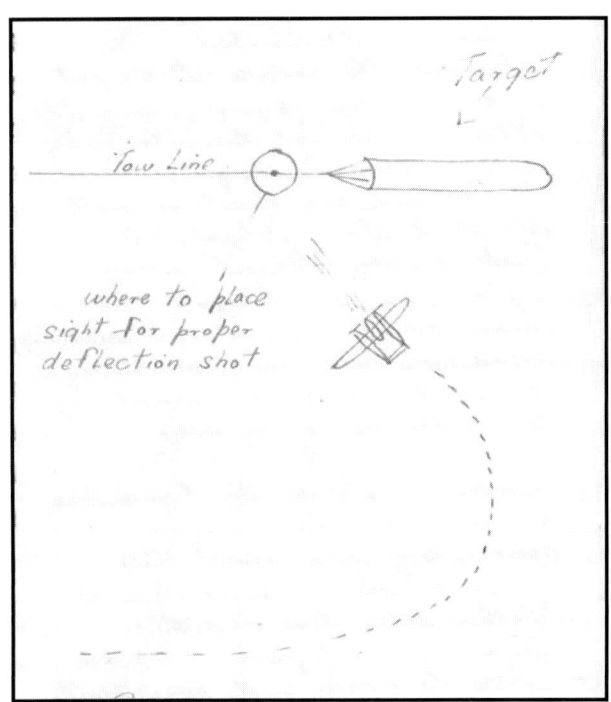

Sketch by Bill

We've been assigned a RAF truck to use while we're here and I had a good deal of fun checking myself out on driving from the left-hand side.

August 31, 1942: The weather was very bad this morning again, so we took our time about getting up, eating, and reporting to the line. By 10:00 AM things cleared up enough to permit the first gunnery mission to start. I took off first and headed for the east coast to meet my tow ship. At first I got too far up the coast and wasted about five minutes before I finally located the target. It was a tight pattern and hard to perform, but I was satisfied that my sighting was good, and felt that I had hit it. Later on the ground I found out that I had hit it only 7 times out of 138 rounds fired. I fired two guns and one jammed, but the cannon worked okay. On my 2nd mission, I went up more determined and paid special attention to my sighting. And again I was disappointed with a poor score.

Shipman and Sorensen seem to be finding the right deal, as each is making very good scores. On the third mission I fired on the West Range. On my first pass I swung too close behind the target and before I realized it I was on top of it. I pushed hard forward on the column and the seat release let go and my head hit the top of the canopy with a bang. This was too close, and I learned my lesson. I did make a few good passes and a few poor ones on the rest of this run, but my score was worse than before, I must be leading too much. Tomorrow I'll try less lead.

I flew two hours and five minutes today and made three good landings. Twice I took off without flaps, and once obtained 140 MPH on the ground. We worked until 6:30 tonight and then we showered and shaved and ate supper. I've been writing in the book for one and a half-hours. Good Night 10:30.

September 1, 1942: Bad weather must be the usual thing in Anglesey because this morning at 7:15 AM it was raining hard. We all stayed in bed for awhile and finally were able to get underway by 10:00 AM. My first mission, produced no score, or very little, as did the two in the afternoon. It seems that I just don't have the hang of it. Also I'm having gun trouble. Two of my guns have broken loose from the mount, and one steel mount is cracked completely through.

Drawing by Bill

Tonight after supper, I read war news from a magazine, did this for an hour and a half while the rest of the boys played pool. I gained a lot of information, and it's all helping to prepare me for what lies ahead.

September 2, 1942: After breakfast we walked down to the flight line instead of taking the truck. I flew two missions today. The first was in Shipman's plane and that didn't help my score any. The second, I made in good old 7650, and used tracers and the camera gun, still no score. However it'll be good to see just what I'm doing wrong, when the film is developed. One thing we've learned down here is how to improve our landings. All the boys are bringing them in slow and short, with the tail well down.

Goebel got a wing tip when he was taxiing by Ziegler's ship. There are very bad taxi conditions due to all the construction work. I hardly ever go out on a mission that I don't have a narrow squeeze between a truck, car or something. It's a wonder there aren't more of these accidents occurring.

We knocked off work a little early today because everyone was becoming a little stale and Mark thought we could stand a change of pace. So I went back to my room and caught a little nap. These English rooms have been very pleasant. We have what they call Batmen, who bring us hot water the first thing in the morning, shine our shoes, and keep the rooms clean.

I've been reading every chance I get, as they have a good many English magazines. This is the first time I've been able to keep up with the news since I joined the squadron. I read about the Dieppe Raid, the Milne Bay Battle in New Guinea and others. Tonight we all went to the post theater and it is very nice. "The Courtship of Andy Hardy" was the feature, and although I'd already seen it, I enjoyed it again. Then our truck wouldn't start so we had to walk home in the rain at 11:30 PM.

Bill is still stationed at Atcham Field but his squadron is doing gunnery and other maneuvers at other places throughout England. His letters home are less frequent and don't contain much information.

September 3, 1942: As usual it's raining and foggy this morning, but today the weather didn't break. We spent the day playing cards and reading at the Officer's Club. Mark and I also saw a few pictures, made during the times we used the camera guns during gunnery practice. With no one to tell us what we were doing wrong we weren't able to learn a whole lot from them.

At 4:00 PM we went up to tea. I had two cups, two pieces of bread and butter with jam, and a

Combat Training in England

piece of fruit. I kept thinking how mother would have gotten a kick out of this.

Mark decided we could make it home so we hurriedly got everybody together and paid our bill, left a tip for the Batman, and pulled out about 7:00 PM. The wind was blowing 35 MPH, and it was a job taxiing and taking off. I watched my air speed indicator on that fast down wind turn.

First we went south down the coast to get around the weather and mountains, and then after the third inlet, turned toward Atcham on 92 degrees and were home within ten minutes. We put on a beautiful eight-ship formation show coming over the field, and later on heard many compliments from the fellows.

Ate a late supper, and then had a surprise by receiving seven letters. It really cheered me up to hear from home.

September 4, 1942: Johnson gave me a list of things to do while he goes down to gunnery with Bing and his flight. They got off about 10:00 AM and landed at Valley about 10:30 AM. There we lost another ship, Bestgen landed short of the runway and completely demolished his plane. Too bad, he's a good boy. Of course he wasn't hurt and I'm glad for that.

I spent the morning working on reports and getting the Operations Office straightened up. This afternoon, Mark led us on a flight of four, to Burtonwood. We had to go through the balloon defended area near Liverpool, and that's far from being any fun. Everywhere there are factories, airports, and you never know if you're going to hit a cable when there's a balloon sticking up through the clouds. The field at Burtonwood is really camouflaged with sod roofs over the hangars and such. We got our pay and made the return flight to Valley by 6:30 PM.

September 5, 1942: Up early this morning and down to Operations where I had to handle the job alone, as Johnson was at Valley on gunnery practice. I called in the 8:00 AM status report, and Mark straightened out a few items with the flight. We put all planes out of commission as all of them are in pretty bad shape from doing the Gunnery Mission. At 9:00 AM we attended a show which warned of parachute raiders. They also showed the Dieppe Raid.

They brought in three German planes that had been captured in England. We spent an hour looking these over after the show. The first was a HE III. We sat in the pilot's seat and worked the controls. The nose is completely glassed in and the pilots look below the instruments and out through the front. Second was the JU-88, really a first class design, but poor in detail and workmanship. Third was the one I liked best, the ME-110. A three place job and really has a clean design, I would really like to check out in that one.

The rest of the day it rained and was miserable, so we eight boys of C Flight studied our intelligence reports and talked over flying problems. Mark and I wrote up a report on how long it would take to completely service four airplanes, with ammunition, film, gas and oil. We only have two gas trucks, so we figured that it would take 40 minutes to do the four planes. The ancient pumps on the gas trucks can only put out so much in a given time.

Legs Carlton of the 49th bailed out of his 38 today. Something went wrong with the oxygen system at 30,000 feet and somehow he was diving 500 MPH, indicated, at 20,000 feet and couldn't pull it out. He pulled the emergency release and loosened the belt. He was evidently sucked out and landed OK. He was then put in jail because they thought he was a Parachute Raider.

A letter from somewhere in England, dated September 5, 1942: I've had an awful time, it seems, in getting started with my letter writing over here. But I can promise it'll definitely be

Combat Training in England

better in the future. We have been away for a few days, and on my return I found seven letters waiting for me. The most I've ever received at one time. It was really a big occasion, no fooling! Several were from you and dated all the way back to July and up to the 20th of August. One was written by both you and Bob, and was sent to my last base in the US. A couple of others are just now showing up from that same base. So you can see I haven't known much about what's going on at home. These letters have been a big help to me.

You said that the car had been sold and you got a check for it. Have had two paydays so with nothing to spend it on over here I've accumulated quite a lot of money. Will cable it home to you, and you can put part of it into bonds. Yes we're really making the money now, and sometimes I think we earn it. We got a 10% raise on base pay for Foreign Service, so that makes $290 a month plus $60 quarters allowance, and they are furnished over here. So really I make $350 a month, unbelievable!

I enjoyed the pictures Bob sent of the three boys in uniform. He's getting to be almost as good looking as I am. I imagine you wouldn't even recognize me now, twenty-four years of age and practically an old man. This game takes it out of you fast. I'm very rapidly approaching a semi-bald state. Still have hair in front, but it's getting mighty thin. Do I worry, well not anymore than anybody else? Keep sending me letters, and I will do the same.

September 6, 1942: God, what a day! The worse one I've had for a long time. Captain Walles told me to have the planes flying as soon as possible, in the morning. That was last night. So at 8:00 AM all officers were at Operations, and not a single crew chief or gunman was in sight. It was Sunday and everybody seemed to have celebrated the night before. Planes were not in commission, batteries were out and things were generally out of shape and disorganized. Shipman and I had a house cleaning all the way around, and the crews were busy at work by 1:30 PM. We grounded all airplanes and let the crews work as long as they wanted, but told them they would have to get them done. They worked right up until dark on the guns, and fired them in, at the pits. Mine was still having trouble jumping the bolts so they ordered new mounts. Yes, the gun department really is amounting to something. I have worked myself to a frazzle getting them that way.

September 7, 1942: Up at 5:30 this morning and down to the line with Shipman and Ziegler. We later came back and got our clothes together in preparation for the trip to Llanbedr. We test flew a few of the ships that were in commission this morning. Shipman swung the compass on Captain Walles' ship above the field, and some of the other boys went up to make movies (combat) of each other.

Captain Watson, and his flight arrived from Llanbedr about 11:00 AM and told us how few hits they had been able to make in gunnery practice. At 5:00 PM I led 8 ships in the flight and we started for Llanbedr. All went well the first part of the trip, until Lawton Control had us climb to 4,000 feet and then they wanted me to take a different course. I decided to disregard and stay to my original course, but by this time we had run into clouds. I became pop-eyed trying to see. First I started down through it, but decided against it as we were above mountains. Calling the flight, I told them we were climbing to the top, which we did. We came out a mite disorganized and I realized that I'd not used good judgment in entering the clouds anyway. We continued on till our time was up in that direction, then turning right, we let down through a hole into an inland mountain valley and saw the coast through a small draw where the clouds had closed completely. We sneaked through that and reached our objective. The other flight let down through a different hole and joined us for a landing. Llanbedr is the most beautiful spot that I've seen yet in England. The mountains come right down to within a half mile of the sea, and it's on that

Combat Training in England

small piece of land that the airport is constructed. The runways are black pavement and the rest of the airfield is heavy green grass. There's such a heavy rainfall here that everything stays very green. You have to take a winding mountain road to reach the barracks area. It passes by a clear sparkling stream and eventually drops down into a draw, goes by a farmer's house and into a meadow.

Bill and P-38

All the fields are completely cleared of stone, and this has happened as a result of years and years of working the same patch of ground. Everywhere there are stone fences, along the roads and dividing the fields. All the rocks have been carried out of the fields to build these fences.

Many houses are of stone construction. The farmer's house, right near our barracks, is made of stone blocks as are the barn and sheds. The roof is even made of slate.

Our work here is tow target gunnery using our own P-38s as the tow ships. We hook two heavy pipes to our bomb racks and a cable leads from them back to the drogue. A wire between the vertical stabilizers prevents them from becoming entangled in the balance weights of the elevators. The drogue is pulled off the ground by attaching the line on the 38, and placing the drogue far up the runway so that when the slack is taken up the drogue will jump into the air as soon as possible, thus not becoming damaged or entangled.

Flying the target ship requires special attention. On the takeoff the engine is run up to 35 inches of Mercury before the brakes are released and then boosted to 41 inches. At 100 MPH the ship is hauled off and kept at 100 until a good altitude is reached. We don't tow over 150 MPH, as the target drogue breaks up too easily.

The RAF uses the same set up as we do and today a RAF enlisted man was killed when the wing of a Spitfire hit him when it was taking off. He was holding the target up so that it would get off better.

Mark and I walked down to the mess this evening and saw a thousand things we hadn't seen before, while riding in the truck. A small herd of sheep coming along the road was being herded by a well trained dog. Some native people up above us were climbing and enjoying themselves in the green, steep pasture. Down at sea level, a small English train was chugging along the countryside. It looked just like a toy. It was a beautiful day and the sun shown out over the Irish Sea and blended with the horizon. Farther along we came upon some wild Blackberries and ate a few before going on down to supper.

September 8, 1942: We seemed to have terrible luck with our targets today. Out of six sleeves, that we towed, we only got back with one. Also we had problems with the tow ships fouling plugs. We could only pull about 21 inches of Mercury in order to keep the speed below 150 MPH indicated. Also we used one-fourth flaps to increase the drag.

Combat Training in England

Frequently our towing grounds were so covered with clouds and haze that we would fly on instruments up to 8500 feet, to get up where it was clear, and then they would fire at the targets. First I would locate myself by the island and then go up through, about 5,000 feet on instruments, to the top, and then fly back and forth 0 to 180 degrees and about 45 seconds each direction while the ship would fire at the target that I was towing. In this way I always remained in about the same spot and had no trouble locating the island when I would drop back below the cloud layer. Did get in quite a bit of time on instrument flying.

One afternoon we knocked off a little early and went down to the beach for a little exercise. Stripped, we plunged into the salt water and had a gay old time. I took a good run up the beach and that I was able to maintain for the whole distance is more real exercise for the whole body than anything else is. It was grand and the whole bunch really enjoyed it.

That night we lit fires in the stoves in our rooms and all the fellows were shooting the breeze in my room when we heard a terrible noise in the adjoining room. We rushed in to find the stove overturned, the back support had given way and the whole outfit was over on its side blazing merrily. All of us had a good belly laugh at the expense of Ziegler and Cole who were trying to straighten the stove. They ruined their underwear and smoke filled the room and they finally had to pour water on the fire to put it out.

Colonel Olds came down to see how we were getting along and decided to fly back in our formation. His radio was out and he didn't believe he could find Atcham without it. It was an uneventful trip; in fact I didn't even enjoy it. The air was rough and visibility was restricted because of the haze.

Back at Atcham we immediately started 100 hour inspections on the planes. Mine had 106 hours, but it is still in fairly good shape.

September 15, 1942: This morning I watched Tech Sgt. Sassman, my Crew Chief, put the finishing touches on my plane after the 100 hour inspection. He hooked up the battery and ran the engines up, tested the mags. And everything seemed to be OK.

A little later on I took it up and gave it a good workout. Had a little oxygen left so I went up to 14,000 feet to get used to wearing the mask. It's handy to have the mike right in the mask, so then you can keep your hands on the controls. Went through a few slow rolls and attempted a loop. I pulled it up too soon at first and stalled out on top, on my back. I kicked it over using the rudder and the plane took its time about coming out and was in sort of a funny spin. It never did shake or shudder, but was smooth throughout the entire operation, even when the airspeed fell down to zero. Everything worked fine except that my turbos cut in rather suddenly and this made them much harder to control than they were before.

This afternoon Mark and I went up and chased each other around a little bit in individual combat. We each learned a little, but never did actually get on one another's tail. After that we tried a little formation flying and then a little follow the leader stuff, through the clouds.

I now have 162 hours in a 38 and the plane still seems pretty good to me, although at times I still feel a little out of place. It's a grand airplane but I'm afraid that it is entering combat about a year too late to do what the designer had hoped it would. Anyhow I'm well satisfied, and would rather fly the 38 than any other American plane unless maybe the Mustang.

The days fly by, and gradually the time is coming when we shall be taking our place in the front lines and doing what we can to defeat the enemy.

Our training has continued for several weeks and now we're getting into the final stages. We've had gunnery, low level navigation, altitude

Combat Training in England

combat interception, in the air and on the ground we've done the Link Trainer, intelligence, aircraft identification, etc.

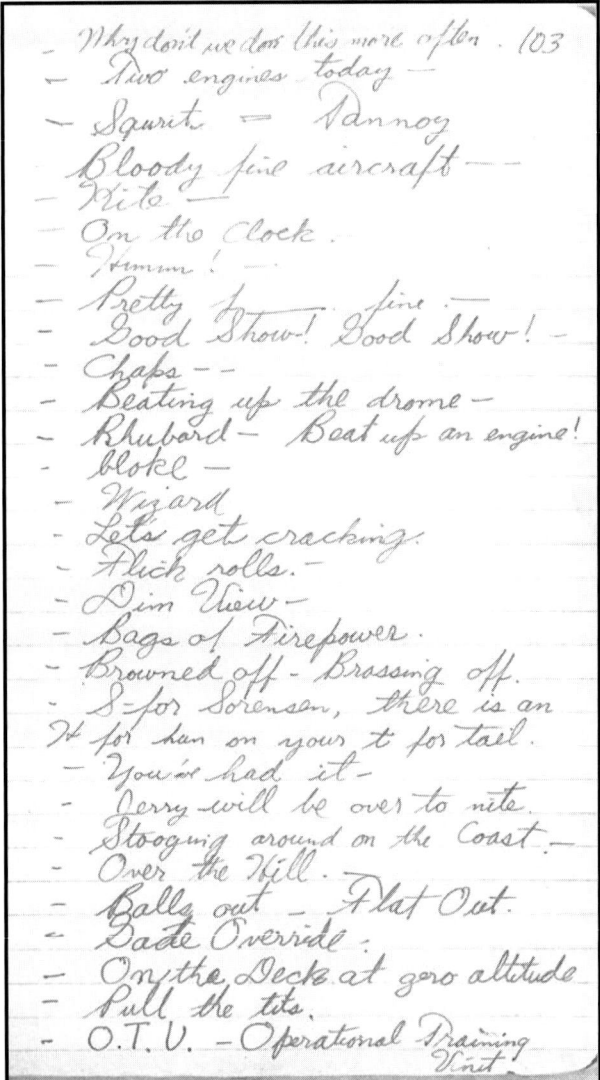

Slang talk that the guys used in England

September 17, 1942: Today we took a 12-ship flight up to practice, Battle Formation. Captain Walles was leading, and there was a great deal of violent maneuvering. Consequently things were pretty rough and there was much throttle cutting and overshooting. However I believe we all learned that there must be perfect cooperation from everybody or else the whole flight will turn out to be a failure.

When I was coming in to land I had quite an experience. My turbo waste gate on the left engine closed, giving me great power with the throttle closed. Consequently I did a lot of skidding, slipping and rolling before I finally got down. A fellow never ceases to learn from experience.

An interesting mission came in on **September 18, 1942;** The British Army wanted a couple of P-38s to try a practice strafing attack on some ground troops. So Sorensen and Yates did the job. It took place on a location right near the field, and we could see them diving and zooming over the treetops. Wally told us that the men were difficult to see, because trees surrounded them. They evidently had a lot of fun.

September 19, 1942: This morning the weather gave out completely, so we started our day by watching a film on the interrogation of English prisoners by the Germans. At 9:00 AM I took an hour in the Link Trainer. Practiced flying on the beam and the blind landing system. I understand the system very well and consider it simple, but the English Link is a problem to fly. My air speed and altitude weren't held very constant today because of this.

Wreken Hill, 1350 feet elevation

We all took the afternoon off, as there wasn't any flying. Mark and I rode our bikes to the top of the Wreken, a hill 1350 feet high and about 10 miles from the field. It was a slight uphill pedal to the foot of the hill and from there we had to push our bikes. Took us an hour to get to the top. Such a heavy workout I've not had for a long time. Once on top we rested, took pictures and watched the

Combat Training in England

planes flying nearby. A four engined Manchester flew over us about 200 feet up. Was all we could do coming down to hold the bikes back, because of the feeble brakes. Took us only 40 minutes from the hilltop to the field.

My Link Trainer time has mounted up by several hours since coming to Atcham. Besides the BB approach, we are also using the "Beam Method". After 3 hours I'm well acquainted with this method.

Ground Crew

Looks like we're not going to stay in England for operations. At least everything would lead us to believe such. Instead of going to Warmwell at the earliest possible time, as we were suppose to, we're now biding our time here at Atcham. Rumor has it that the First Fighter Group is also packed and ready to move. We all believe that it will be a move to the Middle East. They had us turn in all of our winter flying equipment and that indicates a move to a southern climate. Boxes are being packed with equipment, and bedrolls are being marked for shipment. This time we will have to travel as light as possible and I'm double glad that I have only a small amount of equipment.

So we're just waiting to pull out, and at times like these the pilots have very little patience and usually spend their time playing cards or football. When we don't fly, consequently we get on each other's nerves. I've had one flight in the last 8 days. That was a twelve-ship formation flight to altitude, in which we intercepted the 49th Squadron. I made a formation takeoff on Shipman's wing and with full gear on and I could really tell how stale I was.

Censored by Emmett E. Wilson, Capt. AC
September 19, 1942
Somewhere in England
Your latest letter dated Sept. 13, reached me today, which are very rapid connections. The one you sent the 6th reached me only yesterday. So my old friend Bob Ambrose is married! I knew he had been going with this girl for a long time, and I figured that they would be married sometime soon. Looks like the single boys will be in the minority soon, doesn't it?

Tomorrow Bob, will have completed his trip. I would like him to write me a detailed letter on just where he went, all towns, and how the car performed, mileage, etc. The car will certainly deserve a good rest after this trip.

I followed in Bill's footsteps and took the "Dynamiter" on a trip down through Mexico and back up the West Coast. I left for Cadet training immediately upon my return to Missoula.

I received the Birthday card from you folks and also one from Ed, thanks. Well life here goes on as usual. We keep pretty busy and time passes quickly. Today was an exception and for a certain reason, we had a little time off. Mark Shipman and I took a ride in the country on our bikes, just like a couple of sixteen yearolds. Everyone rides bikes over here. Coming home we were passed by two boys on racing bikes, they were really clipping along. Also on the road were a good many motor cycles, but very few cars. By the way Mark's wife, Elaine, wrote him that he could expect to be a father along about next April. He's pretty thrilled.

Ordinarily the English language is pretty much the same whether it's used by Americans or English.

Combat Training in England

Occasionally we say something that the English just don't understand and also the same thing happens to them. They call us blokes, spell while, whilst, and tire, try. I talked to an American who has been over here a year and he speaks just like the English. Getting so we drive and ride on the left-hand side of the road without even thinking about it. Now occasionally I have to stop and think just how we did it back in the states.

Poster of Winston Churchill

I got a letter from Don Tomlinson, which was sent to my last address. I will write him, but I'm afraid he'll never get it, because he moves around so much. Well, I just can't write a decent letter because there's so few things I can write about. I just want you to know that everything is very much OK, and that any worrying you might do is unnecessary, because 99% of the time I'm just as safe as you folks. Well keep the mail coming and I'll do the same. Probably before four or five months go by I'll be coming home.

The 27th of September: I was Base Officer of the Day today. My main duties were to inspect the guard. This I did at 10:30 PM, 3:00 AM, and again at 6:00 AM. Some guards I found were very good, having an exceptionally good method of determining the idenity of the person approaching, and others were very poor. Had a jeep at my disposal and it was fun driving through the foggy mist, early in the morning. I put a good deal of effort into the job and I believe I honestly helped improve the guard detail. Most just skimp through this job.

This afternoon, the **30th,** I watched the girls working in the field as I was coming home from Operations. The men here for the most part are in the Army, so the girls help out in the fields. Around Atcham they raise a little wheat, along with normal garden stuff. The other night Stege and I had dates with a couple of nice English girls. We took them to the show, "The First of the Few", a story showing the development of the Spitfire by the designer Mitchell. After the show, we walked them home. There were no eating or refreshment houses open at that time so we couldn't entertain them with this. No matter I enjoyed the walk holding hands and the good night kiss. Her name was Helen Brooks.

Yesterday I heard some bad news. My good friend Wendal T. Seppich was killed in a plane accident in California. Sep and I went through flying school together and I shall never forget his sense of humor or his easygoing way of life, which he was a master of.

Today there was a 12-ship altitude flight, but I didn't fly in it. Afterwards Johnson and Watson had their usual scuffle on theory. Sometimes I wish I were out of the cursed outfit and in one, that is run and managed by humans.

A 49th boy, class of 41-A, had a forced landing at Llanbedr after both of his engines quit. He landed on the beach, OK. Then he discovered the usual, a plane won't run without gas. He had forgotten

Combat Training in England

to switch tanks.

We find Bill still at Atcham Field. The training is still going on in preparation for actual combat duty. Rumors have all the men guessing where their combat duty will take place. Bill has added things to his diary about things that he must have wanted to remember later on.

England, October 1, 1942: I haven't been flying for some time now, and today was the first chance I had to get in some time since the 25th of September. First I took Miles up on my wing for a little practice on formation flying. He's been a little weak lately so Walles wanted me to have a good workout with him. We did straight formation flying at first but later on made a few passes at Sorensen and Bestgen, who were returning from the coast after firing their guns.

This afternoon I was second element in a twelve-ship flight that went to altitude to intercept some B-24s. Colonel Olds was leading with Miles on his wing and I was third with Ziegler on my wing. Sorensen and Bestgen were the third element. Major Keith, Walles and Bing formed the second flight.

We climbed to 24,000 feet and made a few practice dives and attacks. The B-24s we were suppose to intercept never did show up. We did follow the course as directed by the controller. We went on up to 31,000 feet just for the practice. Coming down we hit 350 and 400 MPH on the clock. Was the best altitude flight that I'd ever been on. The reasons for this was that it was easy for me to maintain my position and I was relaxed and able to look around to good advantage. My plane also ran perfectly and I felt good about that. The new oxygen system is the real thing.

At five fifteen this evening four of us officers and four enlisted men traveled by truck to High Ercall, about 15 miles away, where we were to do some night flying. This place is really nice. First we had to go to the control tower where we were briefed on the field set up. After eating, we started flying around 8:00 PM. Four other pilots brought their airplanes over from Atcham and we eight pilots then took turns using them. I was in the first bunch of four to take off. My plane was one of the new FLOs and there were a few items that were different so this caused me to have a few problems. The first thing that happened was that my running lights burned out and I had to take off without any. The tower called and assigned me a zone, so that the other aircraft would stay out of my way. It has been a long time since I've been up at night, and I found out that I was pretty stale. The takeoff was OK but as soon as I got in the air I could tell I wasn't quite as sure of myself. After 15 minutes I again felt good and when I was called in for the landing I was all confidence again. Entering the light funnel, putting down flaps and coming in was easy. I put down with both floodlights on and it was just like landing in the daylight. Several of the boys landed without using their lights and I could have, but my radio went out after I made the first landing. This finished my flying for the night.

October 2, 1942: We came back to Atcham the next morning, by truck, and it was an enjoyable ride. Everything is so green and fresh that it made me glad to be alive. We passed through Wellington and arrived at the field about 10:30 AM.

Later on a Polish flyer came over to do some combat with Skinner. He was a very merry fellow and entertained us with his tales of flying, sea rescue and what not. Incidentally that afternoon he beat Skinner up pretty good, I heard.

Sorensen and I were on alert today, and about 2:00 PM a call came in from Operations telling us that there was a Hun coming in at 40,000 feet from the south east. We clambered into our flying clothes and rushed out to our planes which had already been started by the other boys. As fast as we could get our equipment on we taxied out and took off on runway three. When airborne and in

Combat Training in England

contact with Lawton, they told us to climb to angles 20 above base. There was nine-tenths cloud cover, so up through the stuff we went and started climbing at 36 inches of Mercury. As usual it was a no go. When we reached 14,000 feet Operations called and said our customer had gone home so we returned to base. Later on I took an hour in the Link Trainer and I now have a total of 11 hours in it.

Bill's diagram of British Operations

This is a report, which we obtained from the First Fighter Group:
"After attempting an interception at 34,000 feet, the leader of an element of two P-38Fs started home by half rolling into a vertical dive from level flight at a speed of roughly 395 MPH; it was not long before the speed was up to 650 MPH, as reported by the wingman. At some point recovery was attempted by the leader ending in an abrupt pull out, approximating 12 to 14 G's acceleration, a wing came off followed by part of the empenage. The wingman, who reported, indicated speeds of near 575 MPH at 20,000 feet effected recovery at about 5,000 feet, blacking out, but doing no structural damages.

The above dives approached vertical speeds of about 1,000 feet per second, or 60,000 feet a minute. With a constant acceleration of 4 G's during pull out, it will require in the neighborhood of 10,000 feet to recover from a dive of 575 MPH indicated."

Promising bigger and heavier raids, he told of a diary found on a dead German soldier, It read:
"The last raid made an overwhelming impression and on everybody's lips are the words Cologne and Essen. Relatives wrote terrible things. Max was informed that life had come off the rails, and people simply could not recover from this dreadful disaster".

"I do not ask you to gloat over the sufferings of the German people", added the minister, "but I say to you that they willed it; they aided and abetted Hitler and his brutal Nazi gang, and to them I would say. Remember Warsaw, Rotterdam and Belgrade, remember Coventry, London and Swansea; and thank your Fuehrer.

Headed by a great gray machine bearing the name of Yankee Doodle, painted in yellow, on it's nose, and carrying Bomber Chief Brigadier General, Ira Eaker, and the raiders attacked railway yards.
Signed:
Major General Carl Spaatz, GHQ

Interrogation:

Combat Training in England

Czechoslovakia's mammoth Skoda Works at Pilsen.

The Dutch Colony of Surinam on the North East Coast of South America, Deposits of Bauxite, vital in Aluminum manufacture. Zandery Field has now been constructed there.

For night fighting the British use a Boston equipped with a powerful searchlight in the nose, and a Hurricane on it's wing. Under radio direction the Boston sneaks up behind the enemy, the Hurricane shoots down the enemy while the Boston keeps it's powerful light on the target.

October 4, 1942: My day off. I spent it cleaning up the room, writing, and generally improving my standard of living. This afternoon I went over to Operations where the British showed us the complete setup. They've done wonders, and this is a perfect example of their efficiency.

Near Atcham there is an Estate of a Lord. Vast lands with magnificent trees and grasslands make up his Estate. Perhaps 150 deer roam it unrestrained. A small stream and waterfall hemmed in by trees, flows through. The Greathouse is 4 stories high and a square block of courts, archways and such. A symbol of the old days.

From a letter home dated October 4, 1942: Censored by Emmet E. Wilson, Captain Air Corps, England: Today is Sunday and my day off. It just happened that I was given the day off, but most of my friends are on duty, so I'm sticking pretty close to the post. Otherwise I would have taken a bike ride or gone into town.

I received your letter mailed Sept. 17th, in which you told about Bob and his leaving for San Antonio, to begin Cadet Training. No doubt he will soon write me. Please forward his address to me as soon as you can. I don't see how he started on that Mexican trip after the setup he knew he was in.

Bill didn't know that the Army had told me that I probably wouldn't be called to active duty for training until Thanksgiving or later due to the shortage of training facilities. I had already enlisted in the Army and intended to be back in Missoula by early September, from my trip to Mexico. When the telegram arrived, Mother telephoned me in San Francisco to let me know. I hurried home about a week earlier than I had planned.

No doubt both of you wanted to spend some time at home getting organized again before he had to start out. Well he little realizes what's in store for him, but I think he'll do all right if he just keeps the attitude that he must be adaptable for meeting and adjusting himself to new and strange conditions. He can't live in the past and think, this is the way I did it back home, that little chapter of his life is gone forever. He must realize this is the future and pitch in to meet it in a manner far different than the way we did it back home. He's young and this is an era of young people. You should see the young people, just kids 15 and 16, in uniform over here. We all know he has the stuff to make good, as he is part of us, and we always do things in a good manner.

Last night I spent about an hour sewing the cuffs of my pants back in place. Made a few blunders, and ran the needle into my finger a couple of times, but when I was through, I was quite pleased. This morning I cleaned up a few items in my room that were getting dirty. I took my ration cans of food off the shelf, plus the toilet articles, and cleaned the shelf. Next I wiped all the articles and placed them neatly back on the shelf. Later on I went to the wash room and laundered several pairs of shorts and handkerchiefs. A day well spent no doubt.

This noon our Sunday meal consisted of steak, mashed potatoes, brown gravy, pickles, bread, butter, tomatoes and lettuce, plus coffee. Dessert was peach cobbler.

Combat Training in England

A few days ago, I was the Officer of the Day, and I had to inspect the guards at 3:00 AM and again at 6:00. A driver took me around in a Ford Jeep. It was awfully cold, but I did my best to improve the guards and make them aware of the important job they were doing.

We have a Clothes Ration Card here, the same as the British, and a few days ago I bought some heavy wool socks, and a few neckties. Yesterday Stege and I went over to the Dental Lab to get an appointment to have our teeth cleaned. I'm expecting I'll have to get some work done, as my teeth haven't been looked at since I left home. They have a nice setup here with all the modern equipment and that makes it nice.

Later we took a ride through a Lord's land. There were magnificent trees and grasslands with perhaps a hundred or more deer running about. After crossing a small stream on an old wooden bridge, we came up to the Greathouse itself, such a place I've never seen. It's about four stories high and a square block in size, with courts, domes, archways and such. The Lords and Ladies must have had beautiful lawn parties and get togethers 10 years or so back. However the day of such things are passing, I believe, even in England.

Remember that I used to mention Wendal Seppich when I was in Flying School. I heard that he was killed in a plane accident out on the Pacific Coast. Too bad, as he was a real pal. His home was in Ogden, Utah.

Tonight, probably the four of us will build a fire in one of the rooms, sit around writing letters, and listen to the radio. It's a pretty good deal over here and we're fairly well contented. Keep the home fires burning.
PS I suppose Shep is really blue these days with Bob gone also. You two will have to keep him contented.

October 5, 1942: At 9:00 AM I had my teeth cleaned at the Post Dental Lab. I was very surprised to learn that I didn't have any cavities. This is the first time I've been to a dentist that something hasn't been bad in my mouth. It's been nearly 18 months since I first entered the service and that's when my teeth were last looked at.

This afternoon we watched a captured German film about their first attacks of Russia. It was awful, showed the Russians being slaughtered and the victorious Germans marching over everything. God! War certainly is awful.

Johnson is being transferred to a different group now, and Watson takes over as Operations Officer. Oh well nothing makes any sense in the Army.

Higher command wants us to be able to completely service the airplanes, as well as be able to adjust the brakes and perform other vital operations. Looks as if we might go somewhere where we won't have many ground crew members to help us. Oh joy to Rumors!! Today we went out to our planes, asking a bunch of questions and generally picked up all the information we could from the ground crew. It all helps.

This sallow dam, still twenty feet high.
Sat stalling it in without batting an eye.
Or using his throttle to ease him on down.
The Flight Surgeon says he'll recover the clown.

The Intelligence Section at Atcham has set up a Link Trainer to practice deflection shooting. The hood is left off and the pilot aims at a model plane that's on a stand on the floor. After figuring the deflection to be allowed for a given speed, the pilot pushes the gun button, that allows a beam of light to shine on the board that is calibrated for correction deflection. The light beam will fall on a line that represents a given speed of the e/a, if the correct deflection has been figured. A regular P-38 reflection gun sight is used. The walls of the room are painted for cloud and sky affect.

Combat Training in England

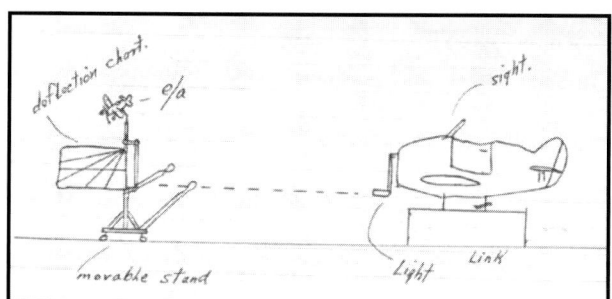
Bill's version of the Link Trainer

October 7, 1942: Today the Medical Department gave us Typhus shots. We're to receive three of these and they will be a week apart. What does this mean if anything? Perhaps a move? A good way to get another rumor started anyway.

This afternoon we went down to the gun butts and fired both the .45 pistol and the .06 rifle. I had a pretty fair score with the rifle, and fired about 25 rounds. As far as the forty-five is concerned, I might just as well throw rocks.

English M9A Miles Master Trainer

Our squadron now has an English Miles Master Advanced Trainer. I checked out in it this afternoon. It's the most sensitive ship, on the controls, I've ever been in. You just have to look at the stick to make it bank. Fast too, about 190 on the clock at 0 boost. It has air brakes and an odd type of stick.

The days go by and the efficiency of our flying isn't improving any by sitting around. They want to save the airplanes until they are actually needed, but in the meanwhile we have nothing but the Miles Master to fly.

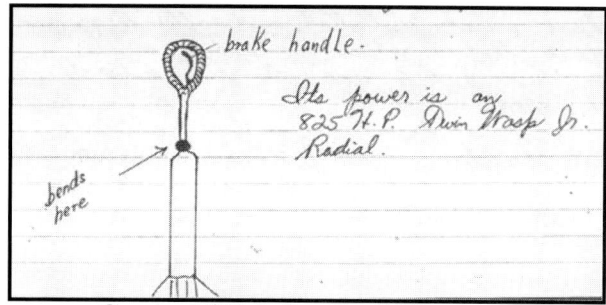
Control Stick for the Miles Master

I used to think that I would like to have a permanent commission, but I can see now the folly of that, for my type of person. Americans make poor soldiers, because they are too independent. Actual military flying is a young man's game. After 30 a pilot would certainly be put behind a desk, this would not be for me. The Army is great, but I would hate to do book work for it. If I am behind a desk I hope it'll be my own business. Also in the Army one would have to attend all types of social functions and could never build a home of his own, because he would be subject to moves at any time.

Being a Reserve Officer is the real thing, if you're young. It takes care of that period in life when a person is restless and wants adventure and travel. Well I have gained just that, and after three years I think that I should be glad to settle down and put to use the knowledge I have gained to use.

We've had a few altitude flights lately. Mostly twelve ship formations, in which we intercept bombers or do escort duty. The last one we had, was a 24 ship affair in which both the 49th and our Squadron, 48th, took part. Our squadron was the top cover at 26,000 feet. We had an interception with some Spitfires. The 49th made a pass at them and we also dove on them. I enjoyed the flight, leading the third element. Everything on my ship worked perfectly, and the Oxygen system is so good these days that I feel perfectly at ease at all times.

A new boy has come to our Squadron. He is

Combat Training in England

Alfonso Segraves, an American boy from Tucson, Arizona. He was trained in Canada, and now or recently, I should say, has been doing instruction flying in Oxfords, a British plane. He has a couple hundred hours in them. Shipman checked him out in a 38 after he had studied the plane for a couple of days. He's a nice fellow and listens with respect, consequently he did a very nice job of landing.

Saturday evening the 10th we had a dance at the Officer's Club. There was excess in our food fund, so they used it to buy all of the free beer and liquor the boys wanted. I went over and had a few beers. It was quite a mob scene, and everybody was quite slaphappy. A bunch of 2nd Lieutenants came over from High Ercall. They are flying P-39s and have just moved in.

Douglas A-20 Boston Bomber

On the **11th of October** the three Flying Captains, Captain Wroten, all the First Looies except Ethell and Eubanks, who are on detached service, and Zeigler and Tollen packed up and took off for Tangmere on the south coast of England. A Boston led us down there for the II Group. We saw a good deal more of England on this one hour trip and it supported our idea or impression of the vast number of airfields that are present in England. Tangmere is east of the Isle of Wight, just north of the point called Selsey Hill. We're about ten miles from the coast. The 49th Squadron is located at Ford, only about 2 or 3 miles from the coast and 10 miles away from us.

The field has two good runways and is completely covered with grass. Our planes are dispersed on the grass near the Operations Hut, where our own little Operations Room is located. Our quarters are nice, adjoining the Officer's Mess and Club. Staying with me in a room is Johnson and Sorensen. The field has been frequently raided and consequently the shelters are large and closely spaced, much more than other posts I've been stationed at. One large hangar has been completely destroyed and is just a bare skeleton standing there. Beside it is parked a Wellington Bomber, a battle scarred veteran.

In the states we heard a great deal about the way the British liked or disliked our aircraft, but now we are able to judge for ourselves. The Wellington is a good design, but a wooded hack, and would certainly go down after a few heavy slugs hit her. Somehow they manage to get performance from their planes, but as far as clean design and quality workmanship is concerned, ours are far more superior.

British Wellington Bomber

Our first night here, Sunday, a party was given and although we were invited to take part, we didn't do much. This was due mainly because of the terrible bags we were expected to dance with.

As usual the weather is bad and our hopes for frequent sweeps have vanished. The UK would be a perfect base to win a war from, if it weren't for the terrible weather.

On the **12th of October** we managed to take a small practice sweep. Taking off at 1420 and flying up and down the coast and about 25 miles

Combat Training in England

out over the channel. We saw a Sunderland Boat and a few other aircraft, but not a Jerry did we see. Later we heard that a couple of 190s had come in while we were gone and dropped a couple of bombs.

Operations, south coast of England, back row: Ziegler, Bill, Skinner, Johnson, Sorensen, Singleton, Smith V. H., Stege, Shipman, front row: Keith, Olds, Bing, Walles, Watson, Wroten

I was flying on Sorensen's wing, Third Element, while Shipman and V. Smith were 2nd Element. Colonel Olds with Johnson on his wing was the Lead Element. Captain Walles, Watson, and Bing lead the 2nd Flight with Singleton, Stege and Skinner as wingmen. We did quite a bit of maneuvering and it was very good practice for me since I hadn't been flying wing for some time.

On landing Johnson got into violent prop wash and landed hard on one wheel, hitting the tail boom, putting a good-sized dent in it. He gave it the gun and went around. Remarking on the incident Colonel Olds said, "Whether you're a Captain, Colonel or Major General, if you've gotten into trouble, admit it was your fault, and do better the next time".

On the **14th** the weather was too bad all day to do any flying. A few raiders sneaked in from France, but were off again before anyone could catch them or before they did any harm.

In the afternoon we all went to town, Chichester, a drive of about 10 miles, and did a little shopping. I got a haircut and some of the boys bought pipes and such. Stege and Tollen had tea at a very modern eating establishment and they induced us all to return in the evening. So at 6:30 PM all of us, except O.D. Skinner, took off for supper. I rode with several others in the Colonel's station wagon. They were expecting us and had a long table already set up especially for us. It is nice to get out like that, all dressed up and it seemed like a spirit of good fellowship existed, and I got the feeling that I'm lucky to be where I am. Incidentally we had a very lovely dinner to the accompaniment of several good musical records. Later on we went to the show, "Song of the Islands", with Betty Grable. I've seen it once, but could watch that gal for a month and not get tired.

October 15, 1942: This morning when I woke up the wind was blowing very strongly and it looked like we wouldn't be doing any flying. Soon things cleared up and the sky was completely blue. We figured there would be a show for sure, and we were right. Soon after lunch we were given our briefing, we were to be the high altitude escort to 12 Boston's, that were to bomb Le Havre, France. We were to be at 25,000 feet and they would have Spits above and below us.

We left all our valuables in our little sacks, took our escape kits with us and started up at 1340. At 1345 we were in the air circling with the Spitfire 9s over Shoreham. They cruise much slower than we do and it was a job to pull only 20 inches and

Combat Training in England

weave behind them. At 1401 we headed out climbing directly across the channel at 190 degrees.

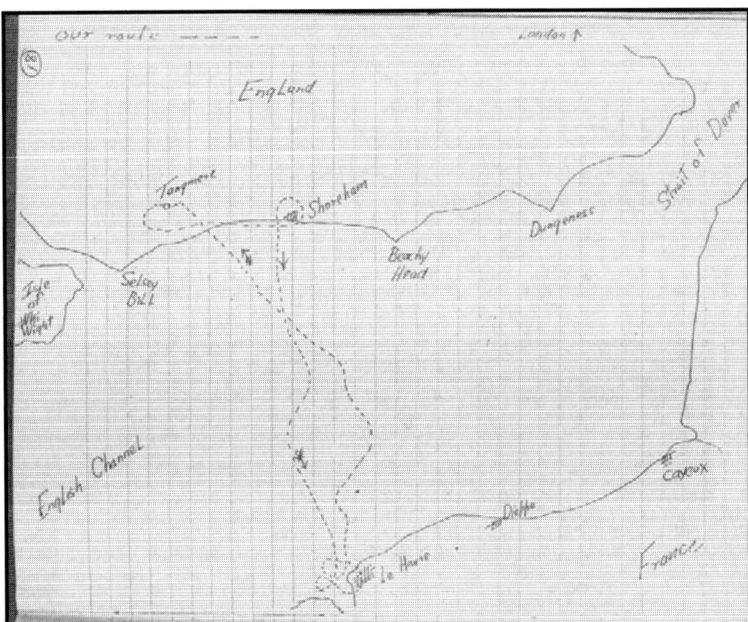

Bill's drawing of their first sweep into France

We climbed too slowly, as low as 130 MPH and this made flying very difficult. We were only pulling 20 inches and even then we had to **S** back and forth to keep from running over the Spitfires. I could see the coast of France about 15 minutes away and from about 15,000 feet, it looked beautiful and peaceful down there in the sunshine and I just couldn't see why people had to fight. By the time we had reached 25,000 feet we were over Le Havre, and the Boston's were dropping their eggs. What I saw of the city, looked very nice and not very damaged. I never did see the bombs explode but I saw plenty of **Flack Bursts** from the AA guns. They were black patches of smoke, and right at our altitude. None came dangerously close to us however!

Soon we started home weaving and gradually diving away at about 350 on the clock. I could easily see both the coast of France and that of England, near Dover, at the same time, from 20,000 feet. Soon we were circling the airdrome and landing. We had taken off on the grass. There had been Spits all over the sky and we came dangerously close to a few.

On the radio, during the sweep, there wasn't a word spoken until we hit the French Coast on the return trip. Then the chatter started!! I heard, "Bloody fine bombing"! "Use your bloody callsign", and "what a formation"! "Good show! Good show!"

Well we learned a great deal and as usual they, the Captains, had plenty to bitch about in regard to formations etc. I think because they are flying element now and not leading, things are a lot tougher for them and they don't like it.

Bestgen and Corporal Robbie our medic, came down in the Miles Master to bring supplies and to give us our second Thypus shot. Some of the boys sure hate to take the shot and Captain Walles said he just wasn't going to.

Group Captain McGregor, the Post Commanding Officer checked out in our 38, and seemed to enjoy it greatly.

Roger, our mascot, the dog that has traveled the ocean by airplane has been found dead at Atcham. He was missing for several days and Captain Walles posted a large reward. However, Roger fell in a construction hole filled with water and drowned. Apparently no one heard his pleas. He will be missed by many in the 48th. They buried him in a regular grave and with a tiny tombstone.

After we returned to our base and a little later on in the evening we learned that one Spitfire had been lost on the raid to Le Havre. Some 190s had come up to 19,000 feet, but we were at 25,000. Evidently some of the Spits flying lower had tangled with them. The raid was very successful.

October 16, 1942: We were rudely awakened this morning at 0600. Evidently there is to be a big show. After eating a hurried meal we rushed down to Operations to be briefed. Ah, we're to be high altitude escort to 92 B-17s that will raid a submarine base on the west coast of France. Just as we were getting the details down pat, a call came from Operations canceling the whole show. Curse, but that's the fighter game.

Today was my turn at Officer of the Day, so I took up the duty of watching the telephone in the little operations room. It was my job to enter all incoming and outgoing calls in the proper ledger. At 1000 Colonel Olds put through several calls to Atcham and Ajax, the Headquarters in London. He talked with General Hunter, our Fighter Command Head.

As there weren't any operations planned for the day, it was decided that we would return to Atcham to install our belly tanks. We weren't told the reason, but evidently it has something to do with a long-range raid. We were given about 20 minutes to pack, and I really threw my things together in a hurry. Back in Operations the zero hour was set and as usual we had 12 planes in the air in nothing flat.

To prevent the enemy radio detection apparatus from picking us up, we flew low level back to Atcham. At first we were barely clearing the hills, but later on we raised to 1,000 feet. Colonel Olds did a nice job of navigation, despite having a strong cross wind, poor visibility and mist and rain squalls. The air was unusually rough and we were all bouncing around badly. I leveled off high and dropped old 7650 in for a hard landing. Too bad as I had been making very good ones lately.

They immediately set to work installing the belly tanks. Also they changed the B channel on the radio, but didn't get finished in time to leave today. I worked on my Oxygen mask, fitting it to the new type helmet, this afternoon. The 2nd Lieutenants here are pretty well disgusted with the whole deal as many of us are. Major Keith is to fly with us now. It looks as though the whole group will fly, and the flight, which did so much training, will be left behind.

Ted Sweetland, class of 41-I, dropped in this afternoon in a Spitfire. He's located at Ajax with Fighter Command. Spent a peaceful evening, alone, in my room, with a good fire, just sort of thinking the whole situation over.

October 17, 1942: Up at 0630 this morning so we could get an early start back to Tangmere. Belly tanks on, radio crystals on B channel changed to Number 1 Group Guard Ten and we were ready to go. Then we learned that on two ships the turbo brackets were sprung, so that kept them out of commission. On another that Major Keith was to take, it was Tollen's ship, the exhaust plugs had become fouled and a change was needed. The Group Captain at Tangmere had checked out in that ship and had idled it excessively, which no doubt explains the need for the plug change.

I led the Third Element in the last flight with Sorensen on my wing. Take off was good and everybody was in formation as we passed over the field en route. We flew the whole distance at 500 feet and occasionally dropped down as low as 100 feet. Never have I had a more enjoyable trip. Steady throttle settings, and fairly smooth air, helped. We flew over towns, farmer's houses, haystacks, etc. It was interesting to watch the people look up at us as we thundered by 200 feet above their farms. Some places, the horses bolted, and sheep scattered for cover.

This afternoon we all went to the briefing room, as there was to be another show against Le Havre. Weather of 9/10 canceled that. A detailed briefing was given however so we could see just how it would be under actual circumstances. Many of the fighter sweeps across the channel are mainly to make the enemy put their fighters at one point and then a bombing raid can be carried out at another place. Lines and courses are drawn to show exact actions in the channel.

Combat Training in England

The briefing room is very interesting. It has maps and charts covering the walls completely. There are notebooks with pictures and information about every friendly and enemy aircraft in operation in Europe today.

We saw a short movie on Air Sea Rescue. I played a game of badminton with Skinner, Shipman and Stege. Oh yes, about the Air Sea Rescue. When a fix is taken on the position of a flyer that has gone down at sea, the rescue launches, the Lysander, and the Spitfires take out. The Lysander is suppose to spot the dinghy and circle above it until the speedboats come and rescue the flyer. The Spitfires protect the Lysander against enemy fighters.

From the Squadron Atlantic Air Route Guide:
Greenland
1650 miles long at the extreme length
800 miles wide at the widest point
827,275 square miles estimated
Disko Island off the West Coast is the largest with about 3,200 square miles
On the ice cap there is a half to two and one half feet of mealy snow resting on a layer of hard packed snow
The border zone is 30 to 50 miles in width
In July the ice pack has been known to move as much as 125 feet in 24 hours
Mount Forel near Angmagssalik is 11,500 feet high
Most of the ice-free land is North of 70 degrees North Latitude
Small settlements are Umanak, Godhaven, Jakobshaven, Egedesminde, Holsteinborg, Sukkertoppen, Godthaab, Frederikshaab, Ivigtut, and Julianhaab. On the East Coast, Angmagssalik Labrador Settlements are Battle Harbor, Cartwright, Indian Harbor, Mokkovik, Hopedale, Nain, Port Manvers and Hebron.

October 18, 1942: Today the right landing gear of a Boston folded up as it was finishing it's landing roll. Very little damage was done, the engine nacelle and prop were all that were damaged. A Spit also landed with its engine on fire. White fumes were pouring back over the cockpit as the pilot climbed out. Early afternoon several of the boys, who were in town, saw someone floating down in a parachute, evidently one of the Spit boys had gotten himself into the sights of a 190.

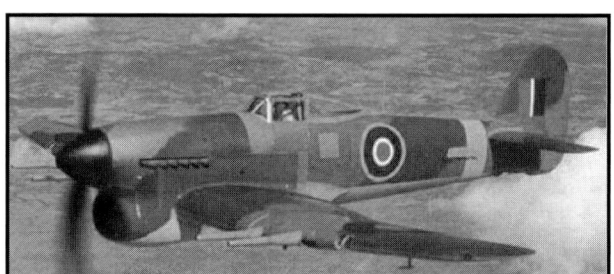

British Hawker Typhoon Fighter

Today I got a good look at a Typhoon Fighter. Five of them landed here and we had a good talk with a New Zealand Sergeant. The plane, much like the P-47, weighs 12,000 lb. and has a 24 cylinder H engine, which develops 2400 HP at 3700 RPM for takeoff. For offensive weapons it has four 20-MM cannons. Two days ago a Lancaster, which participated in the 94 Bomber raid on Le Creuset, France, landed here. It's a clumsy looking affair, compared to our B-17 Flying Fortress, but it's really plenty good and does the work.

Stalin said: "There are three things necessary to win this war, blood, materials and time. The United Nations have all three. Russia has the blood, the United States has the materials, and England has the time."

October 19, 1942: Today we inspected the squadron which takes care of setting off or rendering harmless, bombs that have not exploded when they hit. They showed us a 1100 pound bomb and some pictures of a land mine that carries 750 pounds of explosives. Best of all things we saw and liked was their little black Scottie Pup!! We also saw some propaganda leaflets that the Germans had dropped concerning

Combat Training in England

the Dieppe Raid. Today it's raining very hard. I guess operations for us in the European Theater, will be nil for today.

Tonight we talked to a few of the RAF boys. Some of them, from Canada, are flying the P-51 Mustang. They are wild about them, and praise them for the way they operate. They fly over in two's to do any cooperation work, and despite the extreme danger they usually get back. The .50 Caliber guns are wonders, they claim. One told us of a railroad engine that he blew completely up with a blast from his fifties.

October 20, 1942: Up at 0530 this morning and over to the Airmen's Mess for a bit to eat. After eating we left our valuables with our Intelligence Officer, Captain Wroten, and obtained our escape kits, we were ready to shove off at 0715.

The airdrome was just beginning to get the first light of dawn, when we ran out to our P-38s. The mist and dew had settled on the windshields so heavily that visibility was practically nil. However with the aid of running lights we did OK. The Colonel led us in a low level flight to Exeter, where we were to fill our one and only belly tank, the right one, and prepared to operate a flight from there. I had noticed a slight tendency to swing to one side on landing and a difference in trim of the aircraft, but all in all operating with one belly tank proved to be very practical.

On the Exeter Airdrome were a group of Czechoslovakian Airmen who worked on our planes. They were very nice, worked hard and praised the airplane. One told how he had escaped from Germany, he said that no true Czech would ever fight for Germany. I helped service the planes with gas, oil, and oxygen.

We ate breakfast at 0915 in the Officers Mess, which was an old house that had been taken over for this purpose. In the Briefing Room we were given detailed instructions as to our course, speed, and times for our upcoming operation. We were to escort B-17s at 22,000 feet, to the submarine base at Lorient. This would entail passing over a large strip of occupied France to the northern part of the Bay of Biscay. The complete trip would be a total of 366 miles. As usual the briefing was very hurried and we had to rush in order to make our takeoff time at 1210.

My plane, as usual, ran very good and we started a rapid climb to the specified altitude. I had better luck staying in formation this time, even though the climb became as slow as 130 MPH, indicated at times. I experienced severe prop wash. By the use of cross feed I was able to run both engines on the drop tank, for one hour and twenty minutes. However the weather was destined to give us trouble. We passed through layers of thin overcast at 6, 11, and 15,000 feet, and at 18,000 it was really thick, so we stayed at that altitude.

I sighted the French Coast at 1300, and we flew on for twenty minutes before we were called back. The B-17s didn't get very good protection from us, and although they bombed the objective, they weren't as successful as they should have been. They lost one of their planes.

France looked much like England from 16,000 feet. The fields were laid out in squares in the same manner. At that altitude we experienced heavy flak fire but none of our planes were hit. Going back across the channel we hit 300 MPH on the clock most of the time as we were in a gradual let down. We were lost after we hit England but after a terrible jumble of radio procedure we got a homing. All our planes landed safely

A B-17 landed badly damaged, with three men injured. They shot down 3 FW 190s. The flaps on the B-17 were shot up beyond repair, the gas tanks were leaking, the fabric was completely gone on one side of the elevators, the tailwheel was flat, and there were large holes all over the plane.

After waiting around with nothing to eat for a

couple of hours we finally took off for Tangmere, where we landed at 1745 (5:45 PM).

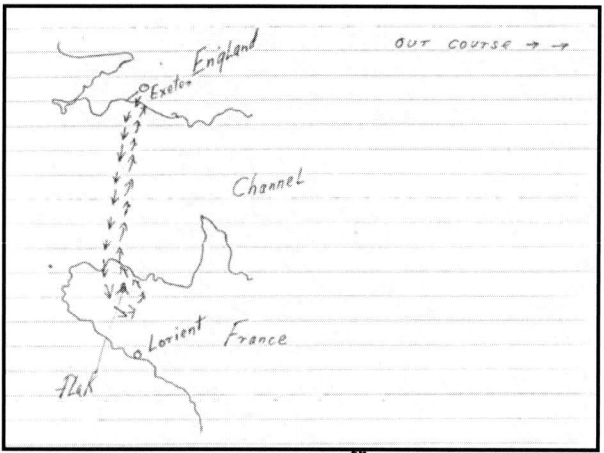
Mission on the 20th of October

Finished a book today, "Readiness at Dawn"--The veil lifted from a Fighter Station's Operation Room--

At Tangmere:
"Hello, hello, hello, this is a test broadcast."
"Telephone call for Pilot Officer McGregor".
Pilot Officer, Flying Officer, Flight Lieutenant, Squadron Leader, Wing Commander

October 24, 1942: This morning when we arrived at the Operations Hut, we were due for a little surprise. Colonel Olds called us out in front and had us fall in, in two ranks, at attention. This included Major Keith and the four Captains. Right face! Forward March! And we were off to town, 3 miles away. We hadn't marched since leaving Cadet School, but I really enjoyed it. Of course, the Bing and the Walles thought it was absurd, but naturally!! In town we had coffee and cakes at a very lovely little shop.

This afternoon we saw 94 Lancaster Bombers as they flew over at an altitude of about 200 feet. They were on their way to Italy to bomb Genoa on a daylight unescorted raid.

October 25, 1942: We were briefed this morning for another Boston Mission to Le Havre. The weather had been very good early in the morning, but was gradually becoming worse as the day progressed.

We took off at 1337, and joined up with three "Spit" six Squadrons over Shoreham. I was on Sorensen's wing, Third Element, Last Flight, which was led by Major Keith. We really had a rough time of it, because we received all the prop wash of the other squadrons and also we had to stay at such low altitudes, (0) to avoid enemy radio detection. We couldn't avoid the prop wash.

English Lancaster Bomber

At 1401 we started out on 181 degrees for Fecamp, which is up the coast from Le Havre. At first, things were going nicely but soon the usual began to happen. Our climb dropped from a comfortable 165 MPH to a mushing 130. At 12,000 feet Smith decided he couldn't go on, as his supercharger wasn't cutting in so he and Shipman returned to base. The clouds were all about but we had managed to keep everyone in sight by good flying. But it was useless to continue so were called back just as we'd reached the coast. This wasn't too soon, as the weather was 9/10 and 1500 feet. As soon as we landed and unloaded, it started to rain and the field closed in entirely.

I was a little disgusted with the 38 after that flight but I know for sure that we learned a great deal. First, the P-38 can't work with other type aircraft, as we must keep up our speed and when we fly with Spits, we have to climb too slowly. We would be slaughtered if we kept up our speed for long at 130 MPH and were bounced. Two there's absolutely no use in attempting high altitude

Combat Training in England

bombing or escort work, unless the weather is clear and unlimited. Yes this winter, on this front, the P-38 is practically useless. I'm ready to move on.

Today is Mother's birthday.

October 26, 1942: This morning was a rainy one. Ceiling was 500 feet. We were sitting in our Operations Hut at 1100 when we suddenly heard some shooting. "Practice firing, I guess", said Captain Wroten. But looking out the window, we could see a plane coming straight for the field, with tracers being fired at it. We all piled out of the windows and watched with open mouths. He came right up the field and suddenly banked right. We saw four bombs drop and a moment later the ground shook from the explosion, flame, dirt, and debris flew from the ground. By this time, ack ack was opening up from all sides, and tracers were flying all over from around the field. The plane a JU-88 replied with rear machine gun fire. We lost sight of him then.

Later on we examined the damage. The bombs had passed through a house and completely ruined it. Then they knocked down a tree, a fence, and slid down a road for 200 feet where they exploded. One left a crater 6 feet deep and 10 feet in diameter. It was quite a little thrill for us but it could've been a disaster if he hadn't turned.

More raiders were plotted, for another hour, and Mustangs patrolled the airdrome at high speeds. We learned from the 49th that the raider had passed over their airfield, Ford, and had killed one man with machine gun fire. Later the raider was shot down.

October 27th--Dad's birthday: We packed up this morning, and Major Keith led us back to Atcham on a very enjoyable flight. The weather cleared, the air was calm and zero feet was our altitude. We buzzed Atcham like it's never been buzzed before. We sneaked in from 10 miles out, barely clearing the trees. They didn't even see us coming until we were over the edge of the field.

Here at Atcham, things have been poppin! All bedrolls have been moved out and the ground crews leave tomorrow by boat. Air filters are being installed on our planes, under the booms, and in the wheel wells. When the wheel doors are closed, when the plane is flying, the normal air intake scoop on the side is in operation. When a landing is affected, and the boom doors or wheel doors are open, then a separate air intake is put into operation by means of opening a butterfly valve and closing the valve to the main air inlet. This second air opening is a screen mesh affair that is about a foot high and two feet long.

October 28, 1942: Fifty percent of the pilots have been given 48 hours leave, so that they can go to London, if they wish. Stege and Shipman took out together, but Sorensen and I decided to stay at home. We've seen London once and there's no use spending $30.00 and freezing on the train.

We went to town and got a haircut, and took care of some business. The weather has been very bad since our return from Ops. Fogged in completely, and extremely cold. We keep our little fire going all the time, and it's not too much.

We got a Tetanus booster and the third Thypus shot at the hospital this afternoon. That completes the works for me. We have had instruction in tropical medical care, water, food, insects, and such. We have special equipment that includes first aid packages, Quinine pills, water purification tablets, etc. We should do quite well if we're careful.

October 29, 1942: Every day we now take a hike for a couple of miles wearing our side arms. This is intended to keep us in good condition, and give a taste of what we might expect in the near future.

While Watson has gone to London I've been taking care of Operations. Not much to do now, but at least I can drive a Ford Carryall and a Jeep.

Combat Training in England

Since we've been issued English parachutes, our list of English equipment is pretty well complete. Formerly we had only the helmet, which provided a quick removable attachment for our Oxygen mask. The new "chute" is mainly used to enable us to attach a dingy, rubber boat, and still provide headroom in the cockpit. We also have new parachute bags and Ziegler and I have been putting names on them.

We've packed our flyers kit bags and they were crated and sent by boat, evidently. Now we'll live out of our airplane again.

Johnson, Tollen, Fulmer and Ethell went to Scotland to get four new airplanes, which are to replace a few which have been damaged around here. We'll get two of them for the 48th and headquarters and 49th will get the rest. They are equipped with the a new high speed flap, which enables the pilot can use as a brake.

There will always be an England
October 31, 1942
Dear Cadet Brother,

I've received your two letters, and they made me very happy. I'm glad to hear that you're getting along so well. You and I haven't heard much of each other since I left home but we've both been very busy I know and could hardly be expected to do much writing. However not that we're both under the same circumstances. I think that it would be of benefit to both of us if we could establish the habit of an active correspondence. You see, things will never be the same for us again. Indeed, it's essential that we keep each other in the know. Here's where I'm at quite a disadvantage, because I can't say what's going on over here, even though I believe it would be fairly interesting material to read. So you'll have to bear with me on my information, while I can continue to enjoy yours.

England is about like home this time of year, that being pretty darn chilly. This makes us keep the little stove in our room working overtime. We get a certain amount of coal to use, but the wood is fairly scarce. We just break up a few old boxes to start the fire and sweat out the coal.

In the course of our stay we've covered a great deal of this island and eaten at various English mess halls. They've a funny way of serving a meal. first comes soup, then fish served by itself, next is a main course of probably some potatoes and more fish. Finally instead of having dessert, they have a savory toast with some kind of burnt fish spread on it. Coffee is served in an entirely different room, sort of a sipping after thought affair. You see, they sort of play around and putter over their eating. You and Mother would get a kick out of having tea. It's a regular habit that takes place every afternoon at four. The table is set all over again and you enjoy tea, cakes and toast, along with pleasant conversation. A far cry from home!

Awhile back I fired my 45 service piston and a 06 rifle. I did OK with the rifle, but when it comes to the 45, I could do better throwing rocks. We can fire, for practice, just about anytime we care to. Of course this is great fun.

Although I can't say in a letter what's going on, I can keep a record of it, which I do. I have filled one book already and am well started in another. This will remind me of things to talk about **if I ever get back home.** I also keep my logbook up to date, and this is something you should do. I have an exact record of all the flying I've done, what type of ship, where and anything else that's important.

Well let's talk about you. All the stuff you've been through since leaving home has been mighty serious business to you. From this distance, I have to laugh at you and your buddies. You should do well for you are a typical cadet. This is the start of a typical cadet; a few highlights in dumbness.

1. Reports for physical exam in a very worried state, imagines that he will wash out if small toe slants more than 20 degrees from accepted plane.

Combat Training in England

Actually very few ever wash out for this reason once they are accepted. There's no reason to worry here, as they're not as strict as one hears.
2. Meets a few buddies on train headed for flying school, they compare notes on experience, etc. Worried cadet supposes that because he's not had Secondary CPT that he has a much poorer chance, one of the biggest misconceptions I've ever heard) With what I know now I would rather enter school with just Primary CPT than with any other state of experience.
3. Cadet hears about co-ordination in flying and imagines that in every move he makes, stick and rudder must go the same way or he will surely spin in. A good theory, and a condition which should normally be worked for but in formation flying, in landings and takeoffs, during a strong crosswind it's nothing more than a theory as I'm still here.
4. Cadet worries about check rides, practiced forced landing and a thousand other such things.

It all boils down to a few simple items.
1. Learn all you can from your ground school and with the airplane, practice them yourself in the air. Experiment! Nothing much will happen.
2. Don't believe all the rumors you hear. The Army is worse for these than any number of women in the back yards. Wait until something actually happens, then judge for yourself. I mean that. I've heard many things that influenced me and then had them turn out to be completely without basis.

Well Bob, just something to put a few ideas into your already confused head, so I'll sign off now.
Love Bill
PS My new APO number is 525. Use that instead of 1255. Just put 0-431164, you don't have to write **Army Serial Number**, they'll know what it's for.

Fog, fog, and more fog!!! We've had several days of heavy fog, this early part of **November**. We've been waiting and preparing to start on our great new adventure, whatever it might be. In preparation we've been getting our planes in good shape. Crew Chief Sassman has completed the 125-hour inspection on my plane and proclaimed it ready to go. We have also been packing the planes and arranging our belongings to best fit in the ship. Our bedrolls have left already and now everything we own must fit into the plane itself. I've put my shoes, toilet articles, steel helmet and gas mask in the plane already.

While waiting we've been taking Marches, having meetings on the explanations of **Italian** aircraft. Sending home money orders, and buying new shoes and pants, at least that's what I've been doing. I bought a nice pair of Army shoes for $3.40 and the pants for $4.88. However the pants will have to be let out before I can use them.

Mae West—The Pilot's life vest.

Wally and I cleaned out the chimney in our room and found that the stove worked 100% better. We did this by dropping stones down the chimney, which cleared out the soot. It's been mighty cold these last few days and the fire really feels good in the evenings. Everyone wants to leave England. It's no place for a flyer in the wintertime.

Cockpit of Bill's P-38

Combat Training in England

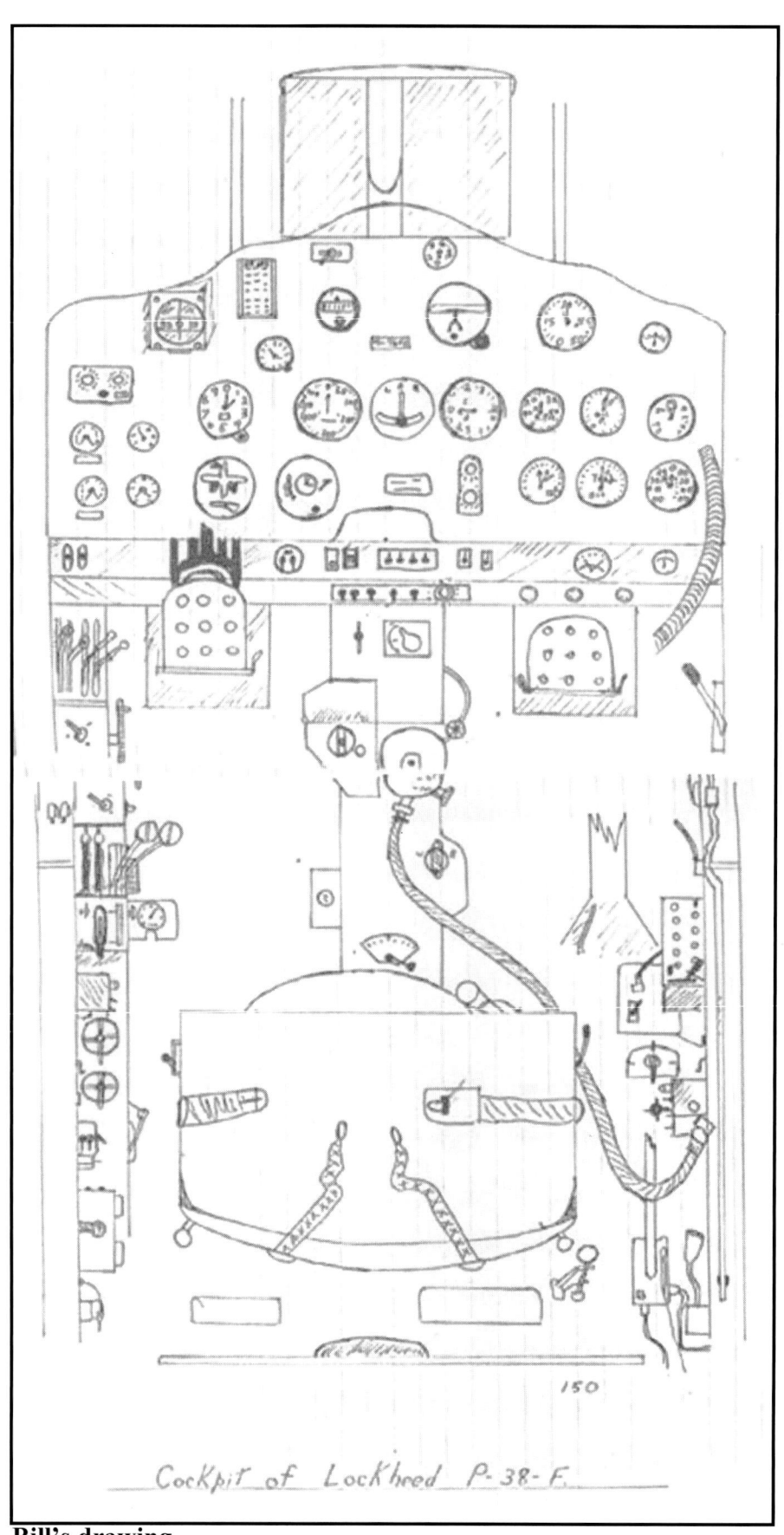

Bill's drawing

England to North Africa

Bill is still at Atcham Field, England awaiting orders that will take him to another stage of his career. Some of their equipment has been packed and sent on ahead while other equipment is packed in their planes. Still they don't know where they are headed.

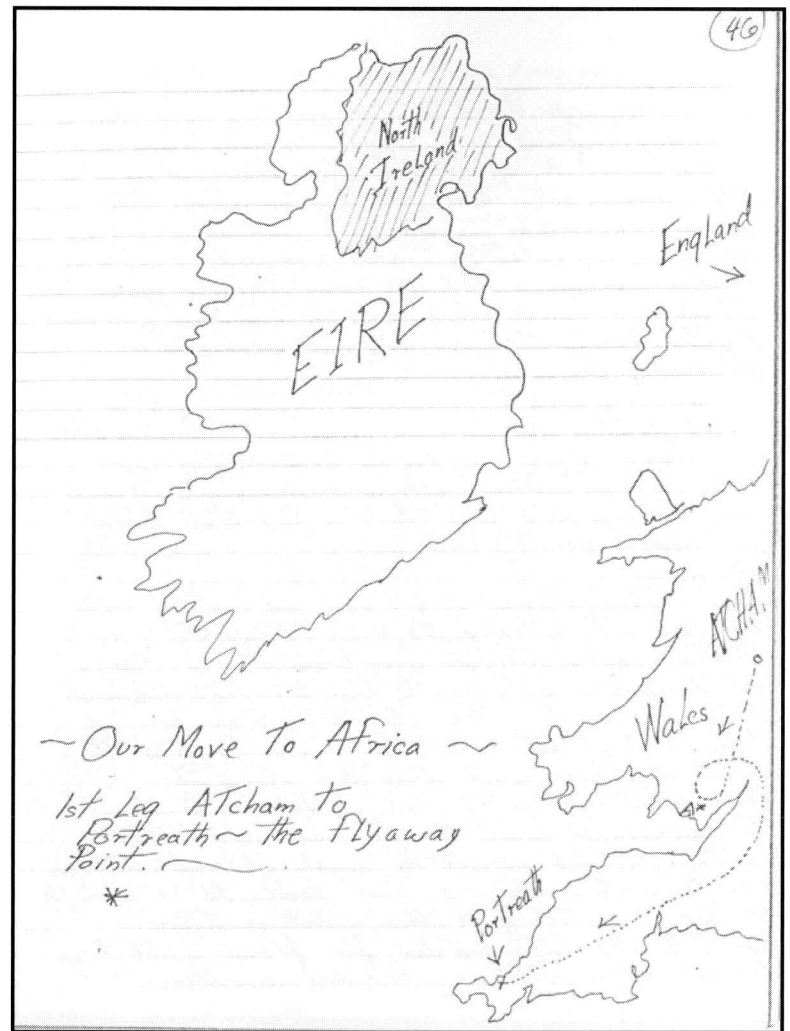

Map by Bill

November 6, 1942: Today, just three months and two days after our arrival, we left Atcham. This morning the fog lifted and the weather cleared. About 0900 we were given instructions to preflight our planes and this started the turmoil off in great style. Lack of transportation was our biggest worry. I had to wait for the second truck going out to the line and this put me way behind, to start things off. The engines were extremely cold and on the first try they wouldn't begin to turn over. However on the second try they did and because the oil was so cold, they had high oil pressures. I ran them slowly to begin with and then faster as they warmed up. Everything checked out fine and I began to unfasten hoods, etc., in preparation for packing the rest of my goods. However, Captain Walles and Sorensen came out in a jeep and interrupted my work, telling me to hurry back to my room and pack as the briefing was to begin shortly at the Operations Hut of the 49th.

So the hour that I had planned to use for packing the rest of my belongings turned out to be a hectic 5 minutes. Then I hurried back to Operations, dumped my things and hurried over to be briefed. I was totally amazed at the co-ordination that is necessary to make this move possible. Radio, supply, parachutes, medical departments all have to be co-ordinated and each one frequently caused problems for the others. Poor Boots, in the parachute department, had an awful time. About three days before we were to go, our English Parachutes arrived and the dinghies had to be attached to them. These were fitted to the seat, then each pilot had to have the chute fitted to him. After all this was accomplished, new orders came through and the old backpack was put back in use. All chutes had to be redone completely and then refitted to each pilot again. Quite a task! The medical department finished with the last minute handing out of Quinine Pills, water purifying pills and Sulfanilamide Tablets.

We were to follow Havas, Bostons to Portreath, a place on the tip of the southwest coast of England. They gave us 15 minutes to get from the briefing to our planes and be ready to go. Rushing back to our own Operations, I climbed into my Mae West, ran to the plane, and hurriedly

England to North Africa

finished packing and fastened down all of the cowlings. Take-off was normal and I flew on Bing's wing. However I noticed as soon as I got in the air that my left engine's oil temperature was climbing rapidly past the safe limit. My first thought was to let my wheels down and go right back in and land. But I decided to see how it would get along. I worked the shutters and tried everything I knew but the temperature ran 95 to 100 degrees, this is 10 or 15 degrees over the normal safe limits.

We set out on our course at 500 feet and skimmed the hilltops. It wasn't much fun for me. My flying was poor, as I hadn't been up for nine days, that combined with the engine trouble made me feel very uncomfortable. The weather turned worse and soon we reached a point where flying at this altitude of 100 feet was getting unsafe. We ran into a solid cloud lying on a hilltop and the Boston started flying straight through it, however Colonel Olds made a turn and started back. I was inside man on the inside flight and it wasn't much fun flying with my wing tip lying right on the hilltop in that turn, especially with all the violent prop wash that I was receiving. We made a very wide turn back into good weather and eventually continued on down to Portreath. We skimmed the hills and made the sheep run and soon the 200 foot high cliffs of the seaside appeared.

Our flight had to circle while the others landed and by the time I peeled off, my hands were so weak that I could barely change the tanks to reserve. As usual the pattern was a long low affair and it dragged on for a great distance. The thing that made it really bad was the fact that we were landing directly into the rays of the sun and my windshield was covered with oil from the guns. With no chance to break my glide, I just cut the gun while looking out the side doing 115 MPH. A terrible landing.

Something happened to Major Russell, I believe he forgot his tanks. He crashed in a field 4 miles from the field. The plane burned but he got out with a broken ankle and a few bruises. A very lucky fellow!

We staked down our planes, put on the covers, locked the canopies and retired to the tower.

Our quarters are poorer on this post than most we've been at, probably because of the crowded conditions, there are four of us to a room. Stege, Shipman, Sorensen and I are together. The club and mess are very nice. Meals usually run a Shilling.

November 7, 1942: This morning we went to the Briefing Room where we learned what the big move is all about. We were right, it's down south to Northern Africa. This will be about 1250 miles in one hop. Radio, intelligence, maps, everything was gone over. The Intelligence Officer is an eager American Captain who went into great detail explaining the Arab situation. This included information on what we were to do with our equipment if we are forced down, etc. He gave us money and a so-called Blood Chit, this contains Arab writing and instructs them to take good care of us. We received our maps and it took a couple of hours, of hard work, to properly draw in the courses that we were going to fly on.

By the time I got out to my airplane the RAF crews had put the camouflage nets over it. We had a terrible time getting it off so I could run up the left engine, to test the oil temperature. The run up produced the same overheating that I'd encountered in the air, so we started to look for the problem. The cuno showed nothing but a small deposit of carbon and everything else seemed to be OK. Bing figured that maybe the oil reservoir had been over-filled and that might had something to do with it. The Allison man said yes, there might even be an air lock in the line somewhere that was causing the oil to ride too high in the tank. We drained four gallons from the left engine and ran it up again. This

England to North Africa

time, apparently, everything turned out OK. However I won't be satisfied until I fly it.

We worked on Carroll's ship next. The rubber hose joint, for the belly tank, was leaking. We had to take the belly tank completely off and do the job over again. A tough job but we had the satisfaction of a hard job well done. There were many signs that the Crew Chiefs hadn't been doing their jobs properly.

I was disgusted to think that higher command was not planning to keep some of our Crew Chiefs with us, at all times. They can't expect 50 complex machines to be moved without something going wrong that will be beyond the scope of the pilot to repair.

Five B-25s came in, as they are to escort us. They carry 550 gallon of gas in extra bomb-bay tanks, and a full crew of seven. The crews are very inexperienced, mostly 42-F boys. Cadets are of a much poorer quality now and the officers reflect it.

November 8, 1942: Again, this morning I spent a great deal of time at my ship just doing little jobs. I checked the belly tank hose connections, tightened all cowl fastenings, connected the detonator for the IFF, radio, packed up the mooring kit and fussed around.

This noon the radio told about American Forces landing in Spanish Morocco near Casa Blanca and Oran.

This was the beginning of **Operation Torch,** *The invasion of North Africa. General Dwight D. Eisenhower was the Allied Commander of this operation. This operation began with the landing of troops in various places in North Africa on this day.*

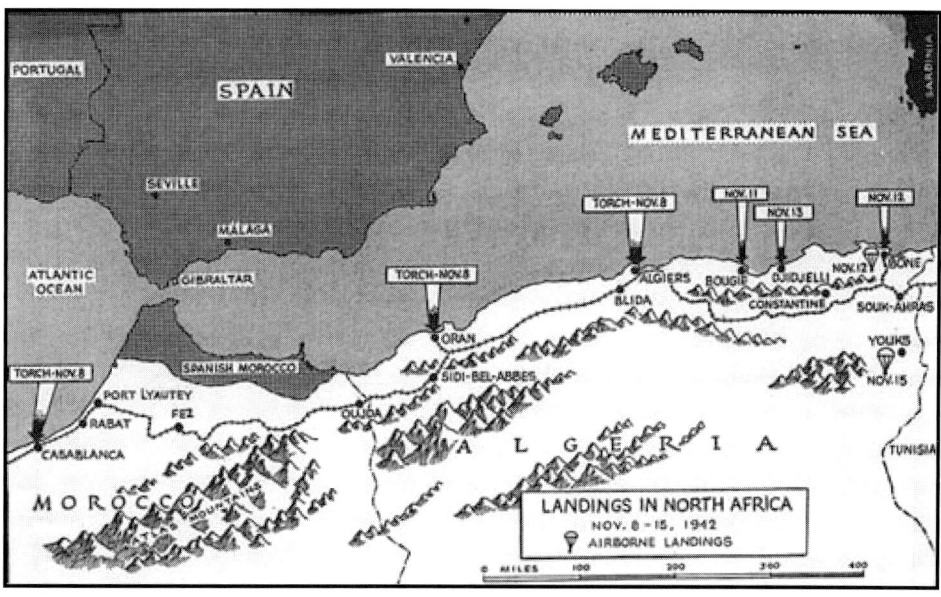

Five more 38s arrived this afternoon, bearing Captain Morin, Bestgen, Warren, Ayes, etc. I worked for two more hours completing the courses on the maps.

November 9, 1942: Today we had hoped to get going but too many things came up. The radios have to be crystallized on a few of the late arriving ships, meteorological information must be gathered, courses and maps must be worked on, oxygen tanks must be filled and countless other little things needed to be attended to.

This morning Wally and I watched a 40-MM ground gun crew go through a practice drill. A man sits on each side of the gun, looking through his sight. The man on the right moves the gun up and down and the one on the left moves it back and forth across the sky. They agree by voice, when to fire.

In the afternoon, a great many B-17s came in from a raid on a submarine base, 60 miles south of Lorient. They raided, and bombed from 7,000 feet causing terrific destruction, however they

England to North Africa

took a heavy beating from **Flak**. They came in, here at Portreath, in a terrible mix-up, as they were trying to land from every direction at once. A Major landed two-thirds of the way down a runway and went over the end and piled up. His Bombardier was already dead from the flak. Two others were making approaches with engines feathered and both had to go around at the last minute. Four of them landed downhill with no wind and burned out their brakes and tires. One came in and landed on the grass and skidded to a halt, after taking out a hangar and two P-38s. This plane had a dead engine that wouldn't feather, another engine that would only give 16 inches, manifold pressure, an aileron shot up, and the rudder was useless. 2nd Lieutenant Bucky, who went all the way through flying school with Ed Halm, was flying it. He says he was in the same flight with Ed at Santa Maria.

November 10, 1942: Today we hiked down to the sea near Portreath. We stopped to look over a couple of Anti-Aircraft units right off the end of the runway, on which the B-17 overshot. The gunners narrowly missed being run down while in their gun implacements. All along the coast, besides real guns there's many dummy ones set up. A gun, which fires out to sea, is located along the 200 foot cliff that runs all along the shore.

November 11, 1942: This morning we had our final briefing and then removed the camouflage from over our planes and ran them up for a final check. Just before takeoff we topped them off with gas and also put in 350 pounds of oxygen.

Take-off occurred at 0915 and we started out on our course, following the B-25s at exactly 0930. Williams and I flew on Singleton's wing. My oil temperature still ran high, but I didn't worry about it as much. We climbed to 8,000 feet and held that altitude. About 1200 we sighted the coast of Spain, we then flew along it about 10 miles out to sea. Mountains seemed to come right down to the beach, and to be about two to three thousand feet in elevation. The beach was wide and consisted of white sand that looked suitable for a forced landing. Near this point somewhere, some of the boys sighted five planes which they though were JU-88s. I didn't see them.

German JU-88 bombers

We passed over several coastal towns, and watched the small ant-like life below. I could see roads, ditches, bays and harbors. It all looked so peaceful that it was hard to realize that if I would have to force land here, I would be interned. One town was especially large and busy, I believe it was Pontevedras. It was located on a harbor and I could see the waterfront and also several factories. All along the coast, rivers ran into the sea from the interior.

At Oporto in Portugal we took a new course of 180 degrees, magnetic, and flew directly across land, maintaining our altitude of 8,000 feet. The climate now was definitely warmer. The land below still provided interesting scenery of mountains and a great many large, muddy rivers flowing toward the ocean. The hillsides were terraced, evidently to prevent erosion, with many areas under cultivation. Neatly lined orchards were everywhere and the houses in the settlements were completely plastered in white stucco, with red tile roofs.

About half way we passed by more populated areas, and the land became more barren and rugged. There still were trees and they seemed to be growing from clay like soil. Now very, very

England to North Africa

seldom did we see any habitations. It was lonely God Forsaken Country! About this time we ran into Cumulus Clouds which became as heavy as 9/10, and these continued to stay with us. At the next clear space we dove through the clouds and came out at 500 feet over a town, which I believe was Beja, anyway it was a fairly large place. From here we flew at 500 to as low as 300 feet along the coast. People in the little, white washed, farms would stop and stare up and occasionally we would burst upon a place so suddenly that the people would just hear our engines as we roared overhead. It looked like a peaceful friendly country, and I would have liked to wander around there, on foot.

Second leg of the trip to Africa

Suddenly we came out over the Bay of Cadiz near Huelva. There was a flat sandy beach and out in the bay were many fishing boats. The weather looked very dark through the strait. The 2nd Lieutenant, flying the B-25, started a radio conversation with Colonel Olds about what action should be taken. We finally started going around the rain squalls. One minute it would look awfully black and then suddenly we would break into a clear patch. It wasn't easy flying in the rain and trying to keep the lead planes in view. Finally we came out completely into the clear and set out straight for Gibraltar at zero feet. Passed over fishing boats and I thought someone would surely fire at us.

Along the coast of Spain we skirted small fishing villages and the ruins of old Moorish Castles, then we came upon the Rock of Gibraltar itself. Quite a sight!! We circled the rock to the right once and landed on the second time around. I made a good slow landing and that made me feel like it had been a very successful trip. Total time that it took us was six hours. We all thought that the rock was a most interesting sight. It was strongly fortified and we could see the guns bristling from many holes and embankments. They told us that 15% of the rock is hollow, by that I mean, it's been mined out and put to use. Inside is a complete modern hospital, a six million gallon reserve water tank and supplies enough to last for two and a half years. At night searchlights shine from holes in the rock and completely light up the area where the planes are parked. Well, we were billeted in a building that had formerly been a stable. We had upper and lower bunks and it was pretty crowded but comfortable enough.

England to North Africa

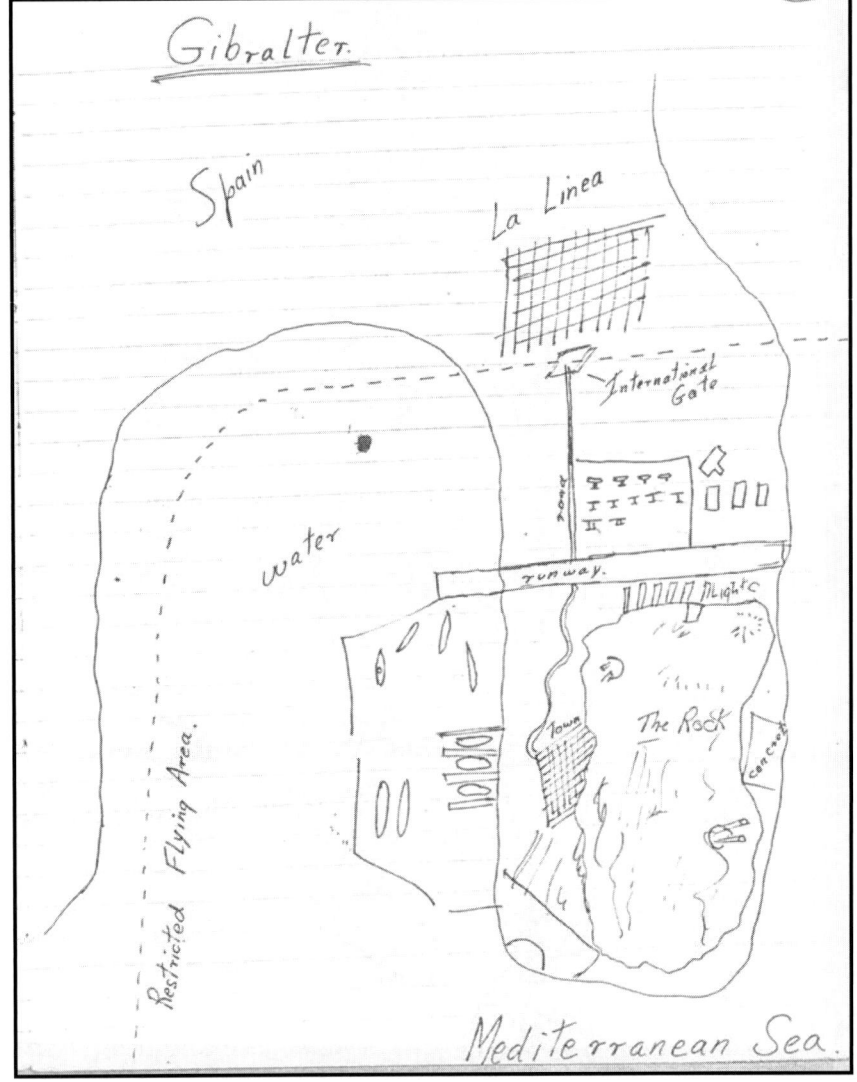

Diagram of Gibraltar by Bill

Our Crew Chiefs came in on five C-47s from England, at least part of them did. One, flown by a Major, got lost in the rain and ran out of gas. He sat it down in the water about 15 miles from Gibraltar. It contained Lieutenant Silliman, Olson, Sergeant Fletcher, etc. The plane floated OK and a boat rescued them all.

The 12th, it rained hard all day, and what I mean it really rained hard. Came down in torrents and the Officers Mess Lounge Room was leaking in several spots and here we spent most of the day. The mess would take silver English coins but not paper money. The town uses special Gibraltar money, which isn't good anyplace but here. There was an especially good band, made up of enlisted men, that played at the mess. We had a few drinks before going to bed.

Salt water for washing purposes was definitely not a luxury and I refrained from using it, to a great extent while we were there. Shipman, Sorensen and I walked into town, about a mile and a half. It was a quaint little place composed of many Spanish-Jew shops that catered to the English trade. Several drinking establishments were going strong and were crowded with rowdy enlisted men of all nationalities. Several fights were in progress.

The people of Gibraltar always refer to it as "Gib". In preparation for leaving Gib, we were divided into several different flights. Captain Bing's flight escorted a flight of C-47 Transports to Algiers. Colonel Olds escorted General Doolittle and General Eisenhower to Algiers, along with six B-17s. I was in a flight that took off for Oran led by Captain Walles, escorting C-47s.

I had 50 gallons of gas in the belly tanks when I took off. Warren was on my wing and I was the Third Element with Sorensen and Cole second. Walles and Tollen were first. We had to circle the rock to get into formation and that made it hard to cut corners. Once I got too close to the rock and got caught in the air currents that we had been warned to stay clear of. It gave me a good shaking up. The transports plodded along at about 140 MPH indicated, and we wove back and forth at about 170 MPH and 20 inches of

England to North Africa

Mercury. It had been cloudy and cold at Gib but as we got farther out over the blue Mediterranean Sea, the sky became clear and the sun became so warm that I took my heavy clothes off, and flew in my shirtsleeves.

As we approached the shoreline we could make out Rashgoun Island and a bit later we were over land. It was a kind of brown hilly country, right from the coast and then turned into more of a flat fertile plain. Could see what appeared to be beautiful villas surrounded by many trees, around Source Blanche, we then passed over a sort of mud depression called Sebkra D' Oran before coming upon the city of Oran itself.

Oran is spread out around a bay, and all the buildings appear to be made of white stucco, a truly beautiful city. We landed at La Senia Airport which isn't much of a landing field, however we managed to land all right, despite the bomb craters and other hazards that were present.

Right after we landed the other officers of the squadron, who had come by boat, greeted us. John Dees (communications), Captain George Wroten (intelligence), White, etc. were a few. They were all completely fagged as they had walked the 14 miles in from the harbor the night before. Dees had huge blisters on his feet. The buildings around the airport, such as hangars, etc. were largely destroyed as the result of shelling from the guns on the hills about 10 miles distant. Destroyed French Pursuit Planes were lying about the field, and also some damaged ones. One BT-14 was still in good shape and a French A-20 was nearly so. We sat out in front of the Administration Building and marveled at the developments. Arabs and ragged urchins passed by picking up what scraps they could gather from the spoils of war. Soldiers that had seized cars were trying to make them run. A full Colonel had seized a black, deluxe sedan, and was using it for his official car. Other old cars and trucks were being pressed into service hauling supplies for our Army. Another full Colonel was speaking French with some natives, evidently trying to get the water supply turned on. A truck came from town loaded with supplies and we managed to get a piece of bread and a few apples.

Soon, we learned that we had landed on the wrong airport and that we were to go to Tafaraoui, a French Naval Airport a few miles to the south. So we started up our planes and dodging bomb pits, we taxied out and took-off. We joined up in formation, buzzed the field and then peeled off over the other airport, as it was just a short distance away.

Tafaraoui has two runways, one concrete and the other gravel. Both are about 3,000 feet long. When we landed there was a group of Spits, flown by American Pilots, already there. We dispersed out on the dirt and then started looking for a place to live. The post seemed to have been quite well designed by the French. However there seemed to be much work to do yet. The French had hastily abandoned the barracks where we were assigned to stay. They had thrown all their trash right outside the doors. Old clothes, books, letters, magazines, notebooks and everything imaginable were strewn about. The old books and notebooks, that I looked through were very interesting. There were books on French Military Policy, math, history, etc. The notebooks had been compiled by French Naval Air Students and were neat and detailed. They contained notes on the Theory of Flight, Gasoline engines, etc. We spent the better part of a day burning all of these old things and burying them in a hole.

As far as eating was concerned, we cooked our own rations in the back yard. Several of us gathered some large Granite stones and made a fireplace. There wasn't much variety in our meals, mostly they consisted of stew, beef, coffee and tea. Water was one of the biggest problems at this field, as we had to stand in line at the kitchen and pump the water slowly with a handle. To this water we added water purification tablets.

England to North Africa

These French kitchens are very interesting. A large room has a centrally located stove, and an iron rail above the stove supports a chain hoist that in turn is connected to a huge iron pot. Evidently they cook up such a huge stew that they need a hoist to put it upon the stove.

All the buildings are a pink stucco with wooden roofs. Our building has a number of bullet holes through the walls and a few windows are out, but never the less we were as comfortable as you could be on a concrete floor. Didn't take us long and we had everything organized and arranged. The building was provided with an iron rail for hammocks, but we just made our beds on the floor. Of course everything was completely mixed up as far as baggage was concerned. My bedroll was at Algiers, and John Goebel was there also, his bedroll was here, so I used it. We have some steel lockers in which we stored our equipment. After we had been in Oran for a couple of days, Major Keith came in with the 49th. They came all the way from England and had been in the cockpit for seven and one half-hours. They were completely played out.

It was here that I thought I'd lost old 7650. I'd had trouble with the left engine, oil temperature running high, ever since I left Atcham. Now that some of our ground crew-men had arrived we were working on the plane getting it in shape. Shorty had worked all morning getting the guns cleaned. Sergeant Smith and his helpers were tearing off the oil coolers in preparation for cleaning them. I was sitting in the cockpit, arranging things and getting the Form One's up to date when suddenly the men found that the left engine block was cracked just above the pan. It was just a fine crack but nevertheless it was there and according to the Inspector it meant the engine would have to be changed. Under the conditions at Oran, this meant that they would strip the plane and use it for spare parts. I cursed, because it'd been the world's best ship. I took all of my belongings out, and, then they started taking parts from it right away. It had 142 hours on it and hadn't had a scratch of any kind since I'd gotten it new at March Field, when it had only 5 hours on it.

P-38s in Africa

Stege and I took a walk one day around the airport. We looked the hangars over and talked to many different men. One service outfit, composed of mechanics, were doing nothing but trying to put the battered French trucks back into running shape. At another place we got a good look at a French Dewoitine Pursuit Plane. Farther along was an anti-aircraft gun implacement. These mostly were 80-MM guns. Here we met a Navy man who was going around taking still and movie pictures of everything, for a permanent record for the government.

While we were at Oran we were on alert for one day before the First Fighter Group came in. We weren't called off once during the day but we did fly an evening patrol for an hour. I got a good look at the surrounding country and was surprised at the number of good paved roads that are in the vicinity. We landed quite late with very little light, but we did OK.

It was surprising to see the vast number of reinforcements, which are arriving by air. On the field at one time there must have been a hundred and fifty airplanes of all kinds, B-17s, B-26s, C-47s, P-38s and Spits. It was a real sight.

England to North Africa

Martin Marauder B-26

While sitting at the end of the runway, on alert, we watched a squadron of A-20s come in. They landed on the dirt way out in the field ahead of the runway to give themselves plenty of room for their landing roll. The B-26 could start their take-off from the field. At this time we started our refueling by means of 5-gallon gasoline cans.

Our enlisted men lived in their pup tents and established their own mess in their area. Captain Walles did all he could to see that they had their share of food and wine, which was purchased in town.

I didn't get into the town of Oran, but those who did said it was very nice and modern. One of the boys picked up a 37' Chevy Sedan at La Sen'a Airport and thus the squadron gained an official car. It was the best one in the bunch that I saw. We nearly lost it to a full Colonel, who eyed it with great interest.

Suddenly orders came from General Doolittle that we were to move to Algiers. This order came in about 2000 hours and the whole squadron was to move by 1200 the next day. We got up early the next morning and unpacked and carried down to the line all that we had worked so hard to arrange before. I had packed everything I owned up to the barracks and I was a bit grieved at having to pack it right back.

Major Keith told me I was to take my old plane, as it was, so I got busy and packed it. Next I had to put on a canopy and nose wheel. We escorted C-47s to Algiers. It took two hours and twenty minutes of flight over beautiful inland mountains, down valleys and around fair weather Cumulus clouds.

There are two good airports at Algiers, Blida and Mon Blanche. We landed at Mon Blanche. Things here were even more mixed up than at Oran. First I sent the nose wheel back to the 49th at Oran, by transport, as I had borrowed it from them. Next we made a gas fire out on the airport using a gasoline can filled with dirt, and cooked some rations. This proved to be the favorite way to cook and obtain warmth for some time to come.

Bill's diagram of the stove

In a lot of entries, Bill had no date recorded, evidently he had kept notes and would go back later and write in his diary. He is getting to be quite an artist and using illustrations more and more.

We had arrived in Algiers on the **17th of November**, having left England on the 11th. Here again they started stripping old 7650. One consolation to me was the fact that my last landing in the old boat had been a beautiful slow, nose high, affair. This is just how I always had hoped to make one.

Landing he had always hoped to make

Zeigler, Shipman, Johnson, Goebel, Bing,

England to North Africa

Skinner, Williams, and some of the other boys, who had arrived here earlier, have been doing a lot of flying. They've been escorting C-47s that are hauling Parachute Troops, as they are trying to capture certain inland airfields. They've flown farther up the coast to Bone and several other points. Bone is where some ME-109s strafed Eubanks while he was on the ground. Four of the six were knocked down, two by anti-aircraft fire and two were shot down by Spitfires.

Downtown Algiers

They've also been escorting B-17s on bombing raids over Tunis. They ran into some ME-109s and Zeigler got his first chance to shoot at one, however he pushed the mike button instead of the gun button. Carl Williams shot down one 109, the first for the 14th Group and the 48th Squadron. He did this on one of the Tunis sweeps.

Most of the squadron lived in the Headquarters Building, until we arrived. Then most of us moved into a low wooden building. It didn't have any beds but we scouted around and found a few iron bound affairs. After we placed cardboard on them they proved to be fairly comfortable. Again I carried all my worldly goods over to the barracks and rigged up hangers, boxes, shelves and had everything in tip top shape.

We had one particularly interesting mission while stationed here. It was an escort mission for some C-47s filled with paratroopers, who were to take over the airport at Tebessa. The weather was bad and we had to skirt down the coast, passing through rainsqualls, mist, etc. Usually we fly about 500 feet above the sea. At one point two Spitfires, on patrol, jumped us and gave us a scare as they look an awful lot like 109s. We flew as far as Bone and then turned inland through a mountain pass for Tebessa. The clouds were right down on the mountaintops and we had quite a time getting through the narrow gorge, all of us at the same time.

German ME-109 fighter

There were 24 transports involved. In order for them to feel their way through the bad weather, they lowered their landing gear and this reduced their speed to about 110 or 120 MPH. In the meantime the rest of us flying the 38s were weaving back and forth, in the narrow pass, trying to miss each other and the transports. To make matters worse the air was so rough that my ship was dancing around like a duck on the North Atlantic. Finally the weather closed right down on the hills, and the transports had to turn around and we went through a different pass. This led us over the town of Constantine and such a pretty place I've never before seen. At first I thought it was an old ruin, but as we approached I could tell it was a modern city of white color. Built on a hillside, and over a deep rocky canyon, it's really something to see from the air. We could see groups of people staring up at us as we passed over at 200 feet. About twenty-five miles out of Constantine, we again ran into a low ceiling and finally we were pinched together at 100 feet, weaving back and forth and really having to look out for prop wash.

England to North Africa

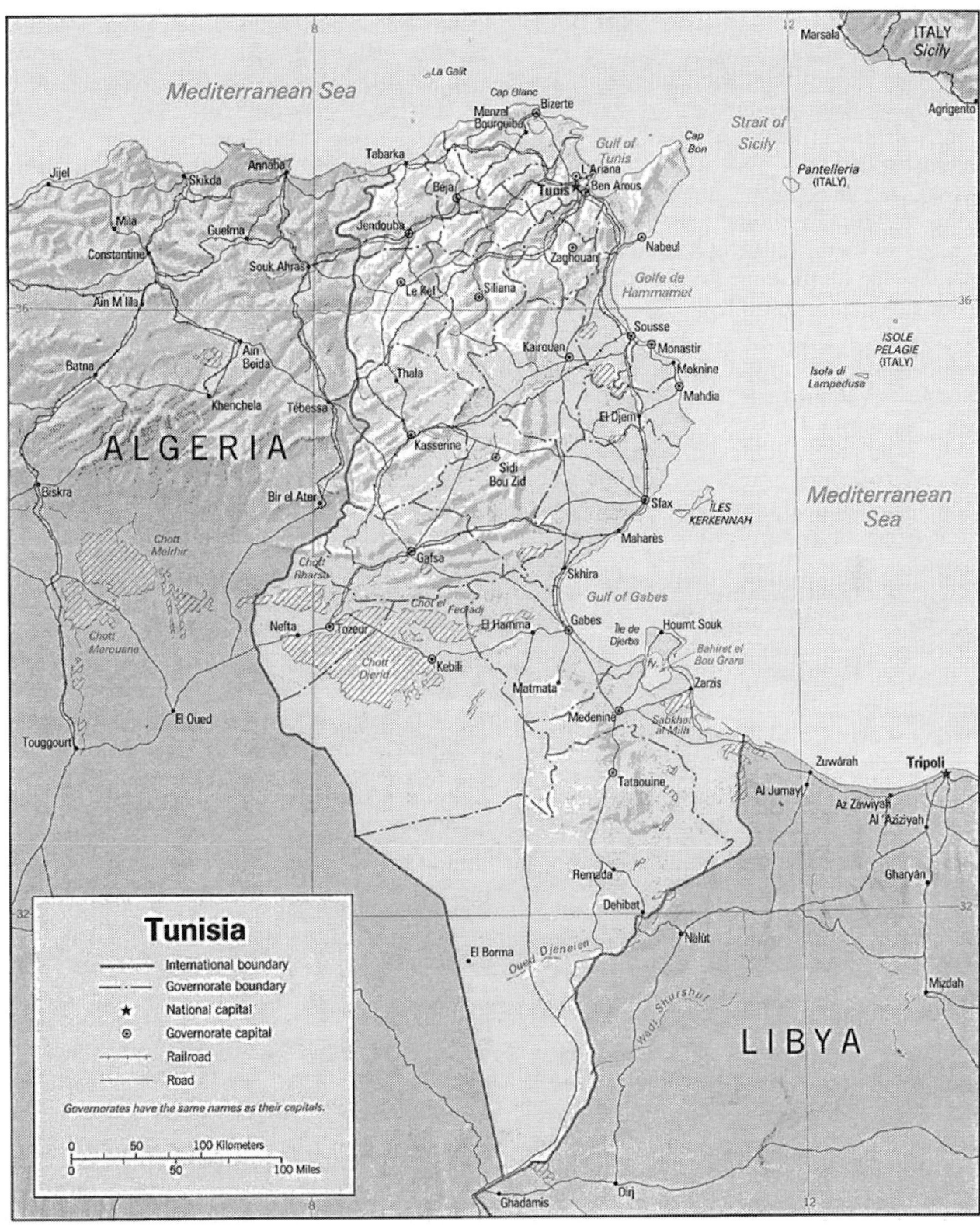

We made a near vertical bank around a hill and over an Arab village and started back. The transports went on but we'd had enough. This inland mountainous part of Africa is beautiful with all the trees and vegetation. This is nicer than the other parts that I have seen. The coastal

England to North Africa

area from Algiers to Bone, near the Mediterranean, is also covered with trees.

At Algiers we had our first real air-raid and bombing experience. At about 2200 one evening when most of us were just getting to sleep the bombs started falling. Such a deadly racket, I've never heard. There's no mistaking as to what's happening. First a whine, then a dead calm followed by the terrific concussion is enough to make the strongest person, quake with excitement and fear, of the highest degree. We all dressed, put on our steel helmets and got in the trench. Nothing else happened and we returned to the barracks. Shipman and I were looking out the window when the second string hit. I dove under my bed and covered my head. I was thoroughly convinced that we'd been hit, and could almost hear the timbers crashing down. Then silence again and I was alone. The rest of the boys had headed for the trenches. The nearest hit was about a block from us, however I thought it had been right on top of the barracks. I hurt my knee getting under the bed so fast. The rest of the night we were jumpy and waiting for another raid. Every time a door closed it sounded like a bomb hitting in the distance.

Next morning we found out that not any of our men had been hurt and that quite a bit of damage had also occurred to the French hangars. They also discovered that the Germans had dropped a number of Personnel Bombs, Pencils and other small objects, which explode when someone picks them up. They were scattered all over the field and several people lost their lives when they picked them up. Later bombings caused severe damage and destroyed hangars. Many of our P-38, B-17 and C-47s were lost in these raids. Ten officers, sleeping in a B-17, were killed as a result of a direct hit. One bomb fell a few yards from our barracks and shrapnel flew through the walls and through my blouse and pink pants, it of course ruined them.

Lieutenant Bestgen was Mess Officer and he made daily trips to town to purchase, bread, oranges, and other food items to add to our rations. This makes eating a bit more tasty.

On one mission that Shipman flew, he had bad luck by losing the left engine shortly after take-off. The intake manifold burned out and set the cowling on fire. He dropped his belly tank and feathered the engine and came in with a beautiful approach and made a good landing.

This next little note had been penned in at the bottom of one page.

When the Germans hastily left Algiers, they left behind a HE-III Bomber. It was loaded with Chicken Eggs, and all the good things they had obtained in the city. Other planes seen here were Air France airliners, all terrible old affairs. Jimmy Doolittle flew back and forth in a B-26 with a Captain for a pilot. ====== Me French Pe Late=======

German Heinkel HE-111 bomber

Suddenly Captain Walles, was told that we were to move south for a couple of days. This news came to us about 2100 at night just as we were going to bed. We were to leave at daylight the next morning. Naturally we had no time to pack and besides we thought that we wouldn't be staying long anyway. Consequently we just grabbed a few essential, log book, diary, ditty bag, pistol and belt, mess kit and our helmets. We arose at 0530, ate a little and then were briefed by Colonel Olds, and Captain Walles.

This was the **20th of November** that we left for Tebessa. I flew on Mark's wing. I was given Warren's plane, a new GLO, number 720 to replace old 7650. Warren was grounded because

England to North Africa

he'd had an operation for Appendicitis. There were just twelve of us going out on this mission. The Crew Chiefs were to come later and bring our bedrolls with them.

Had a beautiful trip that morning, flying a direct route to Gafsa. There are plenty of high mountains in this area and we were flying about 8,000 feet to clear them. Native villages were tucked on the sides of these high places, on cliff tops. Also some very nice homes, which probably belong to wealthy Frenchmen. Good paved roads wound up one side and down the other of the mountains. After reaching Gafsa we dropped our belly tanks, and hit the deck, then we flew along the road to Gabe's at 0 feet, we flew over Arab huts and villages, we were so low that we could see the details of their living. They live in tents with brush windbreaks.

Bill's drawing of the oasis

Soon we passed Menzel and approached Gabe's Just outside of town there's a large oasis and we got a good look at it while flying over at zero feet. It consists of date trees with neatly laid out paths underneath, evidently they have well cultivated vegetable gardens among the trees also and everything is perfectly arranged. After we passed the oasis we came right to the airport at Gabe's. There in the middle sat a JU-52, which had evidently groundlooped. We all fired a burst into it and left it full of holes. This same transport was to be fired at, in the future, by every plane that fired upon the airfield.

After this we took the highway south along the coast looking for a column to blow up. We passed little settlements such as Ketena. We flew as far south as Medenine and then returned between the highway and Goffe De Gabes. Once again we followed the highway and the railway to Gabe's and again we flew over the airport.

German Junkers JU-52 Transport

This time over, a few gun posts fired at us. On up the coast past Cekhira, to the railway junction. All this time we were just skimming the ground and scaring the Arabs and causing a general turmoil, but never actually fired a shot. We had been pulling about 35 inches of Mercury so our gas was running low. We throttled back to 20 inches and set our course for Tebessa. Past El Cuettar, Gafsa, and finally Feriana and through the pass to Tebessa. I hadn't paid much attention to my navigation and found out that I had only 10 gallons left in each tank when we finally limped into Tebessa.

We couldn't find the airport at first and when we did spot it, we didn't think very highly of it as it was a field full of stubble and the boundaries were very poorly defined. We all made it in OK. I came in at 90 MPH, because I didn't have any gas load. The plane rolled over the ground with the shock absorbers hitting bottom. I hardly knew if we were in friendly or enemy territory but I soon learned that we were actually on the Tebessa airport. There were just enough 5-gallon cans of 100 octane gas, piled around, to refuel each airplane. Curious Arabs were standing around smiling at us and a Frenchman and his wife rode by on beautiful horses.
Everyone pitched in, working hard, to get their own plane refueled and have them ready to go. Suddenly a swarm of C-47s came down the valley with about 12 P-38s escorting them. Just as rapidly as we saw them, they started landing. Two of the C-47s overshot the runway and went

England to North Africa

into the ditch at the end. This washed out the landing gears, props and bent the wing tips. Segraves overshot in a 38 and washed it out also. Our Crew Chiefs and our bedrolls were unloaded from the transports, then the planes took off again, in no time, with their P-38 escorts. We then got busy and set up our camp. We unrolled our bedrolls and fixed up a little place to eat. There was a well besides the Operations Building and Doc Bernstein began to purify the water supply. We had several cases of rations and we all had to cook our own meals the first few days.

About two hours after we had landed Colonel Raft, of the Paratroopers, received more information about the column that we had failed to knock out before. Captain Watson, Clark Smith, V. Smith, Leo Yates, John Singleton, and Stege, took off late in the afternoon to try and hit it. They landed at Gafsa to be briefed and then continued on their way to Gabe's. They shot up a French tank, by mistake, and later knocked out about six enemy tanks and trucks. V. Smith was hit in one engine and could only do about 200 MPH on the way home, so he and his wingman, Yates, fell behind and got seperated from the other four planes. Darkness fell upon them, before they realized it and they became lost. Watson, C. Smith, Singleton and Stege all made belly landings at Negrine, a Arab village, some sixty miles west of Gafsa. They were challenged and after being identified as Americans, were taken by a high-class bunch of Arabs and a few French, to a Military Post there. They had a great experience, were well treated, rode on camels, shared in Arab customs of eating and religion and eventually returned a week later.

V. Smith and Yates also had to make belly landings after their separation from Watson. They landed at Kalaa Dejerda, were taken in by French people, given a good place to stay and returned to us the following day, safe and with interesting stories to tell. Well our first day of real operations had cost us six out of the twelve planes. The day after these boys went down, Sorensen made a patrol mission and found the airplanes on their bellies with no-one around, so we knew that the boys hadn't been hurt.

The first night after our arrival at Tebessa, Sorensen was quite sick and ran a high fever. The Doc put him to bed in the Operations Building and in the morning he was OK.

On the **21st of November**, the day after our arrival, Shipman and Cole made a run back to Gabe's, to see if they could learn anymore on the situation there. They found the column for sure this time and gave it hell. However, Cole became a little over eager, and made one of his passes too low. His right prop struck a truck, breaking the crankshaft and raking the whole right side of the boom. It bashed off the Prestone radiator and the projecting part of the horizontal stabilizer. He managed to feather the prop all right and Shipman escorted him back to Tebessa, where he made an excellent landing.

Captain Walles sent Tollen and I out on a little scouting mission of our own. It was the first desert navigating that I had been able to do on my own. I gained a great deal of confidence on this trip. From Tebessa we flew over the highway southeast to the Tunis border and on to Feriana. Following the highway, looking at a map while noting the approximate number of degrees is the real way to navigate in this country. From Feriana we followed the railroad to Kasserine and Sbeitla, which took us away from the nice mountainous country and over more rugged desert country. Flying right on the deck was really fun. We turned and banked as the railroad wound it's way through the pass between Dj (Mt.) Nara and Dj Touil. At one place we came upon a tunnel and had to fly up and over the hill, then out over the plains and back down low again. Went past a little railway sub-station called Pavillier. Kairouan, with its domes and spires, all white, loomed out of the desert just like in the Arabian Night stories I'd read about. We flew over the town at 200 feet while in a steep bank. I was very impressed. Just a magical Arab city as near as one could be to the storybook. The city was completely surrounded by a wall and all the buildings were painted white. We could see bats arising from the various spires. There are no Frenchmen here.

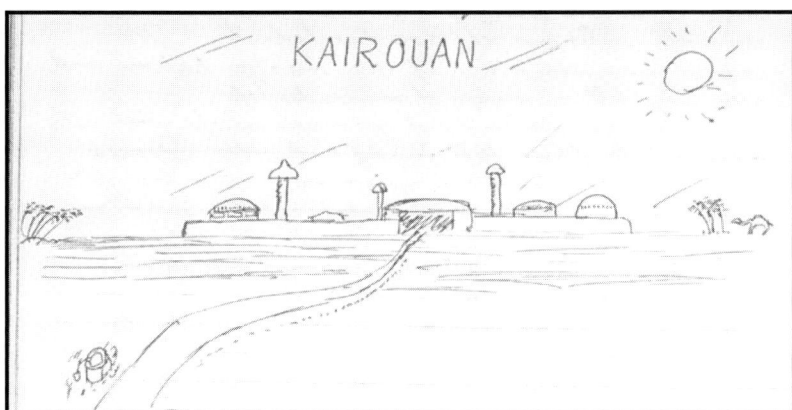

Bill's version of Kairouan

To the west of town sits the airport so Jim and I buzzed it. There aren't any hangars here and just a few little shacks. We returned to base by following the highway and passed over Fondouk-el-Aouareb and Hadjeb-el-Ajoun. Just outside of this last town we spotted three motorcycles with side-cars. I couldn't identify them as enemy so we passed them up, as the riders jumped into the ditch. We didn't have an Intelligence Deptartment at this time, to tell us just where the bomb line was so we didn't know for sure who was friend or foe. We intercepted the railroad again at Sbeitla and returned home by following it by way of Kasserine, Feriana, and Bekkaria.

As the airport at Tebessa was too small, the higher command decided to move us 15 miles up the valley to Youks Les Bains. The Ground Crew and we seven officers, six pilots and Doc, spent the night on the ground outside of the little Operations Building at Tebessa. A little well provided us with water, and Doc purified it. We cooked our meals out of our meager rations and everybody felt a sense of comradeship. Captain Walles didn't get much sleep that night because the phone kept ringing, as the French were trying to contact him to give him messages. In the morning a French Captain took Tollen and me in and served us some coffee, it certainly tasted good.

Jim and I were the second and third plane to land at Youks. I thought that the airport was going to be easy to find but it was only after searching the valley for some time, that I found it. The field was large, very smooth and free from obstacles. Colonel Olds was there, having flown down from Algiers to see how things were coming along. I had been appointed Assistant Engineering Officer, so with the help of Master Sergeant Fletcher, we prepared a list of supplies that we needed for continuing operations. The only other men at the field on the **21st of November,** were about 30 paratroopers, who had taken the field, and a few of our ground crew who came over from Tebessa. Soon the transports arrived, bringing us gasoline, oil and a few more boxes of English Rations. By this time we were becoming quite used to them.

The transports were the things which made possible our movements. We certainly owe them many thanks. The boys flew good formations and peeled off just like the Pursuit Planes.

Our first living quarters at Youks were in the holes that the Paratroopers had dug after taking the field. Weather was good and we were fairly comfortable because we had the extra blankets left by the boys who were still missing in the desert. Smith and Yates came home the next day but not so with the other four. We worked hard, gassing, putting oil in the planes, lugging ammunition and helped in every way we could in order to continue operations.

Captain Walles appointed a cook so then all of us, officers and enlisted men, ate together. Three times a day we were fed stew, crackers and tea. This took place for several days straight. It got to be pretty tiresome and it seemed I was always hungry. In between meals we would get into our rations and cook things over a gasoline fire.

Bill's drawing of a Douglas C-47

About this time a few boys from the 49th arrived, and we started flying joint missions. One of the first missions took us to Sbeitta. Captain Walles led with his wingman, Captain Knapp led the Second Element and I was the leader of the Third Element. Between Kasserine and Sbeitta we spotted a German motorcycle and sidecar speeding along the road. We dove in from his side at 30 degrees and really spilled him. By the time I got to him, the cycle was upside down and smoking. I must have hit the gas tank because the whole thing exploded and burned violently. In Sbeitta we found German amored cars so we proceeded to shoot them up by diving down the streets between the rows of trees. There was a little return fire and I saw one Arab throwing rocks at me as I flashed past at 310 MPH. I don't believe he had the right deflection. It was a very successful mission and we stopped the Advance German Forces from Slax from entering this area.

On the **24th of November,** Jim Tollen and I again went on a mission to Kairouan. My knowledge of the country had improved considerably by now so I was able to take short cuts on my navigation, etc. We followed the road this time and again looked over the town and airport. Coming over town from the direction of Sousse, there was a column of motorcycles and trucks. The cycles got into town and hid before I could hit them but we got three of the trucks. On the first pass I lined up on what I thought was a truck but it turned out to be an Arab cart with two horses pulling it. The first horse just exploded and the other poor beast jumped ten feet. It made me almost physically sick, as I wasn't yet used to the terrible things that happen in war. We then turned south, 180 degrees, and followed a dirt road to join the main road from Safax to Sbeitla. We passed over Faid and just as we were approaching Lessouda, I noticed a plane coming toward us following the same road and about 3,000 feet above us. It was a JU-88.

This was to be the only kill that Bill was to be given credit for in his combat flying.

We did a steep climbing turn to the right and poured on the coal. I pulled 3,000 RPM and 42 inches for about five minutes and after gaining the altitude I had an airspeed of 320 MPH, flying straight and level. The 88 was throwing out clouds of black smoke in an effort to escape. As I approached to about 500 yards the rear gunner fired tracers at me, but they seemed to be falling below me. At about 300 yards I started firing and held everything down in a steady burst. The 88 pilot skidded the plane violently as my tracers ate into him. At 100 yards I was bouncing around in his prop wash, and I waited until I thought that I was going to run into him then pulled straight up and back. Jim then put a steady burst into the left engine and side. At this time his right engine was on fire and smoking badly. The pilot started the plane down but suddenly pulled up the flaming wreck to let the rear gunner bail out. His chute opened OK at about 500 feet. I banked back and forth over the plane as it skimmed the earth just before sitting down in a landing attitude. The right main wheel was hanging down. I could see the top hatch open and two gunners huddling there looking up at me, it was terrible. It plowed a path over fairly level ground and skidded to a halt at a road crossing. The right engine was torn completely loose and was laying some yards distant. I didn't see anybody near and finally saw some Arabs approaching. Jim and I returned victorious.

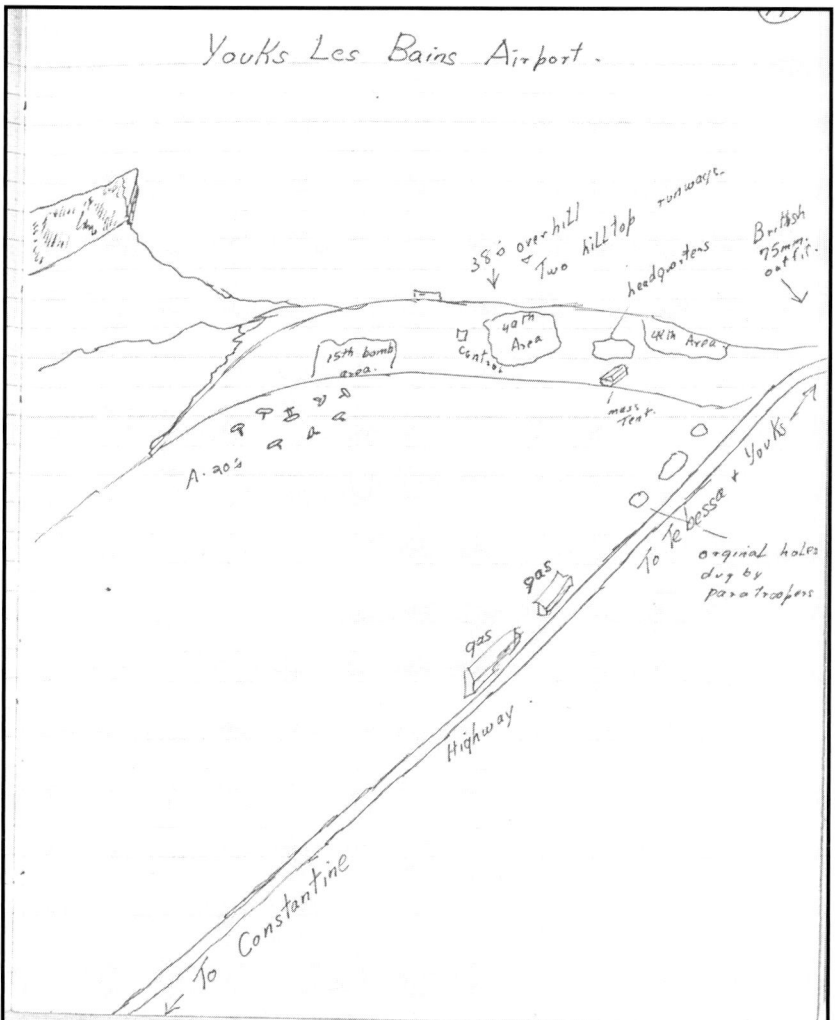

Diagram by Bill

About this time a squadron of A-20s moved into the field and we started doing escort duty for them. One of the first was to Safax, where the bombers did a good job on the airport. Safax is a well laid out affair with miles of neat orchards on the outskirts of town. In town each house seems to have their own garden plots. From the air they're all laid out in neat squares. We strafed the road on the way back.

At this time Lusk Carlton, and Buther of the 49th ran into about 9 Ju-52s along the coast from Gabe's to Safax. They shot down 5 and forced the rest of them to crash-land. Charlie Ernhart was strafing the airport at Gabe's and got pretty well shot up. A direct hit on his windshield caused the bulletproof glass to shatter, and this wounded him in the knee and several other places. He made a safe landing however, and the medics took care of him promptly.

Lusk, Ethell, Butler, Skinner and a couple of 2nd Lieutenants in the 49th went on a T&B run, Tunis and Bizerte, and it ended up in tragedy. Lusk and his wingman had to return early because of mechanical failure. The others were having a field day with some JU- 87s until some 109s showed up and got our boys. Ethell was the only one to return. We've never heard from the other boys again. Ethell shot down four JU-87s.

Several of our trips as escorts for the A-20s were unsuccessful as far as we were concerned. We tried to hit an airfield near Medjez-el-Bab and the A-20s did a beautiful job of bombing some farmer's field. Another time at Safax they just missed the docks and did another beautiful job of raising hell with the water. On all of these missions we received plenty of flak and it was very accurate at our altitude. We would start flying the missions at zero feet and as we approached the target would climb to the bombing altitude of 6,000 to 7,500 feet. We would usually climb up with the bombers.

On the **30th of November**, we started the first of a series of Fighter Sweeps to the Tunis area. The boys named these the T&B milk runs, because of the two names Tunis and Bizerte. We heard that the famous Abbeville Boys had come down from France and it was evident, either we would wipe them out or they would wipe us out.

The Abbeville Boys were a squadron of top-notch German fighter pilots that had been stationed in France. They had many kills to their credit.

German Junkers JU-87 Stuka

I was on Watson's wing and V. Smith and Cole were the Second Element. Walles and Bing were leading other flights. The sky on this fair weather day was covered with Cumulus Clouds at about 8,000 feet over the target area. A 109 was spotted above the clouds, waiting to pounce on us. He did dart down a couple of times and each time we sent him right back up again with volumes of firepower. Soon others appeared and a furious fight developed. We used our full-rated power then, 47 inches of Mercury and 3,000 RPM. We climbed practically straight up with the indicator reading 4,000 feet a minute, made a circle around a cloud, and I noticed that all of us in Watson's flight were still in formation. Watson got a direct shot at a 109 and I had to duck because one 109 was shooting a 90-degree deflection shot at me. Just then one came in between Watson and me and I started firing at him. My tracers fell all around him but he flew right into a cloud before I could get another shot at him. I didn't see him again.

Returning to base, still on Watson's wing, we indicated 325 MPH. Flew this way until we hooked up with Bing's flight. V. Smith and Cole dived down near the deck after a 109 on the outskirts of Tunis. Smith got the 109 but we never saw Arthur Vincent Cole again. Cole seemed to have had nine lives when it came to flying. At March Field he cracked up in a 38, badly, during night flying. Then he had hit the truck while flying with Shipman on the first Patrol Mission out of Tebessa. Then of course, he and Elliot of the 49th had to crash land on the desert after becoming lost on a late mission. That time he sat down with the landing gear extended and nosed over, lucky! The Arabs brought them back to Feriana.

Back on Youks Field, several of us had moved a couple of blocks away from the main highway up into a little community of our own. We called it Beverly Hills. Shipman and I made a little house out of gas cans with a canvas roof. It worked pretty well.

Shipman and Bill's sleeping quarters

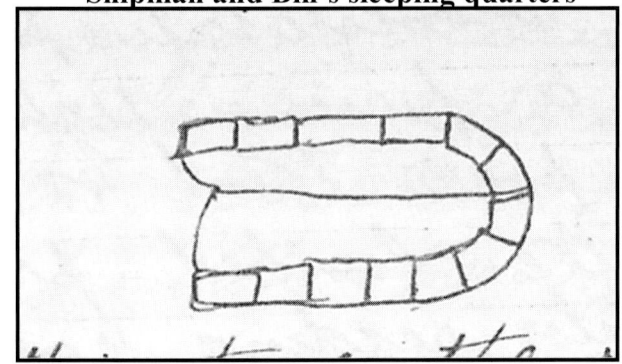

About this time the rest of the squadron started coming in. Ground crews and more pilots flew in. Due to a terrible blunder most of these new men didn't have any sleeping equipment. Mark and I took Ethell in with us, three in a bed. Naturally it was a miserable night and I nearly froze to death. Then the rains came and the camp was a mess for two weeks. Our blankets got wet, clothes were soaked and the mud stuck on the bottom of our feet, four inches thick. To walk a block was a day's work. Nevertheless the work went on as usual. We made an Engineering Hut in which to store all of the supplies that we removed from the wrecked planes. We hauled gas from trucks and filled planes with 5 gallon cans until we were blue in the face. Many times we would have to fill six and seven planes in a row. Sitting in a plane, early in the morning at six o'clock, on alert, with mud in the cockpit, on the parachute, and with frost over the windows was really **Hell**. Taking off was even more dangerous. One boy in the First Pursuit Group, which came to the field for a week's operations, ran into a parked B-25 and mangled both planes.

Fueling with 5 gallon cans

Colonel Olds moved down from Algiers and sat up his Operations Tent along with the British Radio Tent, which was operated by Captain Flemming of the British Army. He was a nice old fellow and I always got a laugh out of him. One morning as I greeted him, wading through the mud and the cold of the morning, he said, "Oh how I detest the squalor of campaigning!!".

Before we started our missions we would be briefed at Operations and then report back again after returning, this was so that the Intelligence Department could record anything that we had to report.

The mess grew steadily better. Occasionally we would get a candy bar and some butter with our bread. The real luxury was jam. Usually we were so hungry that we would cook up some emergency rations over at Beverly Hills. The community continued to grow and soon we received bedrolls, air mattresses, and little green tents. Boy, these things saved the day. I'd had enough of those miserable nights, and from then on I was usually too hot, not too cold. Our community included Captain Watson, V. Smith, Singleton, Shipman, Goebel, C. Smith, Zeigler, Stege, Sorensen and myself. Evenings we listened to Zeigler's radio and sometimes forced ourselves to stay awake for the 2100 news.

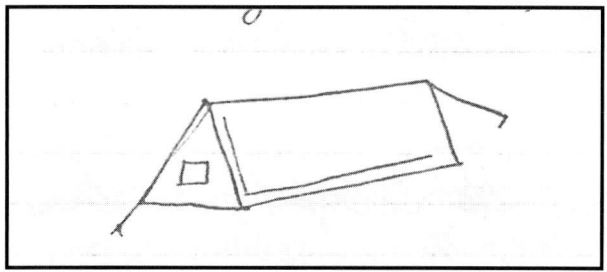
Bill's version of the little green tent

On the **30th of November**, we again made a fighter sweep to Tunis, using 12 planes. Again I was on Watson's wing and Bing and Walles were in other flights. I always enjoy the rides up and back, beautiful country, sun shinning, the French waving us on and nice farmlands. However once we get in the vicinity of Tunis things are different. Right away Bing's Flight spotted a 109 and it immediately did a Split S and dived for the deck. Williams peeled off of Bing's wing and said he was going after him. He did and we never saw Williams again. About a month later some Englishman said that they had seen three 109s on Williams' tail and when he attempted to bail out, his chute caught on the tail of his plane. They identified him by his Dog Tags, and buried him near an English Mission. A good boy, but he had too much ambition.

Watson and I had a mighty hot time on that mission but we never could quite climb up to those two 190s, that were in the sun. After Watson used up all of his ammunition we dived for the cloud layer, at about 8,000 feet, indicating 420 MPH. We leveled off and flew on instruments for about 5 minutes doing 350 MPH. When we came out of the clouds and looked around, there were four of them firing at us. Back into the clouds we went and came out in a different spot. We hit the deck and ran flat out for home, down gullies, over ridges, farmlands and moors.

Mud, Mud, Mud!!

didn't seem to be following the map. However we soon came out at Maktar again and everything was OK. It was a two and a half-hour mission. By the way old 7650 had been refitted with a new engine, at Oran, and I am now using it again. V. Smith is using Warren's old plane, number 720, the one that I had been using.

> **Some pilots are good
> Some pilots are great
> The best of all
> Flew the P-38**
>
> **By: Colonel Al Greibling
> US Army (Ret)**

The **2nd of December** Goebel and I flew a recon mission over a complicated route. It took most of my time navigating but we still saw some wonderful scenery. We picked up the railroad at Youks les Bains Tebessa and followed it on to Kalaa Djerda, Salines, Maktara, Pichon-Kairouan, and then to Msaken. Between this last point and Sousse, we flew at tree level following the road. We spotted a light German carryall and the soldiers, about six, got out and ran for cover in the orchards. We set the car on fire. Over Sousse at 200 feet I didn't see any Army movements. Here the country was very nice, fertile trees and nice houses. We continued on as far as Enfidaville and then turned inland to Dejebibina. We then followed a good road up to Pont du Fahs, which sets in the mountains. Such nice country up in the hills, there were lakes, streams, trees and grassy meadows in the lowlands. Our gas was running a little low so we throttled back and took it easy. At one point I got a little worried about my navigation, as the roads

Arabs scrounging in camp

> **When good men die, their goodness does not perish.**
>
> **-- Euripides**

Combat in Africa

Still in Africa, facing danger, living under adverse conditions, but still able to see the beauty of things, this is Bill

**Somewhere in North Africa,
December 4, 1942:** Dearest Mother and Dad. Today is a beautiful warm day and I will take advantage of it, to write you a note. You might have expected where I am because of what is going on at the present time and this will let you know definitely. I'm sorry that I couldn't let you know sooner but it was impossible. I have been here for some time. I'm enjoying it down here, despite the fact that we've been rushing from place to place and haven't had much of a chance to keep ourselves clean or even wash clothes. All our moving around has been done in the same manner as that in which we crossed the good old US.

Down here now, it's supposed to be the rainy season, but all in all the weather has been very good. However the nights are very cold and I froze before we had adequate equipment that was brought in to remedy this. At first I had only two blankets and a canvas tarp, that made things pretty uncomfortable, when it rained. Now we have great equipment. Each man has a small, light waterproof tent with a floor which is very easily set up. Also we have a full length air mattress and a nice sleeping bag. I've been warm and comfortable ever since these things have arrived.

Today I had one of the boys give me a haircut. It wasn't exactly first class but pretty good, considering the circumstances. Next I shaved, using a canteen cup of water and so now consider myself to be in first class shape. Water is quite a problem here. All our drinking water is treated, just to be certain that it's okay. Washing water just doesn't exist as such. About once a week we manage to take a bath at a hot springs which is not far distant.

The part of Africa, I'm located in, is similar to northern Arizona, like the country just south of Prescott. Not all of Africa is desert, in fact a good deal of it is beautiful, mountainous country, with good highways and beautiful towns.

The Arabs are always coming around, trying to sell us eggs or chickens. Most of them are awfully poor and wear nothing but rags. The little kids run around on the cold ground without any shoes and with just a shawl to cover themselves. Here I've seen Camels for the first time and I can safely say that they're the laziest animals in existence. You can fly right over them at 10 feet and they won't even look up.

In the evenings we can't have fires because of the blackouts. We do a little singing, while Mark Shipman plays his Mandolin and then we listen to the 7:00 PM news on the radio. This lets us find out how **we** are doing with the war. Usually we're in bed by 8:00 PM.

I was thinking of you on Thanksgiving. I could imagine that the Halms were down, everyone talking, all cleaned up and sitting down to that wonderful dinner. Here, I swallowed hard, slung my mess kit over my shoulder and set out for the stew line. You can't stop a fellow from dreaming, anyway!!

December 12, last year, you remember don't you? It seems like an awfully lot has happened since then. Merry Christmas and Happy New Year. My thoughts will be with you on those days even if I can't. Love, Bill

About the 4th of December the situation at Faid Pass opened up. The French and our paratroopers had pushed their way from Sbeitta toward Sfax as far as this pass. They were doing okay but about 5 Italian tanks were giving them a lot of trouble. Walles made a flight and knocked out the tanks. The infantry said that one move saved the day for them. After that the JU-88s started bombing the pass, so we started a constant patrol down in that area. Sorensen and I made one that lasted for two hours. We went on past Faid and located five huge German trucks pulling four wheeled trailers, that were leaving the area and evidently starting back to Sfax for supplies. We put an end to that by making a gunnery pattern right down the road and left all of them on fire. Sorensen also got a staff sedan burning. We patrolled around the pass and watched our infantry laboring up the hill and digging in.

On December 7, we had a high altitude fighter sweep to the Tunis area. We hadn't been having much luck with the low-level stuff, so we tried it high. Major Keith led the flight, low level to Souk Ahras, where we started our climb to 26,000 feet. There was a 9/10 overcast at 10,000 feet and we went through a hole and on up. We did a lot of weaving but didn't see a single thing.

Captain Walles, Bing and Major Keith self-appointed themselves to one tent and made a stove and wash basin, etc. A radio out of the wrecked B-25 furnished the news and in the evenings we would sit around and have a big bull-session. This really crowded their place to capacity.

During some extremely bad weather, Colonel Olds led a flight down to Kebili, way down in the desert. We had to detour around a lot of rain-squalls and I learned another lesson from the old master, Colonel Olds. Heading into the rain it looked bad but it would only be of a short duration, and we would usually burst into the sunshine on the other side. Kebili is really out in the desert. We crossed three rocky mountain ranges and a great desert of nothing but sand before we arrived there. It was the kind of sandy desert that Dad always wanted to see. The town was a large oasis. We saw a few trucks but they and the other things looked like French stuff, not German. So we returned without firing a shot.

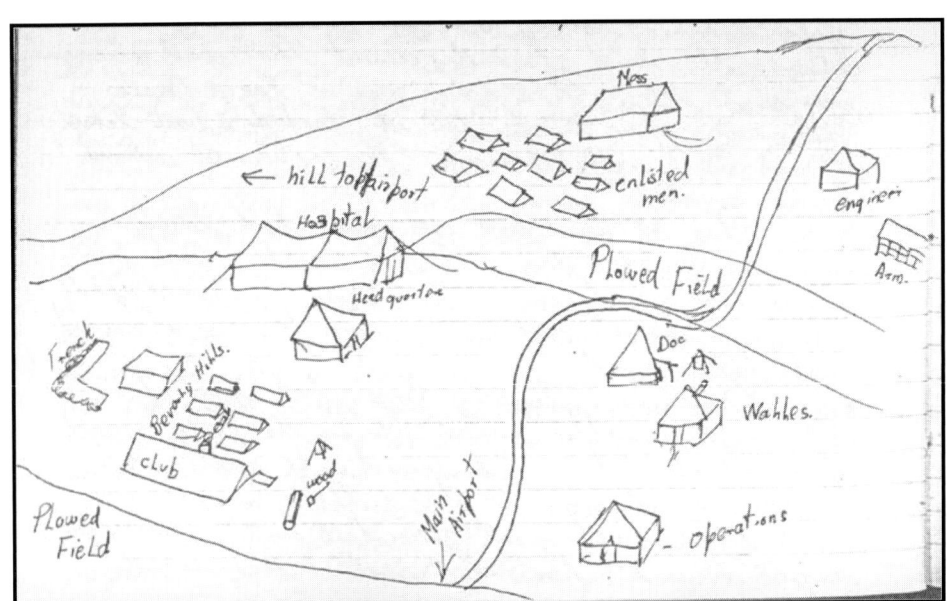

The new camp at Youks les Bains

About this time everyone at our field moved up on the hill at Youks les Bains. We had been living down in the bottom-land but it had gotten too muddy. The hill was more rocky and grassy and the water just sank into the ground. Our squadron gained the choice spot and we pilots gained the new Beverly Hills for ourselves.

About this time two runways were developed on the nearby dry hilltops. One for the 49th and one for us. The 49s is a very short uphill runway but quite smooth. It is easily seen as it parallels a road. Ours is slightly longer and full of dips and ends up in the back yard of an Arab hut. We found the only way to land on it was to drag the ground for a block before touching at zero feet and just fly right on to it. We've had some real cross-winds to contend with also. It was a tribute to our experience that we never have had an accident because of the bad field. The 49th killed two burros that had wandered onto their field. The Arab owner cried like a baby and helped the burros lie down before some men came and shot them.

Beverly Hills

One morning a correspondent from the Army Paper "Stars and Stripes" came to interview Captain Walles. He had been a sports writer on a paper back in the states before he started doing this kind of reporting. After we finished telling about our experiences, on the Tunis front he told us a few things.

He flew over from the states in a C-87, a converted B-24. His route was Florida, the islands of the West Indies, Georgetown, British Guinea, Natal, Brazil, and Ascension Island, located in the middle of the Atlantic, and Accra, Gold Coast Africa. At this last point he spent some time hunting. He showed us a picture of a native who had Elephantiasis of the balls. What a mess, they hung down to his knees. From Accra he flew 1800 miles directly to Oran, over the Sahara Desert, this took 12 hours. Their route took them very near Timbuktu. In the plane they had a Jeep, and several of them sat in it while flying at 10,000 feet. He said many A-20s were forced down in the desert and the crews were rescued by caravans.

Nearly every night a Ju-88 or several would fly over Tebessa or the Youks region. They bombed Tebessa for many nights in a row. They hit the American Twelfth Fighter Command Headquarters, causing the old brass hats to become pretty well shaken up. This included General Blackburn. This kind of gave them the war nerves.

One day three JU-88s approached Tebessa in formation. Another one came over Youks looking for something to bomb also. The British heavy guns opened up and put puffs in right beside him. He ducked into a cloud, came out and dived for the A-20s sitting on the field. We jumped in our trench as four bombs fell from the plane and exploded when they hit. One man was killed because he didn't have his steel helmet on. Three more were in a trench, just 20 feet away from where one of the bombs exploded, they came through OK. A bomb carrier was destroyed and that was all. The 49th boys on alert shot down two of the 88s and the French captured the crews. One was a dyed in the wool Nazi and another was a sort of a devil-may-care pilot who had fought in the Spanish War. The enlisted men were good looking, wore good flying suits that had zipper pockets. Holly and some of the boys went to see them and had some good talks with them.

P-38 getting ready for take off

Another time three 109s streaked over our field at lightening speed, turned around and came down past us, running for home. Eubanks who was on patrol got a good shot at one over the field and finally did shoot one down. Also V. Smith chased after them and got another one.

Combat in Africa

About this time the boys are making quite a few runs down toward Tripoli. They would fly down to Gafsa and then over the desert to the coast, so that they missed Gabes' with all its fighters. Captain Bing led eight of our boys down there and they shot up 21 trucks and cars of an advance force of Rommel's, that was coming up the coast toward Gabes. One of the cars they got was a new Ford V-8, they happily told me. That mission was a surprise to the enemy but the ones that came later proved to be a different matter.

Captain Lewis had led a mission of eight planes to Tunis and only three came back. Captain Lewis was killed and two of the boys, Guske and Earnhart later returned. Earnhart, one of the most skillful pilots in the group, was finally shot down by three 190s. He fooled them for a long time by doing loops right on the deck. What guts!! The Germans wouldn't follow him and he would end up on their tail, but he ran out of ammunition. Finally they hit one of his engines and he made a crash landing.

Fulmer was shot down on his first mission and made a crash landing.

Jimmy Tollen was rear end Charley on one flight when a 109 came up and got in a good burst from underneath. Evidently a 20MM shell exploded in the rear of his canopy and partly stunned him, he then went into a dive and crash-landed. We thought that he had gotten it but he turned up a few days later. He said that his helmet and everything had been blown from his head.

Later Shipman and Tollen were on a two ship mission to Sousse. A lucky burst of flak happened to get Jimmy and he went down in enemy territory. Mark thinks the plane exploded when it hit.

More missions went down to the Tripoli area and a 49th one ran into heavy flak near a seaplane base at el Mejen. The Huns simply put up a wall of fire and let the planes fly through it. Captain Mourne, flying on 1st Lieutenant Tom Morris's wing saw him slump over in the cockpit and crash into the sea. Good old Tommy.

On another mission, Holly was leading a group strafing a column of trucks, when he misjudged and hit a telephone pole with his wing. It cut a third of the way through it but Holly managed to pick it up and fly it home, despite heavy vibrations while flying at 150 MPH. It took all of his strength, 215 pounds, to hold the wing up. He had blisters on his hand when he returned.

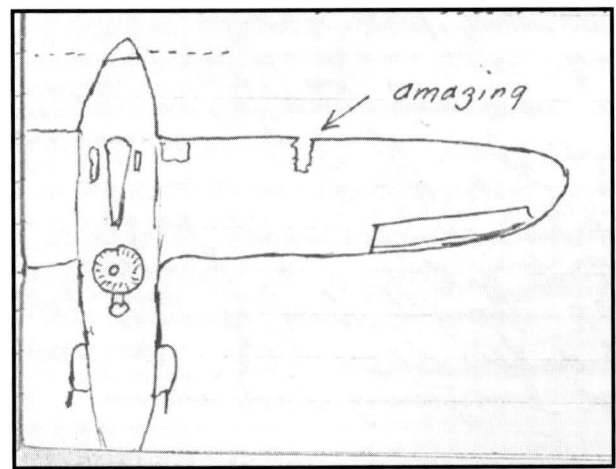

Bill's version of Holly's plane damage

On still another mission, which the 48th took, Johnson flew right into the ground while strafing a car, bounced up and managed to fly 300 miles home with one engine. He didn't even feather the prop on the bad engine. Shipman escorted him back.

While on a Tunis run, led by Colonel Olds, with Sorensen leading the 2nd Element, a German fighter got Sorensen's plane in the elevator trim tab. Wally tried to escape by diving and discovered to his dismay that he couldn't use the tab to pull out. He said he gave up once but then put all his strength into it, cut the throttles and was able to pull it out. He was about 50 feet up and doing 400 MPH when he finally got it under control.

Combat in Africa

On the 14th of December we acted as escorts along with some P-40s to the A-20s. The 40s were close cover and we were high. Just outside of Tebessa we encountered the roughest air that I believe I've ever been in. It was one of those windswept afternoons that mean rough air. I tried to stay in formation, to a certain degree, but the plane just skidded and slipped everywhere and seemed to go any place that it wanted. Planes on the same level as me were going up and down 100 feet, my head banged the canopy several times. On the other side of the pass we circled at Thelepte and picked up the 40s. We encountered some flak over Sfax but our weaving back and forth did the trick for us. The bombers set their eggs right on the docks and railway yards. I watched them explode, spreading ruin and destruction.

After arriving in Africa, Bill had named his plane the Miss Missoula.

On the 15th of December I conducted several test hops with my plane, 7650. The throttles had become very uneven. The trouble was discovered and it was due to dirty backfire screens.

On the 16th we had a nice, well timed mission escorting the A-20s to the Tunis area. There were 12 bombers, we used three, four ship flights. These were led by Walles, Bing, and Watson. Our town was Massicault, which was supposed to be filled with German troops and motor convoys. Bad weather was encountered on the way up and we had to make many changes in our course to get around it. We kept flat on the deck until we were near the target area. The French would come out into the streets of the little towns as we passed overhead and wave their encouragement to us. Twenty miles from Massicault we climbed to 8,000 feet to make the bombing run. The A-20s bombed the town beautifully, all bombs were dispersed to do the most damage possible. A steep diving right hand turn and we were away. The bombers were indicating better than 300 MPH as we wove around covering each other's tails. We didn't lose anyone that day.

On another trip that was taken to the Tunis area at about this time old 7650 received the only damage it has had since I acquired it. Eubanks was flying it, as 2nd Element, in a four-ship flight, with Watson leading. He didn't break when a 109 dived on him and shot a 20-MM slug through the top engine cowling into the prop spinner and it exploded. It made a bunch of small holes in the spinner. Lucky for him everything continued to function properly and he made it home all right. Once before he had crash landed his own plane, in friendly territory, when the one engine he had left failed.

On the 17th of December I was 2nd Element to Spider, on a trip to Gabe's escorting A-20s. On the way out the usual number of 109s, of course, attacked us. Spider and I broke and then found that the other P-38s, 8 of them, had kept going with the bombers. We got in some good shots, and so did the 109s but none of us were shot down. We lost them by diving to the deck. Caught up with the formation and continued our weaving until we were just outside of El Guettar. At this point we settled down to steady slow formation flying. Suddenly black puffs of smoke started breaking all around us. At first I thought it was ground fire and started to weave, looking around I saw two 109s letting us have it with all guns. We broke and they scooted for home, on the deck. Our lack of gas prevented us from chasing them. I simply don't see how they missed us.

On the 19th, Major Keith led 12 P-38s escorting 12 A-20s on an anti-shipping flight off of Gabe's and Sfax. I was second Element in Mark's flight. We hit the coast at 8,000 feet, just north of Gabe's. At 12,000 feet was a heavy layer of haze which made it nice for us as we would be able to see any fighters, that might come up to intercept us. However none did and we continued up the coast to Kerkenna Island and then made a bombing run of Sfax. Beautiful bombing was done on the docks and marshalling yards. Flak hit Segraves' plane and that was the only damage we had. The flights had worked wonderfully on this trip and we had perfect vision, for protection at all times. On the way home one flight patrolled the road and the rest of us stayed top cover. Segraves had to pump his landing gear down before he could land at Youks.

Keith led another 12 ship flight to Pont du Fahs. The French were bravely trying to advance at this point but were being heavily hammered by German columns. They figured if we could knock out the German column the French could continue with their advance. On the way there we passed through country that I was familiar with and this made it easier. We passed Maktar and into the battle area. Immediately two 109s were above us and got a good shot at my flight leader. I pulled straight up and put tracers all around that boy. Making another turn I saw a 109 firing a straight deflection at me, so I ducked him. It was a mad scramble over hills, down gullies and over farmlands at zero feet.

We stayed in the area too long, stooging around, just asking for it. We never did get to shoot up the columns. I hate war! The farms looked so peaceful in that fertile valley, the sun was out and I just wanted to walk around down there and be friendly with everybody. But no, here was a bunch of mad men flying over in machines of destruction and shooting wildly at each other, over these peaceful farmer's domains. One of the boys was escorted back by his wingman and made it home on one engine.

About this time we pilots became a little grieved at not having a place to spend the evenings. We usually spent some time in Captain Walle's tent, getting the latest news about Rommel, from the British and from the German's Lord Haw Haw. The tent would get so crowded that it was no fun and quite a trial for the Captains.

We decided to do something about this so we set to work to build a Pilot's Clubhouse. First of all we had to dig, and the result was a hole thirty feet by fifteen feet and four and one half feet deep. The digging took us four days, with the help of many men, picks, shovels and hard work. While we were doing the digging it rained much of the time. I would go into the Operations Hut to dry out. Sergeant Olson had made a little blow torch heater and had it all rigged up, for a heater. After the hole was completed we began the construction using five-gallon cans. On the backside we piled two layers of cans and on the front five layers. Shipman and Eubank worked on the fireplace and various others built the roof. After the wall of cans were up we used all of the excess dirt to bank against the sides. This made it solid, warm and practically an air-raid shelter.

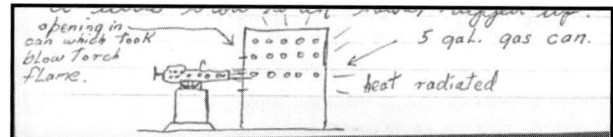

Sergeant Olson's blow torch heater

Christmas day came, and we didn't have the hut finished yet. It was a cold miserable day and besides that there wasn't any mail or anything else. We did have a very good meal. The Officer's Mess Tent had been set up and we actually had turkey, mashed potatoes, etc. Much better than the last few week's food had been and I certainly had no kick on the meal.

We kept at the hut with determination and soon it was finished. The fireplace, due to a great deal of luck or something, drew wonderfully and after everything inside dried out, the room was very comfortable. The Squadron Cat was placed above the fireplace and several signs were painted, black on yellow boards, and placed about the room. The bar was a tropical affair, designed and constructed by the Captain A. J. Bing. Our liquor ration came in and we had quite an assortment of mixed drinks available. A B-25 radio provided the news and the music, which we all called R. A. stuff. On New Year's

Combat in Africa

Eve, Dees ran his electrical line in and we had two electric lights. From the time the club was finished until the time we left, it was in constant use. It certainly made it nice place for us in the evenings.

The Pilot's Club House

On Christmas Day we got in five new replacement pilots from the states. They were flown down from England in a B-17. They are from classes 42-F and H. They have about 50 hours flying the P-38. They all seem to be OK.

On the 31st of December we again flew a mission to Gabe's, escorting the A-20s. This time we swung south of Gabe's and after the bombing run we made a left-hand diving turn off of the target. Twelve P-38s were on this flight. Singleton was leading four, which were the close escort to the bombers. I was on Captain Walle's wing with Shipman leading the Second Element. Watson, C. Smith, V. Smith and Carroll formed the Third Flight. Flak was accurate at our altitude, but the bombing was excellent. We saw enemy fighters but they went after Watson's flight. C. Smith found he could only draw 34 inches and lost the rest of his flight. We heard him call and say that he was alone, coming home on a vector of 310 degrees. We called back a little later and received no answer. We circled to see if we could help, but saw no action. Watson came home alone. We never saw the other three again.

They did find V. Smith near Gafsa, he had been attacked by three 109s, shot up, attempted a landing with his wheels down. He tried to go around, but hit an obstruction, nosed over and was killed. V. Smith was the last of our eager boys. He lost wingmen, right and left, but he did shoot down seven enemy planes.

We had a beautiful little service for him on New Year's Day. Six of us carried his body to the waiting transport plane. He was buried in or near Constantine.

C. W. Smith crash landed his plane and was captured by the enemy and was interned for the remainder of the war.

From a letter home:
North Africa
January 2, 1943
A.P.O. 525 After weeks of not receiving any mail, I'm suddenly drowned by about 10 to 15 letters. I've gotten all of these in the past few days. Your latest letter was postmarked December 13th and I still continue to get odd ones that were mailed in October and November. In fact, this noon I got a stray one that was mailed Oct. 6th. This one told of the visit of Al, Do and the baby. I had just learned this fact a few days ago, in a letter I got from Dinty. You certainly must have had a nice time.

Well there's a lot I want to say, if I can only remember it. First, have you received a letter yet from me, from Africa? I've only written one because I just haven't had the facilities to do so. You've gotten the new APO number I see, but I still think that you believe I'm still in England. I've been here for a long time now. Now that we are a little better organized, I will be able to catch up in my letter writing.

Combat in Africa

What's happened to the "Dymaniter", Bob's car? How many miles are on your car now?

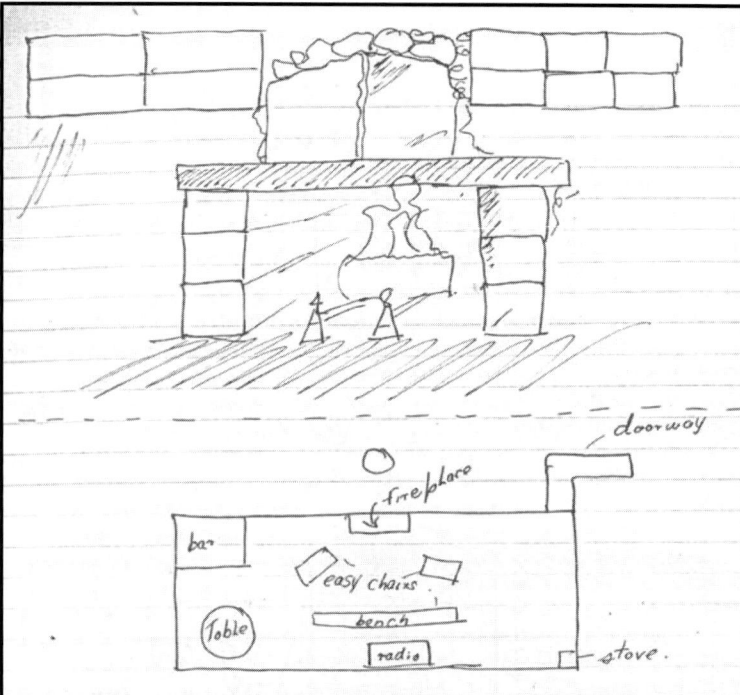
Bill's drawing of fireplace and seating

Haven't received a letter from Bob for quite some time now, but I know he is awfully busy. I'm glad to know that he is to be a pilot and has successfully completed the Pre-flight School.

I want to tell you about the various letters I've received. From Mrs. Halm I received a package of V-Mail stationery and a nice Christmas card. She said Fred Barrett and his wife were home on a short vacation. From Ed, I received a letter in which he told about having Merle for dinner. He also mentioned that Charles, now Sergeant Luedke, had visited them and was going to San Antonio to enter the Classification Center. From Jim Davison, I received a Christmas card and a picture of him in his uniform at San Antonio. Cliff sent me a letter telling me all the latest and be-moaning the fact that he couldn't be home for hunting season. He's a Corporal now.

I haven't heard anything from Bud, but I intend to write to him soon. Is he a Sergeant yet? Mrs. J. H. Miller, of MM, Missoula Mercantile, sent me a nice Christmas card and note and I will try to thank her. Mrs. J. D. Nye wrote me a letter in her typical smiling manner. She said Bill is at Fort Douglas, Utah, and that Joe has a good job, a three and a half year old boy, and another on the way, that's expected in March. She said it's fine to be a Grandma. From Mrs. Centers, a nice card and note. She said that you two seem to be well, and that Dad, had came over to see if Hayden would go back to work at Bell's. I guess Dad is the H. P. at Bell's now, (H. P. = Hot Pilot).

Aunt Ann in Frisco wrote me a V-Letter and extended Christmas greetings. She informed me about Grandmother's death, your letter came later. Also she said Jackie had been to see her, he's now a Naval Aviation Cadet at Livermore, California. Sucker! He will be flying the Navy's terrible equipment, while Bob will fly the Army's **Hot Rocks**. Also that Lynn is in the Air Corps. Also received a letter from Laura in Detroit. Said that Mary married an Air Corps Officer. Don had been to see them and is supposed to be stationed in Great Falls. His letter said he would be coming to see you and Halms soon. Dinty wrote me a very interesting letter telling about Bob's brief visit. Dinty had taken physical exams trying for a commission in various branches of the service but had been rejected.

Christmas day came and is gone and it just didn't seem like Christmas. The weather was bad, rainy, with low clouds. Not a one of us received packages, I guess it was just too much to expect but they will probably arrive soon. There probably wasn't enough shipping space and besides we've been moving around a lot.

Let me see what can I tell you without having it censored? After spending many an evening standing out in the wind, the pilots got together and decided to build a club.

At this point Bill describes the construction of their new Officer's Club.

The fireplace is larger than ours is at home and it'll handle large logs. In one corner we made a Tropical Bar out of Bamboo and Palm leaves. This was a busy place New Year's Eve. A Lion skin lies on the floor in front of the fireplace and there are several easy chairs sitting around it, this completes the picture. Around the walls we have signs painted in yellow and black and saying such thing as this, "The brightest spot in darkest Africa", "Women especially welcome", and of course our Walt Disney Squadron Insignia. Now in the evenings we've got a place to relax and be comfortable. We also aren't going to bed as early.

It's getting quite cold these days. Last night the water in my canteen froze, and there was a heavy frost on my tent.

Our squadron has done some great work and we've been congratulated by Major General Jimmy Doolittle. We've been in the thick of things in this part of the world and everything is OK, so don't worry.

"Miss Missoula", my means of transportation, hasn't been scratched since I left March Field. It's one of the very few original planes still with us.

The Arabs are very friendly as I've said before, and they're great traders. However sometime they get swindled. Someone gave one a shiny English Penny for a chicken and the Arab thought the coin was Gold. When he found out, he came to get his chicken back, but it was already over the fire. He just sat on his Burro, with his feet touching the ground and cried like a baby.

There are many more things I could tell you but right now I will close by saying that we had a very nice dinner on Christmas and New Year's Day. Turkey to be exact. Love to you both, Bill

On the 3rd of January 1943: The situation near Pichon began to develop. The Germans brought in 15 heavy tanks to drive back the French, who were trying to force their way down the draws from the mountains and out onto the plains, near Kairovan. We were sent into the area to stop the tanks. We found them after some searching and made a 12 ship gunnery attack on them. They were huge 30 ton ones and really tough. I could see my .50 Caliber tracers ricocheting straight up in the air after they hit, but I think the 20 MMs were doing a lot of good. Return fire hit Captain Spivy, who was on Captain Walles' wing, on the second pass. With his left engine out, his canopy off and his forehead cut he headed home with Sorensen and Goebel escorting him. We stuck around too long and as we started for home, two 109s hit us from above. We broke and one got a lucky burst into Bing's left engine. The engine burst into flame and Bing cut the gun and set it down on the hill, in a short field, between two ridges. We didn't know at the time if he was safe or not but he returned and this is his story.

He got out of the plane OK and ran about 150 feet then the gas tank exploded. From one hill he could see four Germans running toward him firing their guns. Two others were coming down another hill, so Bing hid in the grass and covered himself up. The two soldiers coming from one direction proved to be French. He jumped up and they brought him back safely.

Sorensen and Goebel were out one morning on a weather hop, when they and a 49th Alert Ship ran across a JU-88 over Tebessa. The 88 shot out one of Goebel's engines and Sorensen saw the enemy aircraft blow up in front of him. However with a flip of a coin the boy from the 49th was credited with the kill. Shipman and others went by truck to view the remains of the JU-88. There

Combat in Africa

were only small amounts of plane left and they found only a little blood and bits of clothing, all that was left of the crew.

We have received about 14 planes from the 82nd Group and already we've lost a good many of them.

The 49th had a bad mission near Kairovan. They Stooged around for a long time and finally were jumped by about 15 109s and 190s. Holly bailed out at 500 feet. Woodard and Kerche were killed and Moffett came in on his belly at Youks. What a mess!

In the town of Youks les Bains there is an old Frenchman who runs a hot springs bathhouse. He is a real old timer, having been at Youks for 41 years. We would sometimes get a chance to go in and have a bath. I had three of them during my busy stay at Youks.

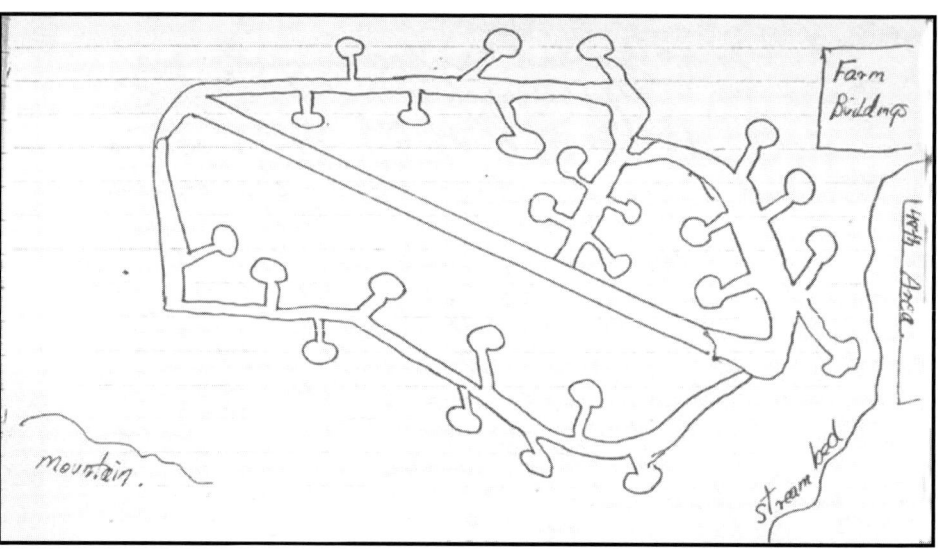

The new airfield

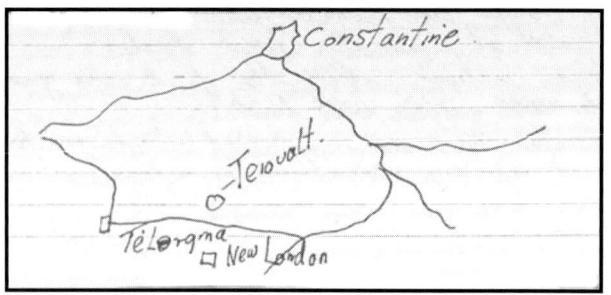

New London

On the 4th of January, we moved from Youks and went backward to a field near Constantine. We called this New London. We flew a sixteen ship in formation, ferry trip, to the new field. Upon leaving Youks we did a good job of buzzing it. When we arrived at the new field we did the same before we landed. They simply took over a big farm that sat on level land and leveled a long, wide, runway down the middle. It has taxi strips plus dispersal areas and all of this work was done with a grader. It has worked out pretty good and proved to be plenty smooth. A B-25 Group was stationed here before we arrived.

We ate at the expense of the B-25 outfit as soon as we arrived. This was our first taste of American rations and boy were they good, especially the coffee and fruit. We didn't have a very good camping site but we constructed our usual little officer's community anyhow. We dug little trenches beside our green tents and used the other little bedroll canvas as a tent affair over our luggage.

At this time our hopes for a trip home were very high but that soon passed from view when we heard that we were to receive new pilots again. However an opportunity came for five boys at a time to go to Casa Blanca on the west coast of Africa for R&R. Zeigler, Stege, Goebel, Bestgen and Eubanks were the first to go.

At first we only had a few patrol missions. From the air I looked Constantine over. One of the most beautiful cities I've ever seen. Everything white, built on a cliff and over a steep gully with arch and suspension bridges. Also while on patrol I looked over some Arab cliff ruins, built on the side of a hill. One hill we have in the vicinity provides an awfully good landmark. It has a thumb sticking up on the top and we can always find our way home using this as a landmark.

The Thumb

On the 9th of January, we started flying bomber escort missions. Our first was with B-25s flying out of our field. We had on two belly tanks. Bing led one, four ship flight and Singleton led another. I was Singleton's Second Element. We passed over our old field, Youks, and then over Sbeitta on the way to Sfax.

Everyone kept flat on the deck, and I mean those 25s were really on the deck, at 10 feet across the desert. The rest of us were weaving back and forth over the top of them and consequently we had to use some good judgement. As we neared the coast north of Sfax, we passed over little houses and nice orchards. The few French in the vicinity would stand out in their yards and wave encouragement. The weather was nicer now and the blue Mediterranean look peaceful with the white sails of fishing boats on the surface. I opened my ventilator and took in the cool breeze. I felt relieved once we were a little way out over the sea. We had passed too close to Sousse for comfort. I still don't know why the fighters didn't come up.

We passed a few small boats but the bombers didn't bother with them. The weather became worse so we had to skirt around rainsqualls while keeping a good lookout around us. As we approached the coast again we dropped our belly tanks, while traveling at 150 MPH. We came in over land at 1,000 feet near Rass Maamoure and made a bombing run on the railroad bridge at Hammamet. There are several towns in this area and considerable flak came up from them, luckily no one was hit. The bombing was rotten as they blew the hell out of a little field near the target. We sneaked out, down on the deck at 300 MPH. Back near home, at Guelma, we became completely socked in and the bombers went up through the overcast on instruments. We left them and sneaked back, through a canyon in the world's roughest air. We finally landed at Youks, gassed ourselves up and got into New London in time for a late supper. We hadn't had anything to eat all day, besides the early morning meal. As we were late for supper we had a cold one. Five and a half hours in the cockpit, now I know what they're paying us for. The bombers couldn't get back to the field so they flew on down to Biskra on a homing.

Some of the boys started out on a mission, which took them to Biskra where they were to meet up with some B-17s. They landed there and as the weather was bad the mission was called off. However they did get to see all of the old boys who we came across the ocean with, Holman, Hair and others. They had a nice visit and talked over old times and what's been happening since they had seen them last.

On the 12th, we escorted some B-26s to La Hencha near Sousse. The mission was poorly organized and the bombing was ragged. I believe a couple of their eggs found the target but the rest of them fell short. Our return was without incident, the flights were working well together. We don't like the 26s as well as the 25s. They are slightly faster but the pilots tell us that they can only climb 300 feet a minute with a full bomb load. This doesn't allow them to fly right on the deck until they're near the target.

On the 14th, we had another mission with B-26s. We had on two belly tanks and headed for Sousse, by way of Youks. The target area was partly obscured by clouds and the bombing, I believe was inaccurate. I had trouble releasing my belly tanks and was just about to turn around when they came off in a tight turn. Going home we passed right over Kairovan Airport at 14,000 feet. I really sweated that one out. I could see planes dispersing there and could also see the dust as they started to take off. We were never attacked however. Yates and I nearly had a collision as we crossed over each other. Rough air – home safely.

Finally made a trip to Constantine. Borrowed the Doctor's ambulance and drove in. It took about an hour on a nice paved road that crossed through the green countryside. All along the way we saw war supplies, truck, tanks, light airplane, etc. It looks like there's going to be a big deal at the front very soon.

A view of Constantine

As I said before it's a beautiful city and quite modern. We parked in the middle of town and found a place to take a shower. After a short wait we got in and what a luxury. That warm water came down over my dusty, hot face and felt wonderful. We paid 6 Francs for the shower and five to some little kids to take care of our clothes and show us a barbershop. I then had a nice shave for six Francs, a shoeshine for five more and I was all set. Sat on a verandah for awhile and watched the people go by. Mark and I took a walk and got a good look over the cliff. It was a scene out of a Fairy Tale Book. Green hills, winding roads, blue sky, dark hills, Oh me!!

A British 40-MM gun emplacement guarded the scene. Up the hill, filthy Arab workers were resupplying modern hotels. Everywhere ran little, ragged Arab kids with sores and smallpox scars on their faces. However a few were neat and had shoeshine establishments set up. Lower down in the canyon, stood modern apartment houses. In the center of town the Citroen Garage had been taken over by the British and they were busy repairing all types of units. In other spots there was evidence of how much was going on and how quickly it had all come about. The best hotels were reserved for high-ranking officers. We returned back at 4:30 PM.

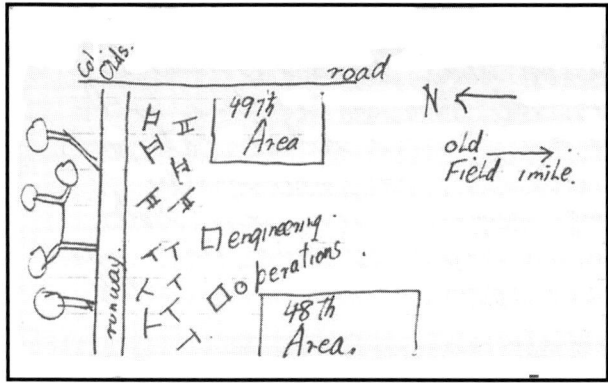

New operation at Teioualt

Again we changed fields. We moved across the road where the graders had plowed a new runway. This field is really called Teioualt. It's a nice setup for camping, as there are a few trees, and an old building to use for the mess and nice grass to set our tents on. All in all it's a much cleaner and nicer place.

The runway is smooth but the bad feature is we have to drag it over a raised road at the end. We of the 48th now have a special mess tent and it certainly is nice. Tables and benches and food is put on the table on squadron plates, etc. No more sweating out the chow line.

On the 15th we had a real mission. Six B-25s, and 8 P-38s. First up to Bone and then out over the water and up the coast, right on the deck looking for shipping. I really sweated this out as we still had our belly tanks on, and if we had been jumped we would have had to drop them and then due to the great consumption, due to combat, we probably would never had made it home. Finally we came upon a large, six

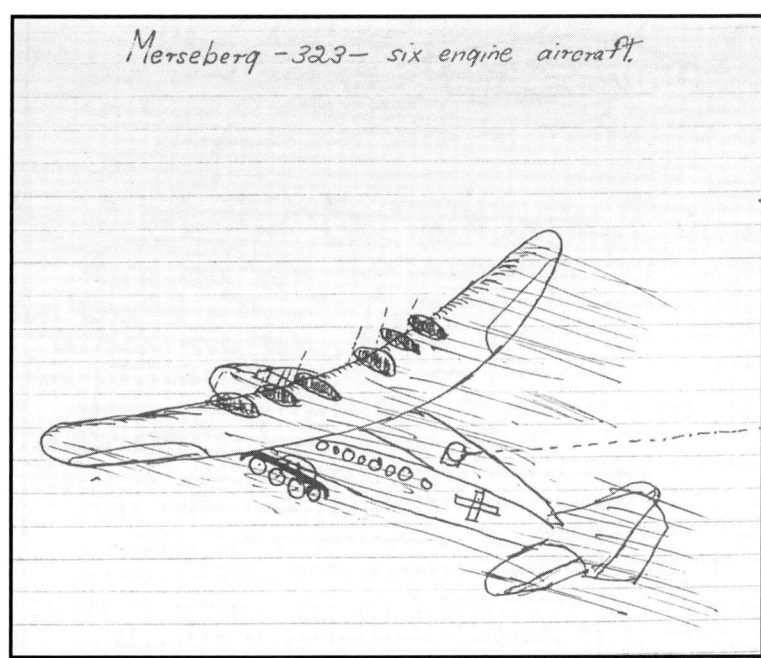

engined, Merseberg 323.

The boys started in and finished it off right away. I led my element out of the way because there were planes going ever which way. When the 323 hit the water a wing broke off, it flopped over on it's back and settled in a pool of foam. I doubt if anyone was able to get out. Later on we ran into three JU-52s and the boys also got these.

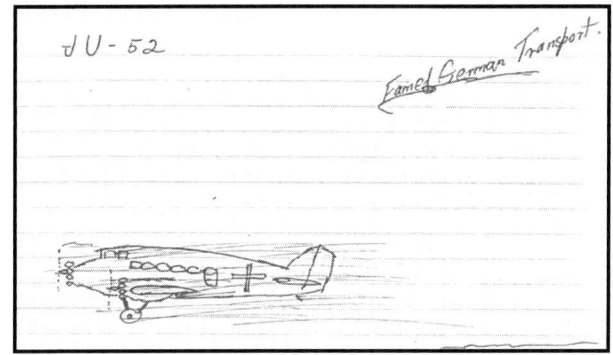

I spotted another in the distance, but could not follow him because of poor visibility in a rain squall. A little later on we ran into a JU-88. He came straight by us at the same level. We were both surprised and neither of us did anything. I could have had a head on shot, but again it was stay with the bombers. Again we sweated out bad weather over the hills. Total time 4 hours and this is simply too long to sit in a cockpit, tightly strapped under combat conditions. A pilot isn't alert enough after two hours if he is bounced.

The water was might rough on this last trip and it would have been too bad for one to have to set down out there. We all returned OK but the 49th didn't have that luck. They started out with an eight ship flight but two had to return because of mechanical troubles. The other six made a mistake, by not weaving, and they just were plodding around while escorting the bombers. They spotted about thirty JU-52s and went for the kill. At the same time some 109s jumped them from above. Fulmer and a new boy went down. Johnson came home on one engine along with the bombers. Blueher crash landed at Bone, with one engine out. The other two landed safely at Bone, both with an engine out. Rather an expensive trip.

Combat in Africa

Again we obtained nine new pilots. Singleton and I trained a group of five, for one day. We gave them the history of the squadron, regulations, combat theory, cockpit check and checked them out on the oxygen system. We did all this on the ground. Afterwards they all got in two to three hours flying the plane. The last flight of the day was carried on just like a regular operations mission. We lined up the flights, gave a take-off time, the channel to use on the radio, briefing, etc. They all did pretty well at this. These boys left the states December 22 and flew across the water by the southern route in C-54s and C-87s.

January 18, 1943, we had 16 P-38s escorting 3 B-26s on an anti-shipping mission. We broke in a bunch of new boys on this flight. Bing led the First Flight, Sorensen second, Singleton third and I led the last. We hit the coast just a little above Sousse and started south. Right away we saw a small merchant vessel steaming south. The bombers peeled off, individually, and made a run on the vessel. I don't believe that any of them made a direct hit on it, but several came very close. The last I saw the vessel was out of commission. We came right out weaving and did have a little flak fired at us. We dropped our belly tanks fairly close to Pont du Fahs, and at this point Warren dropped out of the formation and was never seen again. Slightly later we saw two enemy fighters but they didn't bounce us. I was glad they didn't, because one of my belly tanks wouldn't release. It finally flew off. We came over the field in a stacked down Echelon. I about got minced, as there wasn't room for my flight under Singleton's. However, we moved out to the side and things turned out OK.

20th of January. Captain Holman and Captain Duvall of the B-17 squadron came over today. We had a good talk, going over the trip across the water, about when we flew across the North Atlantic on their wings. They have been doing great work up in the Tunis-Bizerte area, scoring 80% hits. Their biggest trouble is that they can't get parts for their planes and the new Studebaker engines are only lasting for about one mission, or in the most 20 hours. A JU-88 dropped flares near their field the other night but they didn't do any bombing.

McWerter was killed the other day at Biskra. A P-39 landed on top of him as he was taking off. Walles was promoted to Major, and Keith to Lieutenant Colonel. The orderly room and Major Walles each bought a Jackass. They certainly lead a much easier life under us than they had with the Arabs. Pryor, one of our new pilots, contacted Malaria, they believe in Accra, and now he won't be able to fly for at least three months. They will probably send him back to the states.

Major Walles Jackass

From a letter home, dated January 20, 1943:
North Africa: It's been a wonderful day here,

Combat in Africa

one, that makes me glad that we're out in the open, living a healthful life. The sky has been clear all day, except for a ground fog early this morning and this burned off soon after the sun came up. Now the sun has set and I'll take this spare moment to write a few lines and finish it tomorrow. The moon is starting to raise now even though it's still very light out. It's clear now so we will have a heavy frost in the morning, cold enough for ice to freeze. So far I've been very comfortable in my bedroll inside my small tent. All in all, you might say that we've had a very comfortable and beautiful winter.

My last letter, I believe, was written just after Christmas. Well we've moved since then and our new place is more comfortable. While we had no Christmas then, we've since had more than we can handle. I've had packages from everybody, and also Christmas cards with letters. I don't know if I can remember who sent what but I sincerely appreciate it all. I hope that you can thank as many of the folks for me as you can and I'll try to write them.

I received Applets, a real treat, V-Mail stationery, tin of candy, a subscription to "Time Magazine" and more candy including Peanut Brittle. Of course your package was wonderful. I needed and used everything. In fact, I'm writing this letter, the first one, on the stationery. I'm especially enjoying the gum. We all had been acquiring a terrific taste for sweets but after eating all of this we've gotten satisfied.

Ed and his wife sent me a wonderful scarf with their name on it. I'll have to wait a long time to use it however. Ness sent a box of soap and a picture, I'm trying to write him. Have received many letters. The trouble is, these letters never seem to come in any particular order, for instance a couple of weeks ago I received a letter from you dated December 13 and yesterday received one dated November 6, so you see how mixed up things have become.

In your letter of November 6, you asked me a question and wanted it answered yes or no. Do you remember? Here's the answer, at our last place or where we were first when we came across--**some** but not **much**. Down here at this place--**yes** and **how.** **Whew!** One thing I've learned is that you can't rely on what the papers say, as they have the situation pretty well mixed up.

I enjoyed reading Bob's letter that you sent. Also received one from him. He was just becoming an upper-classman at Preflight School. Now I want to write him but he has moved to Primary School and I don't have his current address. Could you please send it to me? I'm particularly interested in knowing what class he's in. 43-F, that's a long cry from mine 41-I. We've been getting a bunch of new boys in over here, fresh from the states, and every time we do, I holler out, "is my brother in that crowd?"

I haven't been paid since October simply because I've had no need for money. We're also going to get $100 in addition for uniform allowance. We got $150 for this when we were first commissioned. This will be a big help to me, for you see my nice, perfect fitting, blouse and my pink pants, seemed to have gotten in the way of some slight activity-a-la-de-enemy, and they're full of holes. Oh well! So when I get home again, I'll have to buy a bunch of new clothes. In fact right now I'm running pretty short on pants and shirts. I just obtained a new pair of shoes, free, from the Quartermaster.

We went into a city the other day and had a bath, the fourth one I've had since coming to Africa. It cost 6 Francs, the present money system we're using. There are 75 Francs in a dollar, so you see that the bath only cost a few cents. The city was quaint and truly a wonderful sight. Sometime I will be able to tell you all about it. Speaking of money systems, we've used four different ones since leaving the states.

Combat in Africa

I'm running short of stamps as the ones I had were ruined when they stuck to a piece of paper. I could certainly use some #620 film too. I hear that you people at home aren't allowed to send us packages anymore. You might inquire about this at the Post Office and if you can, send me a few rolls of film and I will have some nice ones for Ness to print when I get home.

Shipman is doing his washing today and I will do a little more, myself, later on. I washed out my cap and a heavy shirt in gasoline and they came out good. Well, I guess that is about all I will say at this time. Needless to say, I'm hoping for the day when I can sit down with you and Dad and tell the whole story. I know Dad and I will have a lot to talk about. I only wish he could see some of the amazing things, which are going on over here. And Mother, I know you just want me home. We had news the other day that we might go home soon, if the situation develops, OK. Naturally we can't promise anything. Love, Bill. PS The squadron now has two Jackasses bought from Arabs, just for fun. The cooks made jam tarts for dinner yesterday.

January 21, 1943-Well for several nights now the huge tanks have passed here, heading for the coast or the front. They're huge affairs that weigh about 30 tons. The roadbed really shakes as they thunder past.

Spent the day washing clothes, writing letters and just plain enjoying the sun. 49th had a mission. The Germans are crowding into Pont du Fahs, around 5 or 6 thousand of them.

From a letter to Bill's friend Cliff dated January 21, 1943. Cliff sent this letter to Bill's mother and said, "This letter from Bill is in the reminiscent mood of the Round Robin, so I'll enclose it". J. C.

About three weeks ago I received your letter dated December 11 and just recently I received another that was dated October 11. So you can see how mixed up things are. I gobbled up all the news you gave me and eagerly await more. I vow to get letters off right soon to Mick, Bud and others.

We've been moving around quite a bit lately and the ordinary chores of living seem to take up most of my time. Now I have my household in good shape and the sun has been making the days neat. I should have great success with writing now.

Don is a lucky boy to be back home and have a girl. This is a funny game but mostly a matter of luck where a guy is placed. I crave my place but it certainly has a lot of disadvantages, such as promotions, etc. Take Ed, just crying his heart out because he can't go on Foreign Service and fly the hot stuff. Really he's better off where he is, if he only knew it. If I should get through this I will have a lot to tell and if not my complete diary tells everything, from the day I first started over the ocean, July 26, 1942. That makes nearly six months now.

We didn't get any Christmas packages or anything by the 25th but around the 2nd of January they started pouring in and have been coming every since. We had developed a craving for sweet stuff and that has been largely satisfied now.

Your Mother sent me a delicious box of Applets, and they were certainly tasty. I have received letters from Mr. McLeod, Mr. Bunge, and many others. Ed says that Bud is a Sergeant now and also that Brunsvold is an instructor at Mather Field.

Mother said that Bob sold the "**Dynamiter**" for $200 cash. That's pretty good considering that the thing had been to Mexico twice and up to Edmonton, etc. etc.

Bob, Jim, and Chuck are all in San Antonio and Bob is evidently doing OK. His class is 43-F, a far cry from mine, 41-I. We kind of kid everybody that have come in from the late classes. They're being turned out so fast and every time some new boys arrive, we yell, is Schottelkorb's brother in this bunch.

You spoke of the Brawl Book. Well today, I looked over that writing that Bud gave me on the farewell picnic, Remember! Here are a couple of quotations from it. "Dirty fellow Jim will grin right through 3 depressions, the panic of 45 and several bank drafts to come out on top. The Wifey's a good lil manager, you know, and they'll have a snug little bungalow that Jim and Don built--out near the high school field. Remember that Hammering Hearse he got from Don? Well, Murray Motors are going to allow him $12.53 on it toward a new Buick convertible (a sort of Jordon Jade color).

Stiffy-Squid (Bill) will have graduated from the '30 Model A to a comfortable Mercury, (what with his position as Chief Consultant on Accounts at Amalgamated Soap Co.), but otherwise you'll find him little changed, a wife or two, maybe, and several little Johns running about." Well I guess we all hardly realized what was in store for us then, did we? Over here we're having a fairly good life, not as bad as some might think.

You mentioned something about food. Well at first the food was bad, then good and finally bad again. As far as many things are concerned, like milk, we just don't have any. I've had two glasses of milk since leaving the states, but I can't kick too much.

All this traveling causes us to use many different money systems. Four to be exact, since leaving the states. Right now the Franc is our medium. There are 75 Francs in a Dollar. We went to a town the other day and had a bath. It was the fourth one I've had since leaving the last place, and what a luxury. It only cost 6 Francs.

I haven't been paid for the last three months, because there just isn't any need for money. So I continue to coin untold wealth. I'll need it all for Income Tax when I return. They gave us $100 for uniform allowance. I can use that because my neat blouse and pants seemed to have gotten in the way of some slight activity and are now thoroughly filled with holes, luckily I wasn't in them.

Remember all the old sayings we used to use, which were peculiar to our bunch at home? Well I have most of the boys here using them pretty well now. Everyone goes around saying <u>Store</u> tent and little <u>Bead</u> stakes, etc. etc. They all think I'm nuts, however I've found that the best thing a fellow can do during all of this strain is have a good sense of humor.

We have two Jackasses in the squadron now, just for pets. We bought them from the Arabs. They really lead a life of ease compared with what they were used to, that was carting tonnage loads. Well guess I'll close for now, and try it again soon. Yours, Bill PS Rumor has it that if everything goes OK, we old timers might soon see home. We're really sweating it out.

January 22, 1943: This morning several of us went over to the B-17's field and watched them take off on a mission. There's something fascinating about that big boat as it starts on a mission, with complete crew, all ready to do it's job. Such a machine of precision. Later we met up with all of the old boys that we came across the ocean with, Captain Holman, Duvall, Hair, etc. We discussed just about everything with them. They haven't lost a pilot yet in actual combat. We drove over and back in the pilot's old Dodge truck. It was a nice ride on a paved road, however the road is taking an awful beating due to the heavy use it's receiving.

A sudden mission came up this afternoon. Spider led the 1st Flight of four, and I led the Second. We weren't properly briefed and the

Combat in Africa

take-off was slightly mixed up. We finally did get into formation and took out with the bombers. The 82nd Group also had 8 ships with us. They fly a wing tip to wing tip formation and are separated by about 100 yards from one another. We think this is absolutely no good and it certainly mixed us up.

We were escorting 21 B-25s. They flew near the deck until just before we got to Bizerte. There they started a steep climb and we dropped our belly tanks and pushed on up to 32 inches of Mercury for our climb. We didn't have up enough speed to weave back and forth over them as we had done on the flight out, so we each wove on our side within the flight. We were over the Tunis-Bizerte area for a long period of time, making the bombing run at 8,000 feet. Spider's flight got jumped by four 109s and they broke beautifully. Two of the 109s came up on our tail and they were scared away when we broke into them. The flak was simply terrific and I couldn't find the bombers for a minute because of it. It was simply a block of black puffs. I saw the bombs burst beautifully on the Tunis airport. As the bombers made a right hand, diving turn they left the target area and were indicating better than 300 MPH. We again continued to weave over them and diving. The 82nd was completely mixed up and I saw individual planes all over the sky. One of them joined our flight and that made five of us. I saw another one engaging in individual combat with a 109. On both the Tunis and Djedeida airports there were scores of wrecked planes. Pretty soon a 190 appeared just above us and followed as we wove back and forth. Soon he dived on the rear man and I broke hard to the right and was able to get a good burst at him. Miles said the tracers fell just behind his tail as I hadn't allowed enough deflection. Just then my right prop went out, but I got home OK. The rest of the flight was uneventful except for some flak at Medjez-el-Bab. After we returned to the field we saw some movie stars that came to the camp. Carole Landis, Martha Ray, Kay Francis, etc. Quite a day.

This was the last entry that Bill made in his diary as the next day, January 23, 1943, he was shot down while on a mission. On the 28th of January the 48th Fighter Squadron's operations were terminated and the older pilots were sent back to the United States. After returning to the US Mark Shipman and Wally Sorensen flew into Missoula and brought Bill's diaries and other things back to our parents.

Combat in Africa

The following pictures and diagrams are taken from Bill's diary. Not only had he written very good accounts of the flights that he had been on and heard the other pilots tell about, but his pictures and maps were drawn so that he could one day tell his story of what had happened.

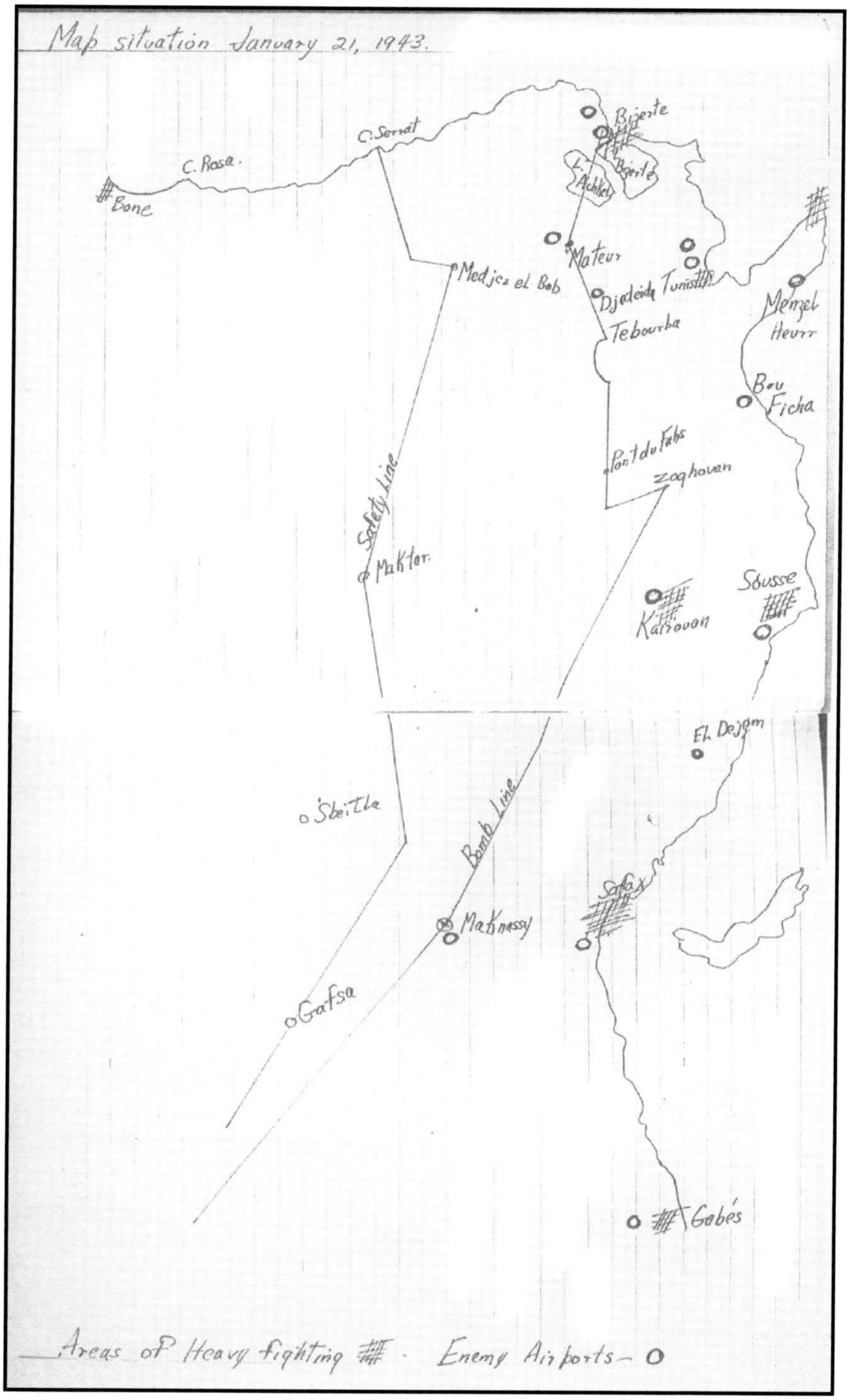

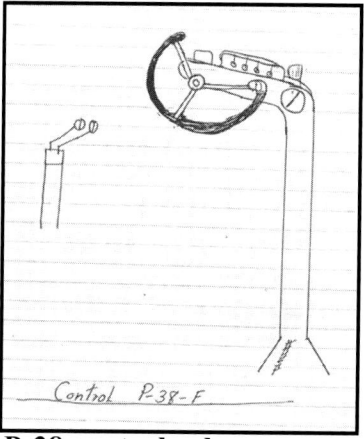

P-38 control column

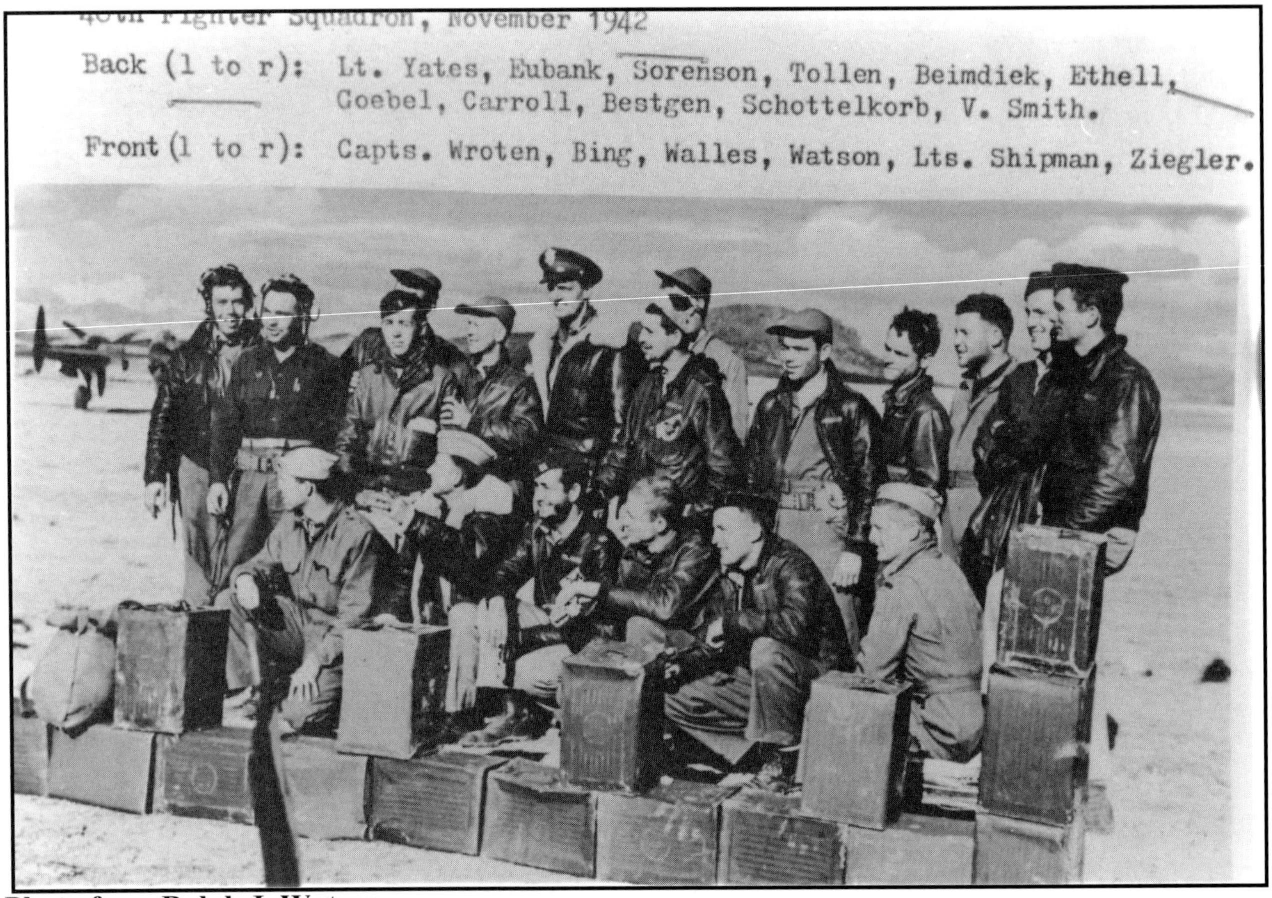

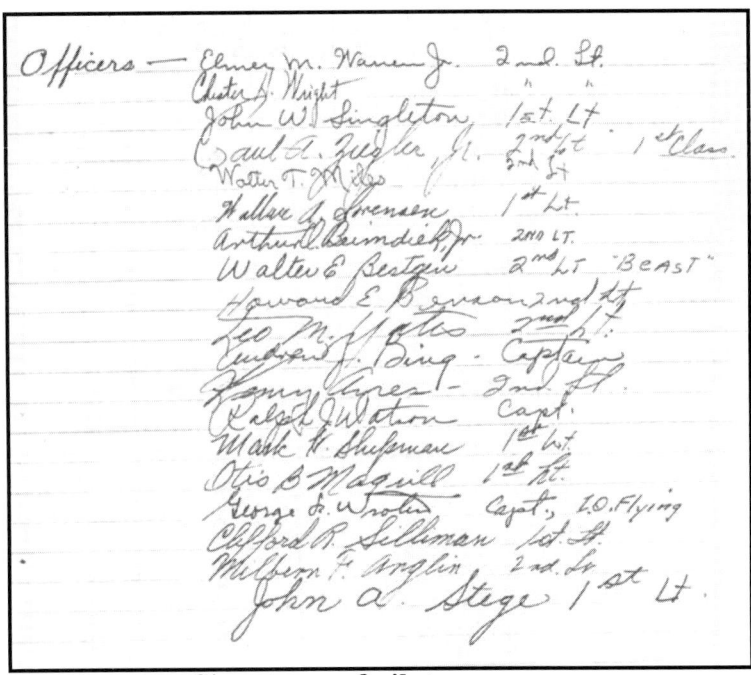

40th Fighter Squadron, November 1942
Back (l to r): Lt. Yates, Eubank, Sorenson, Tollen, Beimdiek, Ethell, Goebel, Carroll, Bestgen, Schottelkorb, V. Smith.
Front (l to r): Capts. Wroten, Bing, Walles, Watson, Lts. Shipman, Ziegler.

Photo from Ralph J. Watson

Officers — Elmer M. Warren Jr. 2nd. Lt.
Chester J. Wright " "
John W. Singleton 1st. Lt
Paul A. Ziegler, Jr. 2nd Lt 1st Class
Walter T. Miles 2nd Lt
Wallace A. Sorensen 1st Lt.
Arthur L. Beimdiek, Jr. 2ND LT.
Walter E. Bestgen 2nd LT "BEAST"
Howard E. Bevan 2nd Lt
Leo M. Yates 2nd Lt.
Andrew J. Bing - Captain
Henry Ayres - 2nd Lt.
Ralph J. Watson Capt.
Mark H. Shipman 1st Lt.
Otis B. Magill 1st Lt.
George S. Wroten Capt., I.O. Flying
Clifford R. Silliman 1st Lt.
Milburn F. Anglin 2nd. Lt
John A. Stege 1st Lt.

Signatures of pilots

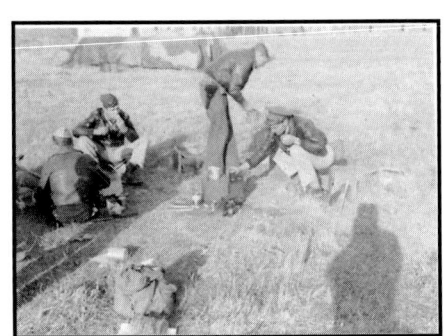

Pilots cooking their rations

Combat in Africa

Pilots from 48th that were lost:
- Carl T. Steiner – Tunis
- Carl Williams – Tunis
- Aurthor V. Cole – Tunis
- Jimmy Pollen – Sousse
- Virgil Smith – Gabés – Gafsa
- Clark W. Smith – Gabés
- Richard (Pappy) Carroll – Gabés
- Elmer M. Warren, Jr. – Pont du Fahs
- Leo Yates – Medenine

Pilots from 48th that were lost

A dry camp with trenches

Pilots the 49th lost:
- Capt. Lewis
- Lt. Woodward
- Lt. W.
- Lt. Tommy Morris
- Lt. Butler
- Lt. Stief
- Lt. Elliot
- Lt. Kirske
- Lt. Mullinax
- Lt. Dryer
- Capt. Fulmer – Headquarters

Pilots from 49th that were lost

The pilots area

Ground crew changing engine

Camp all set up

Combat in Africa

Ground crew checking their plane

Type	Destroyed	Probable	Damaged	Destroyed on the Ground	Number
				48th Fighter Squadron (January 21, 1943)	⑪⑧
Me. 109	7	3	4	Enemy Aircraft	10
Me. 110	1			Locomotives	14
Me. 210	2			Tanks	33
JU-88	4			Vehicles	145
JU-52	10				
F.W. 190	1				
Others	1				
Italian	1				
Total	27	3	4		

Damage that the 48th inflicted

Combat in Africa

What happened to the planes?

- 41-7653 -- lost over Tunis - Williams
- 41-7660 -- one engine out - stripped at Algiers.
- 41-7636 -- hit obstruction - scrapped - Cole.
- 41-7645 - Sousse - Follen. - Flak -
- 41-7655 - Tunis - Skinner. ?
- 41-7654 - 49th. - crash landed Pont du Fahs.
- 41-7648 - Kairouan - Bing - crash landed. L. engine on fire.
- 41-7659 - Follen - Tunis - shot up - crash landed.
- 41-7639 - V. Smith - belly - desert.
- 41-7640 - Stege - belly desert.
- 41-7641 - Warren - Atcham - washed out.
- 41-7643 - Desert - Watson - belly
- 41-7675 A. Singleton - Desert - belly.
- 41-2360 - Yates - desert - belly
- 41-7639 - C. Smith - belly - desert.
- 41-7657 - Segraves - washed out - Tebessa -
- 41-7638 - Johnson - Tangmere washed out.
- 41-7642 - Honk - washed out.
- 41-7644 - Cole - Tunis - ?
- 41-7646 - Eubanks - crash landed.
- 41-7647 - Tomas - Bangor Maine - washed out.
- 41-7671 - Bestgen - Valley washed out.

This does not include any of the new replacement planes which the squadron received & lost. All of the above were orginal planes.

Still running - January 17, 1943.

- 41-7649 - Major Walles - Threw rod. - engines being changed.
- 41-7650 - 272:05 hours. - mine - Schottelkorb
- 41-7651 - engines being changed - Zeigler. 265 hrs.
- 41-7652 - NO nose door. - 24 hrs. - Carroll

Replacements down.
- 720 - V. Smith - Gabe's - Gafsa -
- -------? C. Smith "
- -------? R. Carroll "

Combat in Africa

Bill Schottelkorb, Virgil Smith, Wally Sorensen and Mark Shipman November 1942

One Survived

The following chapter was taken from Mark Shipman's diary. This gives insight into what happened the day Bill was shot down. Mark graciously consented to having his writings put into the book.

Saturday, January 23, 1943 and January 24 I include these two days together for actually, as the following story will verify, the two days were really as one.

At 0600 this morning Wroten gave the "bugle call" for the 16 pilots scheduled last night to hit the deck. It was as usual a cold morning and the sack felt better than usual, so we just lay in our tents, wishing we didn't have to get up. Then Captain Watson came out and soon we were all rushing over to the little mess tent, to get a bite to eat before reporting to the Operations tent at 0645. Tollen was late and therefore kind of held up the deal, but by 0700, Major Walles had told us we're to take off at 0715, on a fighter sweep to strafe Rommel's bunch, between Ben Gardene and Mendenine. We would, after reaching the western tip of Chott Djerid, go down on the deck in order to get an element of surprise on the enemy. Watson and Sorensen would keep their flights as top cover for Walles and Bing's flights, which were to do the strafing and so-forth. At 0715 we were all out on the sod runway, lined up for take off. Navigation lights shown brightly in the half-light of the morning, and soon we were headed into the blue. Due to the poor light the rendezvous was poor. Finally all 16 ships were airborne.

We struck out on a vector of 160 degrees for Chott Djerid, a large dry lakebed, just on the edge of the desert. Going down on the first leg, all was swell – a nice sunrise could be watched from 7,000 feet, the plane was running perfect, the flights looked good, and about 0800 we made a turn to 102 degrees for the coastal road where Rommel was retreating. As we headed easterly over the flat lakebed we all got down on the deck, and there remained until a light layer of ground fog, forced us up to about 200 feet. We passed over one such stretch, found a clear space again, and dropped our belly tanks, that we had been flying on. By that time we were nearing the road, so I trimmed the ship for combat—that is, opened the oil and prestone radiators a little, checked the tank on which I was flying for gas, and took a last minute check of the instruments, made sure the gun switch and sights were ready for use. Again we headed out over a layer of ground fog. As we neared its outer edge, a flak tower, situated on a hill to our left, was seen and as I was watching it for flak, Walles called in 3 fighters over R/T at "12:00 low". I saw them immediately, but as we veered to the right to look them over, we came out directly over an enemy airdrome, a brand new one. Then things really started to happen.

I soon realized E/A (*enemy aircraft*) were in the traffic pattern, preparing to land. It would have been foolhardy to have taken advantage of their slow speed, because ground flak was coming up from all sides. In the course of evasive tactics, we actually circled the air drome and then headed north, along the road to Mendenine. The main road below was absolutely jammed with tanks, trucks, and other lorries, but little did I want to strafe after stirring up such a hornet's nest. First we went about 15 miles from the field, then circled to pick up the rest of the formation. Then Walles went down and strafed the road for about a mile. So naturally, as I was leading his second element, I went down too and shot up about 4 trucks—one of which was a beautiful flamer—before the town of Mendenine was met. There heavy ground flak was experienced from the town. So naturally I broke off and we headed home across the desert. By that time it was too late though for the rear of the formation was already being bounced by the fighters, which were scrambling when we went over the enemy air drome. From there on out it was a hell of a fight and a likewise flight. Everyone raced for the lead position, instead of spreading out, so the flights could protect each other and as a consequence, no proper degree of coordination

One Survived

was received. Sorensen had already called and said his oil temperature was going up and that he needed some help, but it seemed as though his help was feeble. Walles asked Bill to protect him, but Wally said that Bill had been shot down over the air drome, from ground flak. I thought "Oh my God". Finally Bing sent his second element to cover Wally, but still couldn't see Wally or his cover and I wanted to go back myself, but I was afraid Walles wouldn't let me, so I didn't even ask.

Rather I kept weaving and when a ship was being attacked, would ask Walles to break, but the efforts were almost hopeless. I watched the 109s come down, fire, and perhaps get their man. If not he certainly would have to break one way or another and then he would certainly get left by himself, to the mercy of the German Pilots. I begged, pleaded, and did everything I could to get the formation spread out, so that we could handle the 109s, but it remained a jammed up mess. I asked about five times to have the formation break, but each time it was unheeded. I guess my radio must have been out. I just couldn't stand to see the slaughter go on any longer. I had already watched one man get shot up and disappear. I had already seen one man get shot when about 200 feet in the air, go straight on in, and the pilot bolting out of the cockpit as the plane struck the ground and land about 200 feet in front of the crash. It was too much for me and I knew my conscience couldn't be clear if I were to get back without doing my part.

I knew too that if I were to help, it would no doubt mean I would get left back there alone, with 3 ME-109s. I was ready for come what may. I heard Wally call that Bill had been shot down and then recalled a blazing smoke column right over the air drome and I figured that surely must have been him. I heard Wally call for help and didn't know if he received it or not. I had watched 2 P-38s get shot down and so with a silent prayer to God, I prepared for the next attack. And then it came, 2 109s attacking a man on the right side of the formation, (Major Walles as I later found out). I broke to the right and watched them break up to the right, but as they did so I saw their other buddy coming almost head on to me, so I could only completely leave the formation and make a head on attack on him. The range was short—far too short for a successful attack of that type, and we zipped by each other, barely missing wingtips. Then I turned around, saw the formation continuing ahead and I knew that I had had it. I tried to turn with the two 109s just ahead of me. While I was out turning them though, their ever present other buddy shot up my right engine and also damaged the rudders, so I broke to the right into him and made a tight spiral to the right for the desert floor about 800 feet beneath. I knew I couldn't possibly get away from them so I figured I'd better go down and crash land before they hit me.

The flap handle was hit to the down position, I jerked off the canopy and just as I neared the ground I rolled out and belly landed about 140 MPH. At first the ship kept going straight ahead, but as it slowed down it started going to the right. Full opposite rudder kept it from continuing and when the final stop came, the ship was sitting about 40 degrees to the angle of landing. Actually it was surprisingly smooth—my biggest impression was the force the dirt had, which was hammering my left hand on the canopy. I had used this to brace myself. Immediately when it stopped, I popped the release on my safety belt, released the British parachute and got out of the plane. Apparently the propeller shaft broke off as the engine kept running, the landing gear warning horn was blowing and the right engine was smoking violently, but not blazing.

As I stood outside the ship, about 20 yards away, the first 109 came low over the ship and as he passed overhead, I waved. The others followed suit and strafed the ship 3 times each. While they strafed I was kneeling behind a little, one and half-foot high bush, the best cover that I could find and watched them play their game. A mighty fine game they played too, for I knew that they surely saw me there, helpless as a newborn babe, but never once did they attempt to fire on me. Yes, you three German Pilots, you were and still are my enemy in the air, but I hope some day I may be able to give you the same courtesy you gave me, when I was kneeling beside that little desert bush, completely at your mercy. The little ME 109s looked pretty too as they came zooming down, their explosive ammunition exploding and some other type zipping by with queer whistling sounds.

After the little silver planes headed east for Gabes', I went back in the ship, got out my helmet, canteen, pistol, and escape kit. Then started for a mountain, which was about three miles across the level desert floor to the north. About one quarter mile away from the plane, two Arabs that were soon joined by a third party, approached me. As the Arabs previously had treated me quite nice, I asked them the way to Gafsa. They pointed over the mountain in the direction that I had expected it to be. Otherwise they were acting quite friendly to me. Their actions were a bit on the unusual side and they were not speaking French, but at least I trusted them to not give me any maltreatment. Soon however they started going through my things in the escape kit, but I thought surely they were looking for a map, to show me exactly where I was.

First came the Blood-chit, with no apparent impression on them; then came the money in the money pouch, and I was quite surprised to find them put it in their hand. Finally came the little silk maps, and still no impression was made. I really started to wonder what kind of a game they wanted to play. I started to get up from our kneeling position and go on my way, but they made it apparent that they wanted me to stay a little longer. Then came their last breach of etiquette, for they started reaching for my pistol.

At first I warded them away, but back they came, and I knew not whether I should use it or what. I knew that I only had 5 rounds for it, and there were three of them plus a whole field full of them about a mile away. So I decided to let them look at it, in order to show, if possible, my confidence in them. They took it, and then started for the mountains. I figured they merely wanted to carry it for me. However, after we had walked about a half-mile toward the mountain, one of them left us and walked over to our left, just on the westerly side of a little rise in the ground, just out of view from us. Also, the one with the pistol walked a trifle behind and went about 20 feet to our left, and as I would look over at him, he would motion me away.

Obviously, I knew then that I was in for something, and soon it came. The one Arab stood close to me and had me take off my sweater, scarf, shoes, socks and hand over other little items while the other kept the pistol pointed at me. I sure hated to lose all my things, especially the canteen full of water and shoes. I didn't know how well the Arab could use the gun, nor did I know where the third one was, so what do I do? Finally, they seem quite well satisfied with their loot and headed back out into the desert, leaving me only my GI pants and a thin sleeveless, cotton, undershirt to make my way back in.

At the time I felt rather silly too, having been held up with my own gun. Perhaps had I not been amicable the story might have been a different one. At least I was still free, even if my feet did feel awful tender to walk on. On the way up the mountain I followed a streambed which afforded, in some spots, a good sandy patch to walk on, but as the ascent was started it became evident that some means of protection would have to be given my feet. So I cut off my pants, just below the knees, and wrapped them around my feet. This helped some, but goodness knows I certainly could have used more as the creek bed was getting rougher and rougher.

One Survived

About 1300 the final climb was made up the last almost vertical 100 feet of barren mountain, and much to my disappointment there was still a mountain in front of me. I knew that it would be painful, to say the least, if I were to go in a true north direction, as only mountains were ahead. To my right I could see a little valley, stretching down from the mountain, so I started making for it. I hoped, despite my recent experience, to perhaps engage an Arab to take me to Gafsa. My feet were awfully sore by this time, and I figured that I didn't have too much to lose.

Finally one little Arab kid, tending the usual flock of sheep, was sighted and I went over to him, but he insisted so much on having my Boy-Scout knife, I knew that he couldn't have been of good heritage. I journeyed on down the valley, across little plowed areas of desert, which were sown with oats. About a mile and a half from where I met the little kid, just about the time that I thought I was all alone, except for an Arab that I could see ahead, tending a flock of sheep, I heard some heavy breathing behind me. When I turned around there were four Arabs standing there!! I thought surely that this was the end of my freedom, as one had a map wrapped around his forearm and all had on dark green cotton shirts, much the color of the German uniform. This was to say nothing of their hostile attitude.

At first they just milled around, as though they were discussing what disposition should be made of me, but finally asked me if I were going to Gafsa. After my affirmative answer they motioned me down the trail and so we started out, me of course lagging due to the "sore feet and sharp rock" combination. I didn't know how to take them, as they were definitely trying to help me. My position was soon made clear, as after we had gone down the valley about a half a mile, they stopped me and made clear their hostile intentions.

First they gathered around me so that I could not proceed any further and started feeling through my pockets. First came out English currency, then my Boy-Scout knife, dog tags, a picture of Elaine was also taken, but it was returned much to my elation. Fortunately I managed to keep my back to the heathens, so my wallet with about 4,600 Francs, to say nothing of the identification card and so forth remained intact. However, they did get my wristwatch, and despite my objections to the "old man" they insisted it be turned over. One Arab grabbed my wrist and held it, while the other gently unstrapped the jeweled piece. That was the end of a good watch. After all this, they started to take off Elaine's wedding ring off my finger, and that made me so mad, I didn't care what they did to me. One sure thing was that I wasn't going to give it to them. When they would go after it, I would pull away and start down the trail, but the youngest and most damnable of the four, would come up along side me, and make antagonizing hissing sound, and grab me by the shoulder. This cycle was repeated about four times and finally they let me keep on going.

After leaving them I walked on down the valley and soon came to an old dirt road. No doubt the one the Romans had built to get across the mountains. Here and there, traces of hand labor could be seen where the rocks had been cut down, but generally it just wound around, following the easiest terrain. Tracks left by hob-nailed boots made me leery about traveling on it, but it was only about an hour before sundown so I figured I might just as well go along it and make as good time as possible. Primarily I wanted to gain access to the next summit, before complete darkness, so that I could see exactly where I was, but that hope was never realized. I did get to the top while there was still enough light to see, but there was still another mountain between Gafsa, and me so I couldn't see the oasis.

Shortly after I hit the road I met a Camel caravan headed away from Gafsa. They told me, in quite good French that Gafsa was only five kilometers away, and I must say that this built up my hopes. However, another caravan composed of three Camels and twelve Arabs, caught up with me, headed in my direction. They too asked me if I were going to Gafsa, and on my affirmative reply, the elderly one, probably the father, said he would take me to Gafsa if I would give him a 1,000 Francs. He said it was a distance of 50 Kilometers. To the offer I thought, if he were right it would be a good investment, especially if he could get me around the Italians, he spoke of. I quite well agreed to pay his price, so he told me we would have to travel "a la nuit", which again was quite agreeable to me. I knew there would be almost a full moon to travel by. As we walked up the trail, he saw my wedding ring and gold cross and chain that Elaine had given me, and tried to bargain for them. This only made me aggravated by doing so. I told him he could speak good French (not that I could) that my wife had given them to me, so therefore it was priceless to me, but he still wanted them. At least in one sense, decent about the whole affair in that he wasn't aggressive to the point of being hostile.

He also figured that the other Arabs should not have taken my clothing and other items. However, he too made very disgusted, as after he saw that I was having a hard time walking in the poor light, he asked me if I would like to ride on the Camel. "Sure", I told him, expecting to get a welcomed relief for my feet, but then he said, "Give me the ring and vous pouzez mounter l' animal". That was the last straw and when I stopped the next time to re-tie the wrappings on my feet, I just let them go on. They did in a half hearted manner, eventually wait for me, so next time I stopped, I cut down off the trail, it was good and dark by this time, into a little creek bed and that was the last time that I saw them.

By this time it was too dark to travel, especially off the trail, so I went up and then down the little ravine until I found a sheltered spot that I could lay down in, until the moon was up. Several places were tried, one in a hole formed by the stream, one under a little palm tree, but I finally found a place where the water, when it was present, had formed a little ledge underneath the rock. I then waited for the moon. The spot was quite well sheltered from the wind by a sharp turn in the creek bed, plus the overhang ledge of rock. Actually it was just large enough and high enough to crawl under. By taking the wrappings off my feet and throwing them over my shoulders, I could keep comparatively warm. When the two Arabs and three Camels caught up with me I was busy taking another strip off my pants, cutting them off with two rocks to a point, well above the knees. This left my legs rather bare, but so long as the wind didn't get to my chest, I could actually get a few winks of sleep. About 9:00 o'clock the moon came up, so off I went again.

At first a thin veil of high Cumulus Clouds, somewhat darkened the brilliant moonlight, but soon they cleared away and left a beautiful light to guide me by. I kept right to the creek bed for it offered, in spots, good walking in the sand. Just as I got to the base of the mountains, where the desert stretched for about ten miles across to the next range of mountains. I passed by what looked to be a group of tents on the bank of the creek. This, I thought, must be the Italian camp the Arabs spoke of, so I walked cautiously and finally gained the freedom of the desert. About midnight a cool breeze came up and softened the call of the desert owls, but otherwise all was calm and peaceful. Soon though I heard a car in the distance and I knew that I must have been getting close to the main road between Gabes' and Gafsa. Around 3:00 o'clock my belief was confirmed as the black asphalt was seen, even before the telephone poles along the road were sighted.

Then came a hair-raising experience, one that I'm glad that I can reflect back on with joy. While I was walking down the road an Italian motorcyclist came by. As he rode by I could see his dark blue uniform, and watched him give me the once over. I've often since

One Survived

wondered what he thought, considering how I was dressed, only a light undershirt, short pants and rags around my feet. Surely it wasn't similar to the costume of an Arab. Anyway I was glad to hear the noise of the cycle cutting the stillness of the night, as it continued on down the road. From then on I stayed clear of the road, as long as there were vehicles on it.

At first I kept on walking on down the road towards El Gueter, which I thought wasn't too far away, figuring that this Italian was merely a patrol. As a matter of fact, I wasn't sure that Americans were in El Gueter, but I knew for sure that we had Gafsa and thought surely that El Gueter was ours too. At any rate I didn't feel too confident in going much further down the road for fear of hitting a road blockade, either enemy or friend and would then be challenged. So I found a spot about a hundred yards to the north of the road where it had been dug out to provide a place for troops to lie flat, with rifles, and there protect the road. I stayed there until dawn broke. Rather as a dog digs himself a place to sleep, I also rounded out a spot in the soft dirt at the corner of the place and got a few winks of sleep.

Just before dawn broke, I changed my position of one a little further from the road, where I could still identify any vehicle passing by. The first two trucks were painted the familiar desert sand brown, splotched by black for camouflage and I recognized them as of being the same color as the Italian tanks that we busted up at Faid Pass.

From then on I kept working westward along the north side of the road, so I could find another good ravine to hide in, until I could get a good look at the cars. However, after working across a green river valley and gaining access to its western bank, I still couldn't find a good place to stay. When the road was clear, I went across it to the south side and found a little dried up water hole about a quarter mile from the road. There I could rest, as its bottom was about six feet deep and right next to the mountain. Each time a car would come by I would identify it as best I could, but I could still see no definite markings. However, the presence of men in the distance, guarding roadblocks plus the peculiar camouflaging made me sure that I was in an Italian camp. Nevertheless I still couldn't find a logical explanation in my mind for the American jeep and truck tracks I crossed out in the desert, last night. I later found out though that Lt. Pogue had been down to within fifteen miles of Gabes' not long before on a night patrol, but little did I think of that then.

It was nice in my little secluded spot as I could rest and even sleep fairly well in the hole. Its banks not only hid me from sight, but also acted as a fine windbreak, and the warm sunshine made me want nothing but sleep. As a matter of fact I stayed there until about 10:00 o'clock, or some two hours, but soon the urge to keep going hit hard. To the north was a high very rugged ridge about 3,000 feet above the valley, with hardly enough space to sneak between it's base and the road block, so it was definitely out of the question to choose that route. Incidentally it is lucky for me too, that it wasn't attempted, because if I had tried to go that way I would have run smack-dad into another camp. Of course I didn't know this at the time. To my left was another ridge, the base of which I was at, which ran westward for two miles, then swung south to form a large peak, barren and rugged as usual. The base of the ridge went almost down to the road, until it took up it southerly course, and where it turned was practically at the middle of the Italian roadblocks.

From there on there was ample room to go between the road and the base of the peak, I thought, and it seemed a fairly safe route to travel.

Mark obviously had written his account of the mission and his adventures thereafter soon after he arrived back at his base, but didn't record what happened to him in the next few hours. In a personal interview with him at his home in Reedsport, Oregon on September 17, 2002, he added the following information.

"I continued on along the west side of the road but I stayed far enough off it to avoid being seen. As I came closer to the roadblock I was dismayed to realize that there was no way that I could continue without encountering another Italian Army Camp. I decided the latter was the lesser of the two evils so I headed toward the camp. I pretended to be a desert wanderer even though I wasn't dressed like an Arab. I kept my head down and scuffed at any pebbles in my way. There didn't seem to be much activity at the time, probably because it was time for the noon meal. I saw four soldiers standing a short distance away and I knew they were looking at me but I acted as if I didn't see them and continued to slowly walk away and out of their sight. They certainly must have wondered about me but fortunately I was able to continue on through the camp".

"It was a tremendous relief to be away from there and I continued on until I met a American Sergeant on a scouting patrol. He checked my ID and listened to my account of what had happened. After I drank some much-needed water he took me to Gafsa. I gave thanks to God, knowing I had been very fortunate to survive such an ordeal. They put me up there where I enjoyed a meal and a good nights sleep".

Monday January 25, 1943 Pulled out of Gafsa about 1000 in a GI two and a half ton truck and made our way past French Calvary Troops and through rain squalls to Feriana. There we ate lunch, watched the pet monkey climb about the truck, and then went on to Tebessa. There the boys put me up in good style for the night, especially Captain Vessels, and I also got word to Colonel Olds, and later Major Walles that I was safe and sound. A nice fireplace plus some excellent home style eating was thoroughly enjoyed.

Tuesday January 26, 1943 Captain Vessels "commandeered" jeep was piled into about 0830, and four of us headed for Berteaux. Vessels drove the first part, but I was glad when he let me take over, because I didn't care too much for the idea of someone else driving through the heavy rain. Arrived at Berteaux about 1215, after a hard drive through rain and mud, just in time to get in on a big squadron pow-wow.

The pilots were angry after the mission on the 23rd, especially after losing 5 pilots and 6 aircraft, and made some pretty blunt statements regarding it. Major Walles evidently felt it was better to get away from the German airdrome as quickly as possible as the squadron was caught by surprise at a very low altitude by a superior force. No doubt he wanted to fight another day with better odds. After hearing the heated discussion, Colonel Olds decided to have Mark and Captain William J. Holle, commander of the 49th Squadron, give their comments to General Cannon, at the 12th Air Force Headquarters in Constantine. The next day, January 27th, the two pilots accompanied Colonel Olds to Constantine in his staff car and met with General Cannon. Mark didn't know what the General's reaction would be, however he listened to what they had to say and took it under advisement without much comment.

Thursday January 28, 1943 Walles, Bing, Sorensen, Seagraves, and I left for the "rest-cure" on a C-47 today. Arrived after much turmoil at the Tamaris Hotel about 1900. While in Algiers Major Tomkins told us that orders were being cut to send the 14th Group's original pilots home!

Thursday February 4, 1943 Major General Doolittle, seven months ago a Lieutenant Colonel, today presented us with our decorations. Last night Colonel Olds handed out the orders for our promotions, so now we are all set to go back to the **States**.

On Saturday February 6, 1943 the pilots left Algiers by air transport for the trip home. After the veteran pilots of the 48th and 49th squadrons

One Survived

were reassigned the 14th Fighter Group went into a stand down status. The 82nd Group took over their aircraft. By the end of April 1943 the newly refurbished 14th was ready to resume operations after being brought up to full strength for the first time.

2nd Lieutenant Clark W. Smith who was shot down on December 30, 1942 was captured and returned after Germany surrendered.

On January 23, 1943 the five pilots who were shot down and who didn't survive were:
2nd Lieutenant Kenneth W. Harley
1st Lieutenant William F. Schottelkorb
2nd Lieutenant R. H. Soliday
2nd Lieutenant Guy E. Stuteville
2nd Lieutenant Leo M. Yates

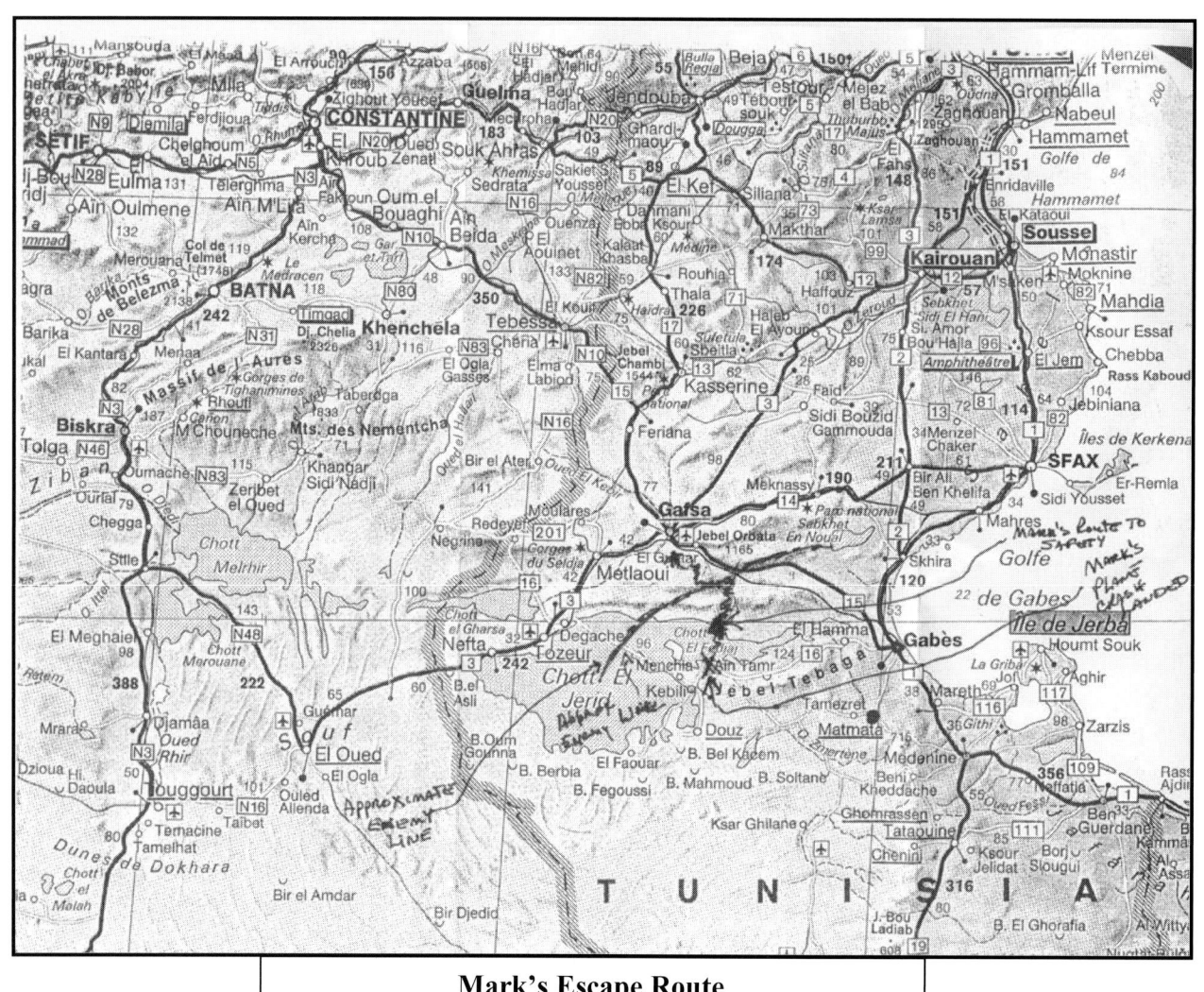

Mark's Escape Route

Beyond Africa

After Bill was shot down, the War Department delayed reporting this to my parents. This was in case that he might have survived or was a prisoner of war, but on February 8, 1943, the dreaded telegram arrived stating that Bill was missing in action since January 23rd. This had to be a heavy blow on my parents, but two days later, Mom wrote me telling of the sad news.

Mom's letter dated February 10, 1943:
How are you? I hope your are getting along fine. You must be about through your Primary School, are you not?

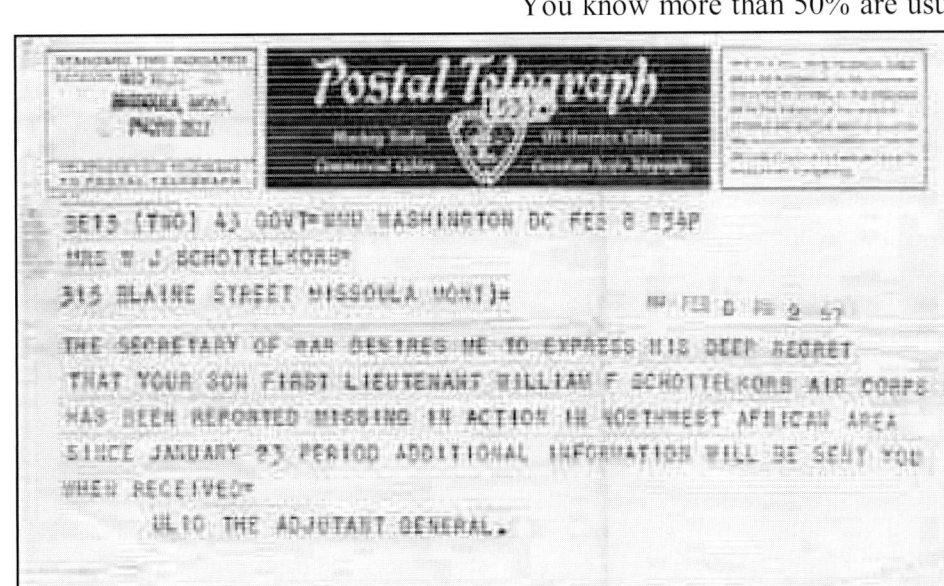

Well now dear, I have a little sad news for you, although I know you are going to take it like a soldier, as Bill would want you to. Monday afternoon I received a telegram from the government stating that Bill has been missing in action since January 23. My reaction was, it is not true. I know it isn't so, but even if it should be, he is missing. He must be OK wherever he is. That is the thought and hope we must bear in mind. We must have hope. I wanted to tell you sooner, by phone or telegram, but I was afraid it would be more of a shock that way. It is hard for us to believe anything but that he is all right. I hope you feel the same. We have to take it standing up just like Bill did.

We are hoping for the best and if anything comes up we will let you know at once. With love to our dear son, Mother & Dad.

Another note was added:
Everyone has been very nice to us. The Halms came over the first evening, as did Mae Heyer. Yesterday morning, Mrs. Barrett came over and in the afternoon Mrs. Stepenson and Mrs. Blanchette came. Last night the Potters and Centers were here.

You know more than 50% are usually safe when they are reported missing in action. Anyway we are going to say he is OK, aren't we? We wish we could be with you.
XOXOXO
Mother

Mom's letter telling about the telegram and the word that Bill was missing in action arrived on Friday afternoon, February 12, 1943. It was the day I completed Primary Flight Training, so I didn't have that to think about along with the news. I was thankful that she wrote, rather than calling me because it would have been very emotional for both of us.

I'm sure it was easier for me to handle than for them, but it was a shock for all of us. I agreed with her sentiments that we had to presume he would be back or was a prisoner of war. We wanted to have hope. As an Aviation Cadet, I had plenty to keep me busy and had little free time to dwell on the news. Mom and Dad had lots of family friends for support, but it was still hard on them, especially Dad, whose health was failing.

MIKE MANSFIELD
1ST DISTRICT MONTANA

Congress of the United States
House of Representatives
Washington, D. C.

February 19, 1943

Mr. and Mrs. W. J. Schottelkorb
315 Blaine Street
Missoula, Montana

Dear Folks:

I have just learned that your son, Bill, has been listed as missing in action by the War Department. I hardly know what to say but I do hope that we will receive news that he is safe and sound. Knowing your boy as I did in the University, I have a great respect for his courage and ability. If I receive any definite information back here relative to your boy I will communicate with you immediately. In the meantime, if I can be of any assistance, please do not hesitate to call on me.

Sincerely,

Mike Mansfield

WAR DEPARTMENT
COMMANDING GENERAL, ARMY AIR FORCES
WASHINGTON

February 25, 1944

My dear Mrs. Schottelkorb:

With great regret I have learned that an official determination has been made of the death of your son, First Lieutenant William Frank Schottelkorb, who has been missing since January 23, 1943, in Tunisia.

The record of Lieutenant Schottelkorb has been brought to my attention and I am gratified to know that he was awarded the Distinguished Flying Cross with Oak-Leaf Cluster. These decorations testify to his splendid service as an officer of the Army Air Forces and climax his worthwhile military career that began at Oxnard, California.

It is my hope that you will not continue to grieve over the loss of your son, but will derive satisfaction from the knowledge that he unselfishly and courageously gave his life for our Country.

My deepest sympathy is with you and other members of the family.

Very sincerely,

H. H. ARNOLD,
General, U. S. Army,
Commanding General, Army Air Forces.

Mrs. W. J. Schottelkorb,
315 Blaine Street,
Missoula, Montana.

Beyond Africa

Missoula Pilot in Valiant Group Bagging 40 German Planes While Losing but Nine in North Africa

BY WES GALLAGHER. 1943

An Adanced American Fighter Base Somewhere in North Africa, Jan. 1.—(Delayed)—(P)—Flying from a mountainside and living on a diet of canned hash, young American pilots fresh from colleges, factories and country towns have proved what a great fighter plane the P-38 is by shooting down 40 German planes with it for a loss of only nine.

The pilots, who less than six weeks ago were upset by the allegation on both sides of the Atlantic that American fgihter planes were inferior to the models of other nations, declared the P-38 was master of the luftwaffe's highly-rated Focke-Wulf 190's and Messerschmitt 109-Gs.

Among the pilots is William F. Schottelkorb, Missoula, Mont., who has one Axis plane to his credit.

This field is so situated on the side of a mountain that the constant rains of recent days have drained off and left the area clear. The flat plateaus are soggy with rain at this time of year.

The first six P-38s started operations here without ground crews, and even without tents for the flyers to live in.

Originally designed only as an interceptor type to protect cities from bombing raids, the P-38 has proved itself capable of every rough job assigned it.

The P-38 has also been used in long-range escort for bombers, and in the last two weeks, while escorting Boston A-20 Douglas light bombers, has not yet let a German plane through the fighter screen to reach the bombers.

"This record has been established against the best the Germans have to offer," said Major Stephen Avery, 48-year-old veteran of the last war, who comes from Hollywood and is the intelligence officer of this outfit.

Avery asserted that the long range of the P-38s enables them to keep up the fight deep into into enemy territory instead of confining themselves to the brief dogfights which have been characteristic of the European theater.

Pilots at this field, who fly every day and stay on the alert against German raiders on their day of rest, labeled as "tommyrot" the opinion of many "experts" that the P-38 was a "hot" ship, unmaneuverable and its twin engines too much for one pilot to handle.

"Our ships were built for high altitude work, but we have been fighting anywhere from the ground up to high altitudes, and our craft have been good at any level," said Lieutenant Virgil Lusk, Santa Rosa, N. M., who has an ace's rating for destruction of five Italian Savoia Marchettis.

MISSOULA FLYER, MISSING IN ACTION, IS AWARDED DFC FOR FEATS IN AFRICAN FIELD

Reported missing in action in mid-January, First Lieutenant William F. Schottelkorb, son of Mr. and Mrs. William J. Schottelkorb, 315 Blaine street, have been informed in a message from the War department that he has been awarded the Distinguished Flying Cross with Oak Leaf cluster "for extraordinary achievement while participating in aerial flights against the enemy on November 11, 1942, January 1 to 25, 1943, in North Africa."

The award to the young Missoula flyer, is a double citation, this being signified by the oak-leaf design, and was bestowed by the commanding general of the Twelfth air force. It will be sent to Mr. Schottelkorb, who has been requested to inform the commanding general of the Army air forces as to his wishes in the manner of presentation. Inasmuch as there is now a unit of the air forces stationed in Missoula at the State University, it is probable that an officer from the detachment there will confer the award.

Lieutenant Schottelkorb who flew a P-38, which he called "Miss Missoula," had written his parents just before he was reported missing, that his plane was one of the few original ones of his squadron, still unscratched. His parents are confident that he is a German prisoner and that they will hear from him. Before being sent to Africa with one of the first groups of American flyers to go there, the officer had served for many months in England and had written many interesting reports on life in that war-torn land.

A brother of Lieutenant Schottelkorb, Robert Schottelkorb, is in the air forces, also, and is at the present time attending officers' school at Pine Bluff, Ark.

Lieutenant Schottelkorb.

Army Air Force Training Detachment in formation prior to passing in review

Reading of awards by Major George Heikes, followed by the reading of the official orders of citation by Captain Joe C. Tyler

Parents of Hero Flyer Honored At Review; Medals Are Presented

A bravely-composed, middle-aged couple, who have sent two sons to the United States Army air corps, stood side by side Sunday afternoon on the green turf of the State University campus oval, as they were tendered the full honors of a military review by the entire air force training detachment here, led by its 30-piece band.

Mr. and Mrs. W. J. Schottelkorb were honor guests of the review, receiving for their son, Lieutenant William F. Schottelkorb, missing in action in the World war, the Distinguished Service Cross and the oak leaf cluster.

Presentation of the decorations was made by Major George Heikes, air force training commandant at the State University, following the reading of the official Army orders of citation by Captain Joe C. Tyler.

With the eternal faith and courage of parents, they hope that some day they may be able to deliver to the son reported missing since last January, the Army Air corps decorations and citations which they received at the review Sunday. The possibility that he may be a prisoner of the Germans is given much consideration.

There was hope in their eyes as they received and viewed the decorations which they will cherish while they wait further word of their first son to enjoy action on the front.

Mrs. Schottelkorb spoke of the other son, Robert, who graduated last week from an Army flying course and was then awaiting assignment. "If he does as well as William, we will have reason to be doubly proud, and we have every reason to believe he will."

The review was executed in approved military style, with thousands of Missoula people assembling to watch the parade and ceremony from the areas surrounding the oval. The entire air training detachment, striding in step behind their musicians, tendered "eyes right" to the delegation in the reviewing stand. During the presentation of the medals, the sprinkle ceased, not resuming until the last company of cadets was swinging off the campus, returning to the barracks. The presentation immediately preceded the parade.

Besides Mr. and Mrs. Schottelkorb, the reviewing line included Major Heikes and his air corps staff, and Colonel Lewis S. Norman and the ROTC staff of the State University. A color guard was provided by the ROTC.

Decorations were awarded Lieutenant Schottelkorb specifically for destruction of a hostile airplane on November 11, 1942, and participation in 10 sorties against the enemy from January 1 to 25, 1943, in North Africa.

These engagements were but a small part of the war zone flying career of the young Missoula air veteran, one of the first of Uncle Sam's fighting aviators to enter the combat areas of the Second World war.

The last letter from him to his parents was mailed January 23, just after Christmas packages from home had arrived.

Born in Stevensville, Lieutenant Schottelkorb came to Missoula when a year old, being reared here. He was attending Montana State University when he enlisted April 25, 1941, being registered then as a junior majoring in history. His brother, Robert, was also attending the State University, when he entered the air corps service.

William took basic training at Camp Oxnard, Cal., later going to Luke Field, Ariz., where he received his commission as second lieutenant. He served at March field and at San Diego, then was promoted to a first lieutenant. He was among the first of the United States Army Air corps flyers to be sent to the North African hostilities and has been in the thick of things.

THE DAILY MISSOULIAN
Founded in 1873
PUBLISHED DAILY AND SUNDAY
Subscription Rates:
Per week, delivered by carrier, 25c
Mail Rates—Postage Prepaid
In Montana—1 month, 90c; 3 months, $2.50; 6 months, $4.75; 1 year, $9.00; Sunday only, $2.75, 1 year.
Elsewhere in the United States or Possessions—1 month, $1.00; 3 months, $2.75; 6 months, $5.25; year, $10.00; Sunday only, $3.00, 1 year.
Entered at the Postoffice at Missoula, Montana, as Second-Class Matter Under Act of March 3, 1879.
500 North Higgins Avenue   Missoula, Montana

To the William Schottelkorbs.

Hundreds of Missoula people watched a military review on the University campus Sunday afternoon, took the salute of the cadet detachment along with the parents of William Schottelkorb, a young aviator whose distinguished career with our armed forces is interrupted by the dread words, "Missing in Action." We say that these Missoula people took the salute with the young hero's parents because, to each and every one, it seemed as if he belonged to them, too.

William Schottelkorb won the Distinguished Flying Cross —and more—but to us he still is the Little Boy Across the Street. When we were lazy or tired, William was available on summer days to mow the lawn or to perform other little chores about the yard. He was a friendly, intelligent, handsome, willing little fellow at the stage of life when energy and judgment often are not well balanced each to the other. We did not dream of war then, but we thought that William surely would grow up to "amount to something." He has—and more. We feel almost as proud of him as his parents do.

But William remains in our memory chiefly the little boy he was a decade ago. To think of him brings the thought that he is typical of all the American war effort, that, after all, this war is being fought by young men who lately were little boys, that to such we owe our future, our chance to live as Americans, our hope for better, softer days to come after the hard, rough, deadly days of war. To these little boys go our thoughts, our hopes—and our prayers, to the thousands of William Schottelkorbs who stand between us and disaster.

May God bless them and keep them!

Missoulian editorial by Mr. French Ferguson, editor

Mr. & Mrs. Schottelkorb at awards ceremony

Beyond Africa

Young Veterans of War in Africa Visit in Missoula

Buddies of William Schottelkorb Tell of Battle in Which Local Flyer's Plane Was Lost

When Captain Mark K. Shipman and First Lieutenant Wallace A. Sorenson, United States Army flyers, circled above Missoula's mountains prior to landing on the county airport Thursday, they were looking upon a familiar landscape even though they were viewing it for the first time. It had been described to them many times by First Lieutenant William F. Schottelkorb, Missoula flyer reported missing in action in North Africa last January 23.

Veterans of the African campaign, the two officers, each of whom is 22 years of age, were returned to home shores last February. Recently assigned to duty at a base in the Northwest Pacific area, their visit here was one planned in Africa on the day that their friend and comrade, Lieutenant Schottelkorb, was shot down in combat over a German airdrome. He went down in "Miss Missoula," officially known as P-38 No. 7850, which he at one time had written his parents, was "one of the very few originals we have left."

They were permitted to make their flight to Missoula to bring to the officer's parents, Mr. and Mrs. W. J. Schottelkorb, 315 Blaine street, such news as they knew of him and to deliver his personal diary. Each of the men had charged the others with the responsibility of taking such messages home in the event that anything happened to any of them. Captain Shipman had agreed that he would take charge of the diary, which is now in Mrs. Schottelkorb's possession.

Hope Is Held

Like his parents both Captain Shipman and Lieutenant Sorenson cling to the hope that Lieutenant Schottelkorb is a German prisoner. Both flyers were participants in the same battle in which he went down. P-38 pilots, they had been in action continuously from the time they had arrived in the African desert from England where they had been based for three months. Shipman, too, was shot down and Sorenson's plane was badly shot up, although he managed to land it at an advanced Allied base.

After he landed his plane, escaping injury himself although the machine was out of commission, Shipman started on foot to make his way through the desert country back to his base. His adventures on terra firma proved to be as exciting as those he had just had in the air, and if anything more unpleasant, he said. He was attacked by Arabs, who, so poor that they will commit any crime for food and clothing, took his clothes away from him, leaving him nothing but his trousers. Without his shoes, he was badly handicapped in continuing his way back to the American lines, but by removing the trousers and converting them into wrappings for his feet, he was able to continue his journey. It was not very hot in Africa at that season, he said, but it was sufficiently warm for him to acquire a fine sun tan in the 36 hours that it took him to make the 30 miles that he traversed before he arrived at camp.

Although the Arabs are not fussy about what they wear on their feet, it is a misconception to believe that they do not need footgear. The officers, to illustrate this point, stated that at one time when a wheel on a plane that had cracked up burst out to expose the tube, a horde of Arabs had gathered round and one of them had made it clear by gesticulations and signs that he wanted the tube for shoes. He was permitted to take it, but Shipman said he felt differently about giving up his own shoes, even though he had no choice unless it was to become very much extinct in the expanse of desert that surrounded him on all sides with nothing visible but Arabs.

Young Vets of African War Visitors in City

(Continued From Page One.)

Graduated Together

Captain Shipman, Lieutenant Sorenson and Lieutenant Schottelkorb were graduated from Luke field, Arizona, December 20, 1941; they had arrived there simultaneously September 30 of the same year. From the time they finished their instruction until the day that Lieutenant Schottelkorb went down in battle they were together. They flew the Atlantic together, experiencing the tremendous thrill of a transocean flight broken with stops in Greenland and Iceland. They enjoyed the sights of England and in Africa shared the excitement, hardship and fun that were their daily fare. All were members of the impromptu club that they built in the desert and of which Lieutenant Schottelkorb wrote graphic descriptions last Christmas. He, his friends said, had done most of the work in building it.

Reticent about their own experiences, the two officers paid feeling tribute to their friend, saying that he was a splendid officer, a true and loyal friend. They remembered that he was in England only a short time when he was out on several operational excursions, presumably with the RAF, over France and that even before he reached the African theater of war, he had won his spurs in battle, having assisted in bringing down at least one enemy aircraft.

In Africa, Lieutenant Schottelkorb brought down his first enemy plane, a JU-88, on December 11, just one month after the P-38 squadron had arrived from England, the flight having been made on Armistice day. Before he went on his last mission he had been out on 45 sorties over enemy territory and had 110 hours of combat flying, his friends related.

One More Flight

By sad circumstance the entire squadron of which he was a member, went on its last mission a day after Lieutenant Schottelkorb was reported missing. "Just one more flight and Bill would have come home with us," said Captain Shipman, stating that all the pilots of the outfit were relieved after one more engagement. All had gone into action a few days after their arrival from England at a base 40 miles from the German lines.

The three friends all won the same decorations for their part in the African campaign. Lieutenant Schottelkorb's parents were presented with his Distinguished Flying Cross and the Air Medal with oak leaf cluster, at ceremonies at the State University April 25. His friends are entitled to wear the same decorations, but they do not tell of winning them; their story is of all the honors and citations that were awarded him.

Mr. and Mrs. Schottelkorb had met Captain Shipman at the time of his graduation, when they went to Arizona for the ceremonies in which their son also won his wings. En route they picked up the young woman who is now Mrs. Shipman and the mother of a small son, in order that she might also be present at her then fiance's graduation. They were married shortly afterward. As he had written them much of his friends, Lieutenant Schottelkorb's parents did not greet them as strangers when they arrived here Thursday to be guests at their home for the brief space before they flew over the mountains to the west in their P-38s to return to their Pacific base.

Captain Mark K. Shipman and 1ˢᵗ Lieutenant Wallace A. Sorensen bring Bill's diaries to Missoula

Beyond Africa

"Miss Missoula," Plane of Local Pilot, Unscathed in African Fight

Africa, once so distant that even the wings of the imagination could not be spread to bring it within bounds of reality, now seems near, and to Missoulians it will come closer still when they know that somewhere in its vast reaches an American ship flown by an American pilot and named "Miss Missoula" is fighting their fight.

Lieutenant William F. Schottelkorb, who has been in Africa for

Lieutenant Schottelkorb.

some time now, has written his parents, Mr. and Mrs. William J. Schottelkorb of 315 Blaine street, one of those soldier letters that do much to give substance and color to the stay-at-home civilian's conception of the far land where so many American men are fighting.

Congratulated by Doolittle.

Pridefully, the flyer reports, "Our squadron has done some great work and we have been especially congratulated by Major General J. Doolittle. We have been in the thick of things in this part of the world and everything is OK, so don't worry."

At this juncture he put in the interpolation about his ship—"Miss Missoula, my means of transportation, hasn't been scratched since I left March field; it is one of the very few originals still with us."

Yankee Ingenuity.

In Africa as well as elsewhere, Yankee ingenuity finds its usual opportunities for display. It was apparently exhibited by the American flyers who, tired of standing in the evening wind, decided to do something about it. The something turned out to be the construction of a clubhouse, of which Lieutenant Schottelkorb wrote:

"After spending many an evening standing out in the wind, the pilots got together and decided to build a club. This is what resulted:

"We dug a hole in solid ground 30 feet long, 15 feet wide, four and one-half feet deep on one side. We made a well four more feet higher by use of empty five-gallon gas cans, using these for the ends and sides. The wall was two and three cans high. Around all of this the dirt was banked to the top. Then two-by-fours and canvas provided a slanting roof, and a double door for the entrance.

"The prize feature of the club," the writer went on to relate, "is the fireplace. This we constructed from large stone blocks. We were very lucky for it draws perfectly. We have a mantel; it is larger than our fireplace at home and we can handle large logs.

"In one corner we have a tropical bar constructed of bamboos and palm leaves."

There was no time lost in putting the club to the use for which it was intended, for the letter goes on to state that "this was a busy place New Year's eve."

Lion's Skin Is Rug.

The club's decor included a lion's skin on the floor in front of the fire. The writer does not say where it came from, nor did he explain where the stones, logs, etc., that were used in construction were secured. "Several easy chairs," he added, "complete the picture, not to mention a short-wave radio with which we get good reception from England and the States.

"Around the walls we have signs painted in yellow and black on wood such as 'The Brightest Spot in Darkest Africa' and 'Women Especially Welcome,' and our Walt Disney insignia.

"Now," the writer observes with satisfaction, "we have a place to relax and be comfortable."

Arabs Out-Traded.

Commenting on the Arabs, Lieutenant Schottelkorb relates an episode that is cut more to the pattern of the average conception of Africa. He wrote: "The Arabs are very friendly as I said before and they are great traders." Here again, however, Yankee shrewdness has been brought to bear, for the letter says, "But once in a while they get swindled. Someone gave one of them a shiny English penny for a chicken. The Arab thought it was gold. When he found out it wasn't he came back to get his chicken, but it was already over the fire. So he sat on his burro and cried like a baby, his feet touching the ground."

Christmas and New Year's dinner menus both included turkey, but nobody got any packages at the African post, a circumstance which the men accept philosophically, the writer stating "I guess that was too much to expect, but they will come some time." Christmas day weather was "rainy and low" and not like Christmas.

Nights Are Cold.

Those who think of Africa as a place of unremitting heat will find contradictory information in the officer's statement, "It is getting quite cold these last few days and last night the water froze in my canteen and there was a very heavy frost on my tent."

Lieutenant Schottelkorb, who was named in a recent news dispatch from the African front as having participated in an engagement, concluded his letter to his parents with a request that he would like a few Missoulians or Sentinels.

Robert Schottelkorb, about whose progress his brother made inquiry, is in the Primary Air corps at Camp Grider, at Pinebluff, Ark., where he went December 14 for special training that will lead to a commission in the air forces.

> The "Missoulian" article at the left came from the January 31, 1943 newspaper. At this time Bill's parents hadn't been notified that he was missing in action.

Mr. and Mrs. Schottelkorb being congratulated for Bill's service to his country

> The following statement is by Ralph 'Doc' Watson from a letter to Robert Schottelkorb on June 2, 1989.
>
> "I knew your brother well, he flew with me many times and was in my flight. I think we called him "Shottle". He was a good pilot and a steady one that you could depend on. He loved Montana and talked of it often and we all planned to visit there someday after the war".

Beyond Africa

Sept. 15, 1943
Muroc, California

Dear Mr. & Mrs. Schottlekorb:

I must apologize for not writing before this, but I've been going pretty hard lately as we all have a nice job, and a busy one.

Your letter was appreciated very much, and I'm glad you sent me the clippings. I know that Shipman and Sorensen gave you all the information, and they told me of the incident. They really did enjoy their visit with you, and after they told me all about it, well, I wanted to visit you too, but my work has held me back, and if by chance I do receive the opportunity, I promise to be up to see you.

In your letter you talked about Bob I believe, well, I know that Bill would be more than proud of his little brother, because he often spoke of him, and he told me all about him. I guess you know that Bill, Shipman, Sorensen, and myself were a click together in all of our engagements. Bill and I had a wonderful time in England, and he and I spent some of our time seeing the bright lights in that country. While we were in Africa it was a business, but we still had laughs during our time while we were not working. I often think of The statement that Bill made to me one day, and here it is: " Stege, I know you want to go home, but just think for awhile, and ask yourself, Who will be doing the fighting when your home???, Somebody has to fight the war." I had all the confidence in the world in Bill, and as I always say to myself, "He's the Best". Even the little girl he went with in England thought he was perfect, and we can all vouch for that. She was a short pretty girl, very intelligent, attractive, and plenty of personality. As I recall the incident, we went to a movie, and saw this picture that is now showing here in the U. S. A. called (Spitfire) or (The First of the Few). We did have a marvelous time.

Most of the fellow's who came back in our organization are now stationed someplace here in the U. S., and they spread out from Florida, Mass., and all the way across the continent to California. Captain Singleton is my operations officer, and my offical job is a flight leader in the training of P-38 pilot's. So far we like our work, and we now are moving to another field here in California very shortly. Lt. Goebel, and Lt. Eubank are also flight leaders, and their still in the same organization as myself. Lt. Goebel and the Mrs. are expecting a new comrade in the family very soon now. Naturally, we want a boy------

Well, I'm sorry I'm so late in answering you letter, but I hope this finds you both in the best of health, and when your write to Bob, tell him to look me up if he's every out here in California.

Sincerely yours,

John A. Stege

P.S. Any information or news on Bill, please let me know. My folks send their best—

Beyond Africa

THURSDAY, JULY 22, 1943

Trio of Army Pilots Fighting War Together

SANTA ANA, July 21.—Together all the way from primary flight training to combat with the enemy is the unusual aerial partnership of three fighter pilot graduates of the Army Air Forces West Coast Training Center here.

The three modern musketeers, who returned recently from North Africa, are Capt. John Singleton, Petaluma; Lieut. John Stege, Lancaster, and Lieut. John Goebel, Grand Rapids, Mich.

Fast friends during their primary phase at Oxnard, the trio stuck together through basic instruction at Minter Field, Bakersfield, and advance training at Luke Field, Arizona. And, as Lieut. Stege puts it, "Darned if we didn't wind up wing to wing in North Africa!"

Fighting, strafing, dive-bombing and escorting bombers in the same P-38 Lightning squadron, the trio won 14 decorations—Capt. Singleton, Distinguished Flying Cross with Oak Leaf Cluster and the Air Medal with three clusters; Lieut. Goebel, the Distinguished Flying Cross and Air Medal with three clusters; Lieut. Stege, son of Mr. and Mrs. Art Stege of Lancaster, Air Medal with two clusters.

They are now stationed in Southern California, training others in combat tactics.

MODERN MUSKETEERS—These three Army airmen trained together and fought wing to wing in North Africa. Left to right, Lieut. John Goebel, Capt. John Singleton and Lieut. John Stege, graduates of the West Coast Training Center at Santa Ana.
Army Air Forces photo

Newspaper article sent to Mr. & Mrs. Schottelkorb with a picture of a Franc note

Beyond Africa

After the pilots, thankfully, returned home and enjoyed their leaves with their loved ones they were sent to air bases to share their combat skills with new P-38 pilots. Mark Shipman and Wally Sorensen were initially assigned to McCord Field, Everett, Washington. While there they were able to fly to Missoula, Montana to bring Bill's diaries and a few personal items to Mom and Dad. They enjoyed the visit and the chance to see Bill's much loved Missoula that he had often talked about.

Mark Shipman

Mark was assigned to the 38th Fighter Squadron of the 55th Fighter Group of the 8th Air Force in England in July 1943. At first their group was the only one that could escort the bombers for extreme long missions. Their protection was critical for the bombers. Later they flew the newly introduced P-51 Mustang fighters that were well adapted to high altitude, long range missions. Mark was promoted to the rank of Lieutenant Colonel and Squadron Commander before returning to McCord Field again. Here he joined five other veteran combat pilots to devise fighter tactics to deal with jet fighter aircraft that were being used by the German Luftaffe in increasing numbers. He was relieved from active duty in September 1945.

In 1950 he graduated from the Colorado School of Mines at Golden, Colorado with a degree in Geology. He then served as Commander of the 149th Fighter Group, Colorado Air National Guard. He attended the Air War College for one year and after he graduated was assigned to the 137th Fighter Wing in Alexandria, Louisiana. There he flew F-84 jets. After the Korean Conflict he retired from the U S Air Force as a Colonel.

At the present time Mark and his wife Elaine reside in Reedsport, Oregon. They have six children, seven grandchildren and eight great grandchildren.

Wallace Sorensen

From McCord Air Field, Wally Sorensen was sent to Alaska and out on the Aleutian Islands. There he had to fly in treacherous weather conditions. Wally attained the rank of Lieutenant Colonel and was separated from the service in December, 1945.

He began a career in banking and retired from that in 1982 as a Senior Vice-President while living in Boise, Idaho. He was very active in several civic and business organizations. He died on October 14, 1990 after suffering a massive heart attack while playing golf, two days earlier. His wife, Phyllis, two daughters, a son and their families survive him.

John Stege

John A. Stege was an instructor of P-38 pilots in Muroc, Salinas and Santa Maria, California. On June 1, 1943 he was assigned to the 13th Air Force in the Asiatic Pacific Theatre. He served with the 347th Fighter Group, 68th Fighter Squadron for fifteen months in New Guinea and the Philippines. He became a Squadron Commander with the rank of Major before he returned to the United States. He was separated from the service on January 24, 1946.

He was the owner-manager of retail liquor stores in VanNuys and Encino, California. He and his wife, Charlene, had one son, four daughters and seven grandchildren. Charlene died in June 1999. John continues an active interest in the 48th Fighter Squadron Association and the P-38 National Association.

These three served their country well and received many awards and medals for their bravery. Bill would be proud of them.

Bill never made it back to his "Peaceful Valley" in Missoula but he did so, many times in his mind.

Beyond Africa

As Always, Just Plain Bill